David Whitehead, Henning Klattenhoff
London | The Architecture Guide

Edited by Markus Sebastian Braun

David Whitehead, Henning Klattenhoff

London | The Architecture Guide

Edited by Markus Sebastian Braun

The Deutsche Nationalbibliothek lists this publication in the Deutsche
Nationalbibliografie; detailed bibliographical data are available on the internet
at http://dnb.d-nb.de.

ISBN: 978-3-037680-30-8

© 2010 by Braun Publishing AG
www.braun-publishing.ch

1st Edition 2010

Editior: Judith Vonberg, Hereford
Design: port-d Burgold & Neumann GbR, Berlin
Layout: Manuela Roth, Berlin
Reproduction: bild1Druck GmbH, Berlin

Contents

Preface

London is both big and old and has been so for a very long time. It is one of a handful of geographical locations in which such a wealth of life histories have been concentrated. Like other such places it has a density and richness of association that is palpable and that lend it tremendous glamour and appeal.

The city's architecture is the principle physical artefact of two millennia of progress from a damp northern trading outpost to a world centre of civilisation. Little but archaeological remnants remain from the Roman and Saxon times. Norman, Gothic and early classical buildings are few after a history of disaster and endless redevelopment, but fine buildings from these periods do remain. The matrix of the existing city dates from the Georgian period. In the centre and at the heart of the villages overtaken by the city, the buildings of this period form the nuclei around which later development has taken place. This fabric is dignified, humane, often very modest and more quintessentially 'London' than that of any other period. The Victorians began where the Georgians left off as far as the everyday fabric of the city was concerned, but strayed ever further from grace and good sense as the period progressed. It fell to the Victorians to build the fabric of a modern state. Their record is mixed, with many fine buildings and many whose whole conception seems inherently flawed, even comic. If the taste and good sense of the Victorians can be questioned, no one can doubt their energy and ambition. The legacy of the 20th century is likewise mixed, with much that is wonderful alongside much that looks disastrous. The damage caused by some road, mass housing and retail schemes of the last seventy-five years is a long way from being repaired.

2000 years of growth have presented challenges. Beyond the ceaseless background growing pains there have been specific problems requiring drastic re-orderings. Deficiency of water in the 16th century and foul drainage in the 19th threatened the very viability of the city; contemporary transport and housing provision problems can be seen as equally serious threats. Canals had to be accommodated in the 18th century, trains, drains and gas in the 19th and electricity, motor vehicles and telecommunications in the 20th. The city's economy also drives changes to its fabric. London has been a major industrial power and the world's largest port. Nearly all such activity has now retreated to the fringes of the city and beyond, replaced by knowledge and service industries. One aspect of London's economy that is constant is the central role of trading. The Venerable Bede in the 8th century described London as 'a mart town of many nations'. There is no change there but trading is by nature volatile and fluctuating.

The difficulties presented by London's growth have prompted administrations from the 16th century onwards to try to curb expansion rather than accommodate it. These attempts culminated in the 1950s when the whole city was circumscribed by a 'green belt', in which development was proscribed. In fact the city simply leap-frogged the green belt with towns ever further afield succumbing to dormitory status. 'Protean' is a favoured cliché for describing London; it is suitable insofar as nothing does check the city's expansion or settle its changefulness. London is by turns beautiful and repulsive, exhilarating and grindingly wearing; few cities can pretend to be its equal and few have its wealth and variety of architectural interest.

David Whitehead

"A mart town of many nations" (1)

Venerable Bede, Historian and Monk (*673, †735)

There is evidence of temporary camps in the London area from as early as 13,000 BC. Settlements proper appear around 4,500 BC. Just prior to the Roman incursion in AD 43, the London area was near the intersection of three British proto kingdoms and stood at the periphery rather than the centre of anything. By AD 50 the Romans had recognised the value of London's location at a point where the Thames was both navigable and bridgeable. The settlement they established fulfilled a largely logistical role, supplying the legions of the conquest from its location at the nexus of the river and various routes into Roman Britain.

The city was destroyed by rebelling British tribes in AD 60 and again by fire in the AD 120s. Despite these setbacks the new city generally thrived in its first 300 years. Sometime in the 2nd century the city became the location of the provincial governor's villa and an arch-bishopric, confirming the city as the de facto capital of Roman Britain. Its name, Londinium, was a latinisation of a British place name, its meaning obscure.

The Romans built a bridge, a forum, an amphitheatre, a basilica; all the amenities of a Roman town. Traces of these have been found by archaeologists as building work has uncovered them along with artefacts. The only standing structures are sections of the Roman Wall from about AD 200. The most impressive sections are in the Barbican by St Giles-without-Cripplegate and the Museum of London. The enduring legacy of the wall can be seen on a map of the City; Ludgate, Newgate, Aldersgate, Cripplegate, Bishopsgate and Aldgate are named for gates in the wall and all are where the Romans put them.

Hurried by incursions of Angles, Saxons and Jutes the Romans abandoned Britain in AD 410 when the City declined to the point of total desertion. The East Saxons did establish a settlement they called Lundenwic just to the west of the walled city, around Covent Garden. This was the East Saxon Capital by the early 8th century. King Alfred the Great created a unified Anglo-Saxon kingdom, beat off the Danes and reoccupied the old City in 886. It is known that the Saxons built a cathedral,

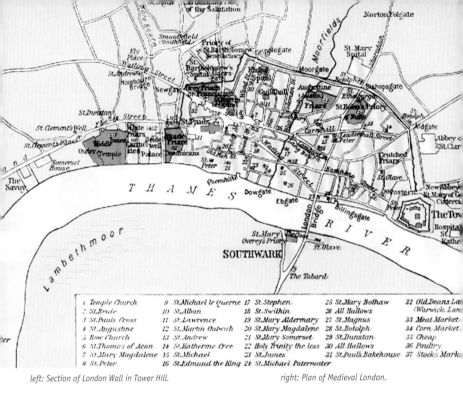

1	Temple Church	9	St.Michael le Querne	17	St.Stephen	25	St.Mary Bothaw	32	Old Deans La
2	St.Bride	10	St.Alban	18	St.Swithin	26	All Hallows		(Warwick Lan
3	St.Pauls Cross	11	St.Lawrence	19	St.Mary Aldermary	27	St.Magnus	33	Meat Market
4	St.Augustine	12	St.Martin Outwich	20	St.Mary Magdalene	28	St.Botolph	34	Corn Market.
5	Bow Church	13	St.Andrew	21	St.Mary Somerset	29	St.Dunstan	35	Cheap
6	St.Thomas of Acon	14	St.Katherine Cree	22	Holy Trinity the less	30	All Hallows	36	Poultry
7	St.Mary Magdalene	15	St.Michael	23	St.James	31	St.Pauls Bakehouse	37	Stocks Mark
8	St.Peter	16	St.Edmund the King	24	St.Michael Paternoster				

left: Section of London Wall in Tower Hill.   *right: Plan of Medieval London.*

9

a bridge, quays and laid out roads, but all that remains of Saxon London are scraps of fabric in All Hallows Barking (no. 21).

The Normans' first capital was at Winchester but it is clear that they valued London, which they immediately fortified with two castles as well as the Tower (no. 3). By 1200 the royal treasury and records were moved to London restoring its de facto capital status. By 1300 many of the features of the City that were to persist for 700 years or more were in place, including St Paul's (no. 2), (Old) London Bridge (no. 8), St Bartholomew's Hospital (no. 94) and Westminster Hall (no. 15) and Abbey (no. 12). The city housed 80,000 souls in mostly wooden buildings on a dense network of streets and alleys interspersed with dozens of parish churches. Outside the city were a scattering of aristocratic houses in extensive grounds; to the south was Southwark with its Priory.

The city bumped along like this for 300 years, its population kept down by repeated outbreaks of the plague. The Great Plague of 1666 was the sixteenth. In 1533 King Henry VIII broke with the papacy starting a series of wars with France and Spain which persisted into the 19th century; wars were also fought in Ireland and Scotland to unite the crown. 1541 saw the dissolution of the monasteries; there were some architectural losses but half of London's land came into more entrepreneurial hands. Whitehall, and St James's Palaces, Christ's and St Thomas' Hospitals are all on monastic lands as were Henry's deer parks that were to eventually became St James's and Hyde Parks.

London's commercial importance increased in step with its naval reach. A new outward looking confidence can be seen in the formation of the joint stock trading companies. The East India Company founded in 1600 was one of many. Increased trade greatly increased aggregate wealth. Clean water shortages were partially addressed by the construction in 1613 of the New River, a canal, between Hertfordshire and Clerkenwell. The construction of a dozen theatres around the outskirts of the City in the late 16th century is indicative not only of increased popular wealth but also a consolidating English speaking culture and Renaissance.

with Inigo Jones, who classicised the nave, transepts, and west façade between 1633 and 1642, and further works were underway when the fire struck in 1666. The damage was so extensive that the decision was made to start afresh, to build a new kind of church for a new world.

Tower of London (3)
1077–1377
Tower Hill, EC3; tube: Tower Hill

There is no doubt that the ogee roof-capped corner towers of the White Tower, the hall keep of the castle, make a delightful picturesque addition to the London skyline and riverscape. Designed as much to defend the ruling elite against the citizenry as to defend London, the tower was started in 1077 and completed by the end of the century. The central tower is surrounded by a double curtain wall. Most of the inner wall was built between 1275 and 1285 and finished along with the outer wall during the following century. All of this has the usual appeal of great masses of masonry but it has been worked over so many times that it now appears almost faked. There are two buildings within the inner ward that are of interest. The Queen's House of 1540 onwards is a pleasant if incongruous array of gabled, half-timbered, black and white Tudor domestic buildings. St Peter ad Vinicula (St Peter in Chains) by William Vertue (1599–1629), is a spare and pleasing Tudor chapel with excellent fittings, its contemporary serenity at odds with its gruesome past.

Old St Paul's Cathedral (2)
1087–1240, 1256–1314
St Paul's Churchyard, EC4; tube: St Paul's

`DEMOLITION` On the site of the existing cathedral the old church itself was a successor to three previous churches dating back to 604; not much is known about these earlier structures. The old church had Norman and Early English elements and was noted in its day for the beauty of its décor and its great size, being 178 metres long, thirty metres wide and thirty metres high internally, with a spire on the crossing tower making the total height 140 metres. It is this size that forms the basis for the enduring image of Old St. Paul's, contemporary images of the city show the City's other churches, houses etc. clustered around its great bulk as if for protection. By the 16th century however, the fabric had been allowed to decay, the spire was lost to lightning in 1561, and puritans and commonwealth forces had caused deliberate damage. Restoration started

Chapel of St John, Tower of London (4)

1077–1100
Tower Hill, EC3; tube: Tower Hill

This Early Norman Chapel is an absolute delight. On the first floor of the south-east corner of the White Tower, seemingly hewn out of a single large chunk of tawny stone, it is heavy and very plain with almost no decoration and consists simply of a short four-bay, barrel-vaulted nave with galleried aisles and a semi-circular apse. Its weight conveys an unchanging permanence, while at the same time exuding a luminosity and sense of the otherworldly.

St Bartholomew the Great (5)
1123
Cloth Fair, EC1;
tube: Barbican/Farringdon

In terms of surviving fabric St Bart's is probably the best contender for the 'oldest church in London' title. What remains is about half of the original medieval Augustinian priory that was attached to the nearby hospital. Almost the whole of the nave was demolished in 1543 after the dissolution of the monasteries, the extent of which can be judged from the remaining 13th-century fragment of the west front which now serves as an entrance way from Smithfield. A Lady Chapel was added to the east end in the 14th century, a brick tower in the 17th, and massive restorations were undertaken by Aston Webb between 1864

and 1928. The external façade is mainly 15th-century Perpendicular restored by Webb and is an amiable enough jumble adorned with picturesque chequered flintwork. Inside, the original Norman choir remains, wonderfully gloomy, atmospheric and fine, the consistency only interrupted by an incongruous but charming Elizabethan oriel window inserted into one of the bays on the south side.

St John's Priory (6)
12th Century
St John's Square, EC1; tube: Farringdon

St John's was the head church of the Knights Hospitallers in Britain. The original church was rebuilt, much reduced and very simply, in the 1720s in the Georgian fashion but utilizing some of the medieval fabric; this in turn was rebuilt and augmented after bomb damage by Seely and Paget (1955–1958). The pleasant undemonstrative neo-Georgian extension forms a new entrance and staircase down to the crypt, all that is left of the original priory and one of very few bits of 12th-century London

11

that remain. It is plain and weighty in the Norman manner though it feels well scrubbed up and not as old as it ought. There is a fine effigy of Juan Ruiz de Vergara, a Spanish proctor of the Knights of St. John.

Today the building functions as the chapel of the Most Venerable Order of St John of Jerusalem, the fanciful Victorian reinvention of the sinister old order as an upper class social club and charity.

St Helen's Bishopsgate (7)
"you owe me ten shillings"
12th Century
Great St Helen, Bishopsgate, EC3; tube: Liverpool Street/Monument/Bank

A Benedictine nunnery was established on this site at the beginning of the 13th century. The chapel for the nunnery was built onto the side of a pre-existing parish church, presumably as some kind of priest-saving exercise, which explains the most unusual arrangement of two naves,

side by side, separated by a screen of arches. Much of the external architecture dates from 1475 and is in a Perpendicular or Tudor style with the tower added later still, although traces of the earlier church can be detected. Certainly it all coheres most picturesquely, especially in juxtaposition with the mammoth structures around it. The interior is plain but light and airy and contains important, interesting funerary monuments and brasses. The building has been recently restored and reordered after suffering damage from two IRA bombings.

Old London Bridge (8)
1176–1209
Fish Street Hill, EC3; tube: Monument

DEMOLITION Immortalised in the children's song, London Bridge may be the most famous London structure. To an extent, London owes its very existence to the bridge, which focused trade and traffic on this part of the river. The first bridge was built by the Romans and followed by several Saxon and Norman attempts, which had a habit of collapsing, until the third Norman bridge eventually achieved some sort of permanence. Much repaired and altered,

it survived until replaced in the 1820s a little to the west. This longevity is surprising given that the bridge was so narrowed by the houses, shops and chapel built atop it that passage could take an hour, and that the obstruction to the flow caused by the 18 piers in the river created a drop so large that 'shooting the bridge' might well be fatal and was usually avoided.

Temple Church (9)
1195–1240
Temple, EC4; tube: Temple

The Temple Church sits hidden within the atmospheric lanes and courts of the Temple. It consists of the circular 'nave' and the rectangular or 'oblong' 'chancel' and originally served as the English headquarters of the Knights Templar. The nave, which is modelled on the Church of the Holy Sepulchre in Jerusalem, dates from 1195 and is in the Romanesque style, while the chancel

was rebuilt in 1240 and shows the development of Early English Gothic. It has repeatedly been the subject of renovations and alterations through the centuries with additions by Sir Christopher Wren in the 17th century removed by Victorians and reinstated after World War II, during which the chapel was damaged. The building contains ten effigies of medieval knights and interesting sculptural decoration around the Norman doorway but no sign of the Holy Grail.

Southwark Cathedral   (10)
1220–1420
London Bridge, SE1; tube: London Bridge

Southwark is neither big enough nor grand enough to be a proper cathedral and was only promoted to this status from an Augustinian priory in 1905 in a doomed attempt to bring some piety to South London. Always quite modest and plain it suffered a series of drastic 19th-century restorations and rebuilding. Perhaps the most blameworthy was Sir Arthur Blomfield, who completely rebuilt the nave at the end of the century in a bloodless mechanical take on the Decorated Gothic of the original. The best of the latter are the 13th-century choir and retrochoir. Southwark's charm lies in its contribution to its jumbled and evocative location; there is something bravely cheerful about the

way the tower, with its chequered flint panels and encrusted be-flagged finials, pokes up into the light through the welter of infrastructure and looming commercial hulks, with which the church is beset.

Lambeth Palace   (11)
1230 onwards
Lambeth Palace Road, SE1;
tube: Lambeth North

The London residence of the Archbishop of Canterbury is strangely isolated for such an important complex of buildings so near the centre of the city. So divorced is it from the public consciousness that references to 'Lambeth Palace' suggest an organisation or concept more than a physical reality. The Early English Chapel and its Crypt of 1230 are the oldest structures, although the Chapel itself had to be rebuilt, not wholly successfully, after the war. The Crypt however is authentically,

13

impressively Gothic in feel. Still more impressive is the 17th-century Great Hall with its mighty hammerbeam roof built in a late Tudor Perpendicular style with just hints of Renaissance detailing, rather late for its date. Extending north and east from the Chapel, the cloisters and ranges incorporate some medieval material, but are mostly Victorian built by Blore (1829–1833). There is a new atrium space between the main building and the Chapel completed in 2000 by Richard Griffiths Architects, mostly glass and entirely modern, very polite but by no means bad. The Palace has a very enjoyable garden, though the bishops gifted much of their land to the people of Lambeth in 1901; this is now Archbishop's Park located to the north of the Palace.

Westminster Abbey (12)

1246 onwards
Henry of Reyns, John of Gloucester, Robert of Beverley

A church has stood on the site of the existing Abbey for nearly a thousand years and has been endlessly subject to rebuilding, repair work and alteration throughout that time – the story is by no means simple. However, the bulk of what can be seen now is Henry III's church by Henry of Reyns (1246–1259), who was followed by John of Gloucester and Robert of Beverley. This was built over Edward the Confessor's earlier church with the aim of creating a shrine to the Confessor and a suitable resting place for Henry. By the time Henry died in 1272, the polygonal apse, transepts, part of the cloisters, the chapter house and nearly half of the nave were completed. The cloisters and the nave were finished during the 14th century in a style unusually respectful of the preceding work. The result is one of the most consistent and homogeneous of the major English churches and certainly the most French, being directly influenced by the cathedrals of Amiens, Reims, Notre Dame and the church of Saint Chapelle in Paris. A prominent manifestation of this influence is its height, which, at thirty-one metres, greatly exceeds that of any other English medieval church. It makes for a striking, slightly exotic presence on the skyline and a strikingly lofty interior. 19th-century clean-up operations have left it feeling a little sanitised in places and perhaps a little too consistent, but it remains impressive nonetheless.

A Lady Chapel was added to the east end by Henry VII in the early 15th century. Robert Janyns and William Vertue are credited with the design. Aisled with four bays and a polygonal chancel, this is an absolute gem of the very English Perpendicular Gothic with extraordinarily rich filigree pendant fan vaulting, massive traceried windows and much rich carving. It has a luminescent and transcendental quality the designers were surely aiming for.

It was only in the 18th century that the will and the money were found to complete the rebuilding with a new west front. By this time the world had changed out of all recognition from that in which the main body of the church had been conceived. Nonetheless, even a designer as headstrong and wayward as Nicholas Hawksmoor felt compelled to be polite and try to fit in. Constructed between 1735 and 1745, the west front is variously described as the first significant Gothic Revival building in England, or as the very last gasp of the old tradition. The former seems most likely because, fine as it is it lacks the authentic Gothic spirit.

The Abbey is the venue for the crowning of British monarchs and has become the burial place for many of the early ones as well as a Valhalla for British 'greats', particularly writers, but also scientists, soldiers, statesmen and the man who invented the postage stamp.

Stained Glass Window from the 18th century.

Westminster Abbey, West front.

St Olave Hart Street   (13)
1270 onwards
Hart St./Seething Lane, EC3;
tube: Tower Hill

This church is an engaging and atmospheric Gothic survivor crammed into a tiny site in the heart of the city. The earliest of the visible fabric is from the 13th century but the overall appearance is mid 15th-century Perpendicular. The vaguely classical tower is from 1732 and designed by John Widdows, whilst the Curvilinear Decorated east window is probably from the 19th century, during which the church received the attentions of both Scott and Blomfield. Considerable rebuilding was required after war damage during the 1950s. Cramped though it is, it still manages a lovely little yard with a sinister skull-bedecked gateway. Diarist Samuel Pepys is buried at the church.

St Etheldreda   (14)
Late 13th Century
Ely Place, EC1; tube: Chancery Lane

St Etheldreda's was originally built to serve as the Chapel of the Bishop of Ely's London palace. It is unusually dedicated to an Anglo-Saxon saint and one-time Abbess of Ely. The palace itself was finally demolished in 1772. The chapel had a chequered history after being relinquished by the bishop in the 16th century, serving variously as a Chapel to the Spanish ambassador, hospital, prison, tavern and Welsh church until, finally, it was bought by the Rosiminian order, making it one of very few medieval churches to find its way back into the hands of English Catholics. The cloister-like entrance passage and the timber-roofed unaisled upper chapel are simple attractive spaces; the crypt below is plain and was substantially altered in the 19th century.

Westminster Hall   (15)
1394–1401
Palace of Westminster, St. Margaret Street, SW1; tube: Westminster

The Palace of Westminster was originally, from the 13th century, a royal palace. The first parliament, with very limited powers, met there in 1295. The Hall was part of the palace, first completed in 1099. The masons for the 14th-century remodelled Hall were Henry Yevele and Walter Walton and the carpenter was

16

Hugh Herland. It served principally as a court with some additional ceremonial uses and has the largest surviving medieval hammerbeam roof, which, at nearly twenty-one metres in span and seventy-three metres in length, is truly magnificent. Even so, externally the Hall is dwarfed by the Victorian parliament building, its simple, direct Perpendicular architecture a mute reproach to the Victorian crocheting frenzy looming above. St Stephen's Cloister and the Chapel of St Mary Undercroft are the other surviving medieval elements in the current palace. The very plain Jewel Tower nearby on Abingdon Street was also a part of the original palace and now houses an exhibition about Parliament.

Guildhall   (16)
1411–1429
Guildhall Yard, EC2;
tube: St. Pauls/Bank/Moorgate
John Croxton, Horace Jones,
Giles Gilbert Scott

At the centre of this complex is John Croxton's great Perpendicular hall, a massive, most impressive space and at forty-six metres long and more than fifteen metres wide second in size only to Westminster Hall. The gables are almost fully occupied by Perpendicular traceried windows. It is not known for sure what form Croxton's roof took since this was damaged by the fire of 1666 and rebuilt with hammerbeams and a flat soffit. These were replicated by Sir Horace Jones in the 1860s, who, like many Victorian architects, felt that Gothic buildings were not Gothic enough, a failing which they were only happy to correct. To this end Jones added the crocheted finials and the flèche to the outside. Jones' roof structure was destroyed in the war and replaced by Giles Gilbert Scott with a series of transverse stone arches connected by flat arches over a clerestory, which may or may not emulate Croxton's original, but certainly works well. Also impressive internally are the east and west vaulted crypts, the former by Croxton and the latter a remnant from an earlier Guildhall of the late 13th, early 14th centuries. The south façade of the hall is dominated by a deep four-storey 'porch' added by George Dance the younger (1788–1789) in a bizarre 'Hindoostani Gothic' style; 240 years later it still looks strange and weak. Unfortunately, this alien aesthetic seems to have been the inspiration for 20th century additions to the historic Guildhall Yard. Robert Gilbert Scott's library and offices with its Flash Gordon styling and upturned concrete pyramid mushroom-columned cloister might well make you laugh. The bulky and incoherent art gallery completed in 1999 will surely not.

17

Inns of Court (17)

15th Century

Gray's Inn.

ENSEMBLE The four Inns of Court occupy an almost uninterrupted swathe of land to the west of the City between the river and Bloomsbury. The earliest extant records of them are of 1422, though it is thought they predate this. Probably lodging houses for barristers originally, they became responsible for legal education in England and Wales, a function removed in 1852. Today they are professional associations, of which every barrister must be a member. Their physical form is a series of chambers (offices) along with a hall, a chapel and a library. The most interesting buildings are noted separately (nos. 20, 31, 36), but the general urban landscape of the courts is charming and even if many of the individual buildings are of no great interest, they are a pleasure to wander around. The layout is still medieval with lots of little courts and passages, which are all very expensively maintained, monopoly having its own rewards of course. The Inns are, it has been noted, most reminiscent of the public schools and Oxbridge colleges, in which the bulk of their tenants were educated.

19

Middle Temple Hall.

left: Lincoln's Inn, New Hall and Library.

Crosby Hall (18)
1466–1475
Cheyne Walk, SW3;
tube: South Kensington

The Hall was first constructed for Sir John Crosby as the centrepiece of his courtyard house in the City on Bishopsgate. The rest of the house was demolished in the 17th century and the Hall was set to follow in 1910 when it was salvaged by Walter Godfrey and Patrick Geddes, who dismantled it and rebuilt it on the river at Chelsea. Mostly it is as it was, although the stone facings, dormers and entrance are from 1910. These Elizabethan magnates certainly did themselves proud; the Hall is twenty-one metres by eight metres on plan and high with an elaborate pendented arched timber roof and beautiful vaulted oriel window. The Hall was originally re-erected as a dining hall for a women's university hostel and in the 1990s it was incorporated into a very convincing but far too 'clean' neo-Tudor private house.

Eltham Palace, Great Hall (19)
1475–1480
Court Yard, SE9;
train: Eltham (from London Bridge)

All that remains of a 14th-century royal palace is the Great Hall; the Palace fell out of favour in the 16th century and was mostly demolished in the middle of the 17th. The Hall served as a barn for some time and was deteriorating badly until antiquarians 'rescued' it in the 19th century. It was fully restored and incorporated into a rich man's house in the 1930s. The Hall, thirty metres by eleven metres, is very plain from the outside with six large bays and pairs of simple, high level Tudor windows in the five easternmost bays. The last bay has deep projecting bay windows with full height glazing. Inside is a large and refined hammerbeam roof with pendants, perhaps the third largest in the UK. The bay windows are vaulted with a lot of rib showing. The dais and panelling and the 'minstrel's gallery' are from the 1930s by Seely and Paget. The original mason is thought to have been Thomas Jordan and the carpenter Edmund Graveley.

Lincoln's Inn Old Hall (20)
1489–1492
New Square, Lincolns Inn, WC2;
tube: Holborn

Not as grand as the Temple Hall but still a noble structure, Lincoln's Inn Old Hall has high level mullioned Tudor windows over panelled walls with full height bay windows at both ends and the roof is arched, braced roof beams with collars. The exterior is in stone-dressed diapered brickwork with crenellated parapet walls and (what look like) Victorian Gothic pinnacles.

20

All Hallows Barking (by-the-Tower)
(21)

15th Century
Great Tower Street, EC3; tube: Tower Hill

Very obviously not in Barking the Church is named for; it is in fact named for its mother church, Barking Abbey, which established this London outpost in the 11th century. Some fragments of this original Saxon church and a Roman pavement can be seen within, making All Hallows another contender for the oldest church in London. If making sense of the rest of it presents difficulties it probably should, for the church has an unusual history. The aisle walls are the most straightforward – 15th-century Perpendicular – but the clerestories in the style of the aisle windows are from the rebuilding of 1949–1957 by Seely and Paget. Most of the interior dates from that time when it was boldly treated to 1950s late Gothic arcades supporting a vaulted concrete roof. Further adding to the assortment of styles, the 17th-century tower is topped by a fantastic baroque copper spire from the 1950s, while the north-west perpendicular porch is by Pearson (1884–1895). It all works surprisingly well. Inside there is a jaw dropping carved font cover by Grinling Gibbons and a small, quite interesting museum in the excavated undercroft.

Barnard's Inn (22)
15th Century
Holborn, EC1; tube: Chancery Lane

This Inn is an absurd survival but most charming, almost like a village hall. Ground floor brick walls support the first floor, which is a continuously glazed timber frame supporting the steeply pitched tiled roof topped by a lantern; it is all very simple and pretty. Originally attached to the Inns of Chancery it passed to Gray's Inn and became a school hall (1894–1959). It is now in the hands of Gresham College, a long-established educational institution that stages free public lectures at the Inn.

Fulham Palace (23)
1480
Bishop's Avenue, SW6;
tube: Putney Bridge

This fairly modest domestic palace was the 'country' residence of the Bishop of London from the 11th century until 1975. The house is formed of two courtyards. The western courtyard is from the late 15th, early 16th centuries and includes a much altered medieval Great Hall and other reception rooms. The eastern, Georgian courtyard was built in the 18th century by Stiff Leadbeater and contains further reception rooms and bedrooms. A chapel by Butterfield was added in the 1860s. It is all executed in brickwork, diapered to the west courtyard and chapel. All is pleasant but unexceptional; of greater appeal are the 18th and 19th-century landscaped gardens by the Thames. They are not in the best condition but still very enjoyable.

The house and gardens are currently undergoing extensive renovations.

St Margaret's, Westminster (24)
1482–1523
Parliament Square, SW1;
tube: Westminster
Robert Stowell, Henry Redman

The 'parish church of the House of Commons' inevitably looks a little redundant in the shadow of its mighty sister; the Abbey however was very much a royal church and it is no surprise, given some of the history, that the Parliamentarians wanted a church of their own. St Margaret's is a substantial and handsome late Perpendicular parish church in its own right. It was designed by masons Robert Stowell and Henry Redman, who also worked on the Abbey. The tower was substantially remodelled in the 1730s by John James. Like most such Gothic architecture of the period it looks a bit thin or at least not properly Gothic. The chaste timber-roofed interior is illuminated by large windows with good examples of stained glass from various periods.

St Giles Cripplegate (25)
1545
Lakeside Terrace, Barbican, EC2;
tube: Barbican/Moorgate

The current church was totally rebuilt in a Perpendicular style after an earlier 14th-century church was destroyed by fire in 1545. It is thought that the new church was built on the foundations of its predecessor as there is some stonework from the earlier church still visible in the chancel walls and the base of the tower. The topmost brick section of the tower was added in the late 17th century. Further repairs were required after a fire in 1897 and it was eventually necessary to rebuild the whole structure after the church was gutted in the Blitz. Not surprisingly after this unlucky history, it now has a somewhat scrubbed-up appearance. It sits very nicely, if a little surreally, in the central public space of the 1960s Barbican development.

Chelsea Old Church (All Saints) (26)
13th and 14th Centuries, 1667–1674
Church Street, SW3;
tube: South Kensington

All Saints is very happily located on a bend in the river in an upmarket residential backwater. The chancel dates from the 13th century and the chapels from the 14th while the nave and tower were rebuilt in the 17th century in brick. Lawrence Chapel, to the north, was owned by Chelsea's Lord of the Manor and the one to the south was rebuilt in 1528 as Sir Thomas More's private chapel. The church was heavily bombed during the war and painstakingly rebuilt by Walter Godfrey (1949-1958). The effort to retain this wonderfully atmospheric old country church, now overtaken by the city, was surely worth it. The church contains interesting early Renaissance carved column capitals and a good number of worthwhile monuments, including one erected by St Thomas More for his wife. The Lord Chancellor, scholar and martyr, intended to be buried here himself, Henry VIII had a different idea! There is a small public garden to the west of the church containing a sculpture by Jacob Epstein and a memorial plaque to the author Henry James, who lived nearby on Cheyne Walk.

23

Henry of Reyns
†1253 (27)

Medieval master masons are elusive; it is rarely possible to match the names that we know with the portraits that we have. Beyond their job title, their job description can only be conjectured at. Master Henry even lacks a nationality, since no one knows if 'Reyns' is Raynes in Essex or Reims in France. Frustratingly, what they lack above all is a voice; there is no personal account explaining why they did what they did the way that they did. That they had their own ideas is clear from the continuous evolution of the Gothic style over time and across

space; ideas were borrowed and adapted, new things continually attempted.

The Gothic is identifiable by the use of pointed arches and vaults rather than Romanesque round headed ones. It was brought to England from France by William of Sens at Canterbury Cathedral around 1174. The impetus for the change can be seen as both aesthetic – it is more graceful and dynamic – and practical – a pointed form allows units of differing widths to be joined while keeping the arches' apexes and springing points at a constant level. This allows for far greater flexibility in plan and section forms.

Early Gothic works are in the Early English style characterised by simple, undivided, pointed headed 'lancet' windows and simple four part ribbed groin vaults. From the middle of the 13th century, this developed into Decorated, involving larger windows subdivided with tracery and more complex vaulting. The Decorated period is usually subdivided into the Geometrical and the Curvilinear. The former employs tracery based on circles of part circles and the latter swirling return curves reminiscent of vegetal or leaf forms. The final phase of Gothic, unique to Britain, is Perpendicular. The windows get bigger still, to the point where interiors feel like stone lanterns or cages, with flatter arches allowing for much simpler tracery at the head; the ceilings become fan vaults where the ribs have multiplied but are much smaller resembling a tracery of fine twigs. Two buildings in London illustrate these phases. The Temple Church's (no. 9) western circular section is Romanesque or Norman and the eastern rectangular section is Early English. Westminster Abbey (no. 12) is largely Geometrical while Henry VII's Lady Chapel is assuredly Perpendicular. A Curvilinear window can be seen in the east end of St Olave's Hart Street (no. 13).

Tracing the development of Gothic hints at their creator's aspirations. The overall progression is clearly in the direction of more lightness, both in terms of more window and less stone and in terms of dividing the stone into smaller units to lessen its visual weight. There is also a clear progression of structural achievement; vaults became bigger and higher as the style matured. These trends in the direction of dematerialisation towards the ethereal and celestial have suggested that in some way the builders of the cathedrals sought to represent the Kingdom of Heaven on earth; they certainly did not lack ambition.

More is known about the way the masons worked than the way they thought. The mason and client had to agree a design and a price. Some drawings and models which could have formed the basis of this agreement have survived and it is reasonable to assume others have been lost; a prospecitve client, who had to be very wealthy, would surely want a good idea about what was to be build for so much outlay. Once agreement was reached the mason was responsible for obtaining the materials and directing the work of all the other craftsmen. Craftsmen did have some scope for individual expression but only within the context of the agreed design. Large works involving so many hands required strong direction if chaos and disaster are to be avoided; the fact that the master mason paid the wages of the rest no doubt helped with discipline. Direction was given via drawings and full sized templates, some of which survive.

The masons moved from job to job but, given short lives, long apprenticeships and slow building, they would not have worked on many buildings in a career. Master Henry is thought to have worked on Binham Priory and Clifford's Tower in York. He is known to have been at Westminster Abbey (no. 12) from 1246 and was succeeded by a John of Gloucester in 1253. The Abbey's Choir, transepts, Chapter House and the east end of the nave were built on Henry's watch. One of the few things we know for sure about him is that we have a lot to be grateful to him for.

left: Medieval Masons.

bottom: Interior of Henry VII's Chapel, Westminster Abbey by Giovanni Canaletto, 1753

St Andrew Undershaft (28)
1520–1532
St Mary Axe, EC3;
tube: Liverpool Street/Aldgate

A very fortunate survivor of fire, the Blitz, terrorism and development, St Andrew Undershaft is a good-sized, if plain, six-bay aisled Perpendicular church. The tower is 15th-century with a final storey added in 1695; it stands in the south-west corner allowing the clerestory to run the length of the nave. Inside, the nave has a shallow timber soffit divided by ribs into square panels with gold painted bosses. The church's unusual name derives from a maypole that was erected annually nearby until a firebrand preacher persuaded his puritan congregation to destroy this pagan relict in 1547; the church is now very much 'Under Gherkin'.

St. James's Palace (29)
1531–1540
Cleveland Row, SW1; tube: Green Park

St. James's Palace remains the official residence of the British royal family and foreign ambassadors are still attached to the 'Court of St. James's'. It was probably never intended for such a grand role,

however, and has not actually been used for this function since the 18th century. It was built by Henry VIII on the site of a female leper colony and only used as a royal palace after Whitehall Palace burnt down in 1698. It is a meandering piecemeal affair now. The principle Tudor survivors are the diapered brick gatehouse with its half octagonal corner towers (the clock and cupola are later additions) and the adjacent chapel, a simple hall with high Tudor windows and ornate Italianesque ceiling.

Charterhouse (30)
1545–1564
Charterhouse Square, EC1; tube: Barbican

A Carthusian monastery originally stood on this site (1371-1414). Following its demolition after the dissolution of the monasteries, only fragments remain, but the site has maintained the name ever since. A manor house was constructed over the latter half of the 16th century, which was converted two centuries later into a charitable founda-

tion, Suttons Hospital, housing eighty pensioners and forty boys; the school moved out in 1872. Seely and Paget were in charge of rebuilding in the 1950s after extensive war damage. The complex presents a most picturesque, medieval appearance to the Square. Beyond the outer gatehouse with its 15th-century arch and the Victorian porter's lodge an archway leads through a much altered and heavily rebuilt 16th-century wing into the Masters Courtyard. Herein lies the 16th-century Great Hall with two large Tudor mullioned windows, a full height bay window at the east end and high level, flat topped windows between the arching members of the hammer-beam roof. To the west of the Masters Courtyard lies Washhouse Court, which was originally the service court built in the 16th century and includes a nice mix of things. To the north are the Pensioners' and Preacher's Courts where the residents have their rooms. Originally built by Pilkington and Blore in the mid 19th century in a neo-Tudor style, some of these were destroyed in the war and finally replaced in 2000 with two blocks by Michael Hopkins and Partners in brick and oak after Louis Kahn.

Middle Temple Hall (31)
1562–1570
New Court, Middle Temple, EC4;
tube: Temple

Constructed as a meeting and dining hall for the members of the Middle Temple, a school of law at that time and today a monopolistic barristers association,

the Hall is still used for its original purpose. The exterior, set amongst attractive courtyards, is handsome with stone dressed brick walls with chequered buttressing and crenellated parapets. The steeply pitched slate roof is topped with a Gothic louvre by Hakewill (1826). The interior is much more than handsome; thirty metres long, twelve metres wide, and eighteen metres high, it has seven bays well-lit by plain mullioned windows. Across the entrance end is a very fine Elizabethan carved timber screen. Above all this is a fantastic and spectacular double hammerbeam oak roof, a complex three-dimensional fantasy of arches and pendents. The creator of this wonder was carpenter John Lewis.

Staple Inn (32)
1586
Holborn, EC1; tube: Chancery Lane

Like Barnard's Inn, this building was connected with the Inns of Chancery and later Gray's Inn. Also like Barnard's Inn, it is a surprising survivor – a row of half-timbered black and white Elizabethan houses. There are three jettied storeys plus attic rooms in the seven gables with numerous oriel windows below. Although it has been subject to much intervention and alteration, it is the most authentic remnant of the fabric of Elizabethan London. An archway leads to a largely 18th-century brick Georgian courtyard of three storeys plus dormered attics. At the end of the courtyard is the 16th-century hall with its elaborate hammerbeam roof and 18th-century Gothick door cases.

Charlton House is a substantial three-storey Jacobean house in brick with stone dressings. The plan is 'H'-shaped and the ends of the wings have large mullioned bay windows while the central entrance bay is very highly wrought. There are tiny towers with ogee roofs in the middle of the outside wall of each wing for extra picturesque effect. Inside, the central connecting block is dominated by a great hall. There are fireplaces, staircases and plasterwork ceilings. The pleasant grounds have stables from the period, a pretty summerhouse with a convex 'Chinese' roof and a very old mulberry tree. The summerhouse is sometimes attributed to Inigo Jones.

Holland House (33)
1605–1614
Holland Park, W14; tube: Holland Park/
High Street Kensington
John Thorpe, Casson Condor

All that is left of a very substantial rambling Jacobean house, designed in part by John Thorpe for Sir Walter Cope, is the west wing and most of the south façade. The rest of the house sustained heavy damage in the war and was demolished in 1957. What is left, with its stone dressed brick gables and mullioned windows, is charmingly characteristic of the period. The House now serves as a youth hostel; the charmless 1950s extension is by Casson Condor.

Charlton House (34)
1607–1612
Charlton Road, SE7;
train: Charlton (from London Bridge)
John Thorpe

Inner Temple Gateway (35)
1610–1611
Fleet Street, EC4; tube: Temple

28

These Jacobean half-timbered black and white houses are almost unique survivors in the city. The façade is elaborately carved with canted oriels on the first and second floors, the latter jettied a little beyond the former, with two rendered gables behind a timber balustrade on the floor above. The ground floor was recessed somewhat when the building was refurbished by London County Council in the early 20th century; this exaggerates the jettying but the fabric is of the time. The extensions to the rear are by the council in the Arts and Crafts manner. The archway leads to the enchanted world of the Temple.

Lincoln's Inn Chapel (36)
1619–1623
Old Square, Lincolns Inn, WC2;
tube: Holborn

The rebuilding of an earlier chapel destroyed by fire was undertaken at the beginning of the 17th century. It seems the members of the Inn knowingly elected to have what, by this time, was an old-fashioned design, which would harmonise with the rest of the Inn's fabric. So the style of the chapel is the Perpendicular of around 1520; such an anachronism might have appeared strange at the time but it matters little now. Samuel Salter added an additional bay and some ancillary accommodation in 1882 and he also designed the timber roof. The body of the Chapel is raised up over an open undercroft supported by massive stone columns and heavily ribbed vaulting. This is the highlight of the design and is strangely reminiscent of a forest of oak in an Arts and Crafts tapestry or an Art Nouveau book illustration.

St Katharine Cree (37)
"maids in white aprons"
1628–1631
Leadenhall Street, EC3;
tube: Liverpool Street/Aldgate

St Katherine's is both interesting and a little unsettling. The first church on the site was started in 1280 by the prior of the adjacent priory known as Christ Church. ('Cree' is understood to be a corruption of 'Christ Church'.) The tower, to which a pedimented door and cupola were added in 1776, is the only surviving part of the earlier church and dates from 1504. The church's strangeness comes from the peculiar melding of styles attempted or stumbled upon. Externally, the aisle windows are late Tudor Perpendicular in a somewhat classicised surround while the west window (boarded-up) is pedimented, albeit most feebly. Inside, the nave and aisles have flat ribbed vaults in the Tudor manner, but they are supported by partially Ionic corbel brackets and two rows of Corinthian columns carrying round keystoned arches. It is by no means ugly but it is strange and uncouth. What interests is pondering the meaning of this incoherent melange of motifs for its creators; what unsettles is the sense of people having dropped the threads of the past without yet understanding the future.

CHAMBERS & PARTNERS

HERMÈS   HERMÈS   HERMÈS

"A much more beautiful city than is at this time consumed." (38)

Charles II, Monarch (*1630, †1685)

The man who brought the architecture of the Renaissance to London had his roots in the theatre business; Inigo Jones designed the scenery and costumes for royal masques. He had also spent seven years in Italy acquainting himself with classical and Renaissance architecture and was most impressed by the work of Andrea Palladio. With contacts at court and a good knowledge of classicism, Jones was well placed to revolutionise English architecture, which he did with three small commissions for King Charles I: the Queen's House (no. 39), the Banqueting House at the Palace of Whitehall (no. 40) and the Queen's Chapel (no. 41). The clean spare forms, the chaste regimented decoration and the sheer whiteness must have seemed like something from another world to the majority of Londoners. After the Civil War and Interregnum (1641–1669) the impact of these buildings was immense, and enduring.

That these buildings should have startled and impressed is unsurprising but that they should cause the abandonment of a 500-year-old tradition and completely upset the course of architecture needs some explanation. Firstly, the general tenor of Renaissance thought vaunted classical ideas above medieval superstition and classical architecture therefore benefited from the thrill of the new and the authority of the ages. Secondly, its origin and supporters – the Continent and the Royal Family – were both viewed as glamorous authorities on artistic matters. Practical and economic factors also played their part. To a modern eye classical buildings might appear ornate and highly wrought but compared to the intense richness and detail of a Perpendicular Gothic structure they are the soul of simplicity, repetition and reason. A classical building requiring less labour would certainly be quicker and cheaper than an equivalent Perpendicular one; circumstances arose such that London had a great need for quicker and cheaper.

It is to be hoped that London never suffers two more years like 1665 and 1666; the first saw the outbreak of the Great Plague which killed 100,000, a fifth of the population. Just as the outbreak was subsiding, the city was

Great Fire of London by Unknown Dutch Artist, 1666.

devastated by the Great Fire. Flames swallowed four fifths of the area inside the old city walls. As many as 200,000 people were displaced and, along with many other buildings, 13,200 houses, eighty-seven churches, forty-four livery company halls and St Paul's Cathedral were gutted. London lost a large proportion of its shelter as well as all its commercial and manufacturing heart. If the twin scourges of flame and disease were not enough, the country was at war with the Netherlands.

The city had to be rebuilt both quickly and better. Wren, Robert Hooke and John Evelyn were amongst many who submitted plans to this end. Most plans envisaged a Baroque axial city of wide straight streets radiating from important nodes. Desirable as such a rational new city might be, it required all property to be surrendered and plots reallocated on some as yet unknown formula and disputes arising from any such procedure would be time-consuming. Time was lacking so the city was rebuilt on the old street plan. The 1667 Rebuilding Act did however regulate the heights of buildings in relation to the size of street and prescribed fire proof materials (brick or stone) for the external walls.

The housing was mostly rebuilt, plot by plot, before the end of 1673. As the King's surveyor, the rebuilding of the cathedral, the lost churches and the Custom House fell to Wren. He was supported by a talented office, but most of the designing is believed to have been done by Wren himself. Before 1700 the office built fifty-one new City churches, of which twenty-four remain, as well as the magnificent new cathedral (no. 65).

The rebuilding of the city consumed the bulk of the available building capacity in this period. Resources were found however for major new buildings for the navy at Greenwich (no. 44) and the army in Chelsea (no. 64) and Woolwich (no. 84). In the Monument (no. 50) and the Royal Observatory (no. 56), Wren and Hooke designed the first two buildings dedicated to scientific research in Britain. Further churches were built outside the City in the new suburbs including six by Hawksmoor, two each by Gibbs and Thomas Archer and one from Wren.

The Queen's House (39)
1617–1637
Romney Road, Greenwich Park, SE10;
train and DLR: Greenwich
Inigo Jones

The Queen's House was started as a home for Queen Anne of Denmark, whose husband James I was happy enough by this point to see her living separately. Construction stopped for ten years upon the queen's death in 1619. Charles I finished it for his queen and it eventually became the home of the Ranger of Greenwich Park and later part of the Naval College. It is now part of the National Maritime Museum. Jones' house consisted of two parallel two-storey blocks connected by a central bridge at the upper level. Two further bridges with screen walls below were added by Jones' son-in-law, John Webb, in 1662 and the colonnades and outer wings were added by Daniel Asher Alexander in the early 1800s. The house is seven bays, rendered with a parapet; it is white, serene, studied, well-proportioned and to the modern eye unexceptional. To understand its pivotal, iconic place in British architectural history, it is necessary to try to imagine seeing a building with these qualities for the first time. An unimaginable future had just arrived.

Banqueting House (40)
1619–1622
Whitehall, SW1;
tube: Westminster/Charing Cross
Inigo Jones

The Banqueting House brought Jones' Palladian revolution into the City of London proper; again, to the vast majority of citizens who had never been to Italy, it would have seemed entirely unprecedented, alien and presumably very exciting. The basic elements are the same as the Queen's House (no. 39); a cool, plain, well-proportioned rectangle of white stone, some of which is detailed in a distinctly Palladian fashion. There appear externally to be two high storeys over a basement. In fact the upper storeys are one large volume with only a small upper gallery on three sides. Originally this great double cube room, used for banquets, receptions, masques and so on, was accessed by external wooden stairs. The current staircase on the north side was added very respectfully by James Wyatt (1808–1809). The huge and elaborate panelled ceiling inside is adorned with a series of famous canvasses by Rubens, painted between 1630 and 1634.

Queen's Chapel (41)
1623–1625
Marlborough Street, SW1;
tube: Green Park
Inigo Jones

Constructed for a putative Spanish Catholic wife for Charles I, the chapel was later used by foreign Protestants at the court before returning to Royal Chapel status in 1938. Externally the building is very modest; a rendered pedimented rectangular box with very simple details, it could almost pass for a domestic structure. Inside is another Jonesian revolution – a simple double cube space with a gold and white painted, coffered, elliptical ceiling. The large windows with their clear glass flood the interior with light, creating an atmosphere of calm and clarity. Clearly this is a very different sort of church from its Gothic predecessors, for a very different form of worship and worldview.

St. Paul's, Covent Garden (42)
1631–1635
Covent Garden Piazza, WC2;
tube: Covent Garden
Inigo Jones

The church was the focus of a new urban square, the centrepiece of a residential development by the Earl of Bedford. Like all developers since, the Earl was nervous about his architect's money burning potential and instructed Jones that he was only looking for a church like a barn. Jones retorted that he would build the 'handsomest barn in England'. The simple pedimented rectangular volume is in fact somewhat barn-like, but it is also handsome with a forceful primitive simplicity. The great Etruscan/Tuscan pediment does not contain the entrance but only a focus and sheltering place for the square; Eliza Dolittle famously waited out a storm there. The true entrance is at the other end via a charming garden. Little of the interior is as Jones left it but it is pleasant enough.

Eltham Lodge (43)
1664
Court Road, SE9;
train: Eltham/Mottingham
Hugh May

The Lodge is a well-preserved example of a gentleman's home of the period. Hugh May was an influential designer who has been unlucky in that so few of his works have survived; his client in this instance was Sir John Shaw, a powerful banker at the court of Charles II. The two-storey house is of seven bays in brick with limited stone dressings. The entrance elevation has double height Ionic pilasters under a pediment with swags. Inside, the rooms are elegant with fine stairs, ceilings and fireplaces. The house is now the clubhouse of the Royal Blackheath Golf Club, which promotes itself as the oldest golf club in the world and has a small museum on the upper floor.

Royal Naval Hospital (44)

1699–1752
Christopher Wren

The current buildings were started as a Royal Palace for Charles I and the King Charles block (designed by John Webb in the 1860s) was the first third of an intended three-sided courtyard facing the river. Predominantly two-storey with attics at the ends, it is in stone with rustication, attached Corinthian pilasters and a central pediment; it is large without being impressive. The house, however, was never fitted out during Charles' reign, and his successors, William and Mary, did not wish to live there. It was decided that this would be the site of a hospital for the Royal Navy, an institution of growing national importance. Wren eventually settled on an arrangement of four blocks disposed symmetrically around the axis between the Queen's House and the river with the existing block forming the core of the north-west block, which is mirrored in the Queen Anne block opposite. The two southern blocks (named after King William and Queen Mary) step in somewhat and are open three-sided courtyards with the fourth side, adjacent to the axis, formed with Tuscan colonnades. At the northern inward ends of these are raised domes marking the locations of

the principle rooms, the Painted Hall and the Chapel. These blocks, while similar to the earlier pair, have a lighter, less stolid feel, there is less rustication and areas of render have been introduced for economy. The more eccentric elevations to the west range of the King William block are generally credited to Wren's assistant Hawksmoor and they are certainly not typical of Wren. The interiors are quite plain apart from the Hall and the Chapel. The double height Painted Hall with its giant Corinthian pilasters and columns and Baroque painted ceiling by James Thornhill (1708-1712) is very grand indeed. The Chapel was badly damaged by fire and splendidly rebuilt in the late 18th century by 'Athenian' Stuart, in the neo-Greek style current at that time, with a shallow segmental vault and narrow cantilevered galleries.

The overall feel of the place is light and graceful, despite the mighty masses involved, and the riverside location certainly adds to the architectural charms. In 1869 the hospital moved out and the Naval College moved in and in recent times the buildings have been given over to civilian educational institutions.

View from North bank of Thames.

Royal Naval Hospital, Greenwich, Painted Hall.

Temple Bar   (45)
1670–1672
St Paul's Churchyard, EC4;
tube: St Paul's
Christopher Wren (?)

`DEMOLITION` It was and is the policy of the City of London Corporation to mark the entry points to the City proper; these days the chosen marker is a metal casting of a Gryphon, the heraldic symbol of the City. At the west end of Fleet Street in front of the Royal Courts of Justice is a particularly fine, spiky Gryphon rampant on a carved pedestal. This is the site of Temple Bar at which some kind of gate had stood since the 14th century; the Renaissance gate was an elaborate carved stone archway with three narrow passages and a room over the central passage under a segmental pediment. It is traditionally ascribed to Wren, though with little certainty. By 1878 the narrowness of the passages was proving a nuisance to traffic and, amid much controversy, the gate was dismantled. The pieces were bought by the wealthy brewer Henry Meux and re-erected as the gateway to his house in Hertfordshire. In 2004 the developers of Paternoster Square, by St Paul's, no doubt realising that their gorilla needed some lipstick, paid for the monument's relocation back to the City to act as a gateway to the new Square.

St Mary-at-Hill   (46)
1670–1674
Lovat Lane/Mary at Hill, EC3;
tube: Monument
Christopher Wren

A church has stood on this site since the 12th century. Thomas Tallis, the Early English composer, was the organist in the late 1530s. After the fire, Wren incorporated much fabric, unseen, of the earlier church, and further alterations have taken place in the 18th and 19th centuries. The church is enclosed on all sides in one of the most atmospheric parts of the City, and the tiny courtyard is approached along crooked little alleys. The little that can be seen of the exterior is of only minor interest though some charm. The equally charming interior has the form of a Byzantine chapel with a central coffered dome on four freestanding Corinthian-ish columns with four near equal barrel vaulted arms intersecting with the dome, the areas between the arms have lower flat soffits.

St Mary-Le-Bow   (47)
"I'm sure I don't know"
1670–1680
Cheapside, EC2;
tube: Mansion House/St Paul's/Bank
Christopher Wren

On the site of a church since pre-conquest times, Wren's post-fire reconstruction is notable chiefly for its tower and spire erected at almost the cost of the rest of the church. At sixty-eight metres it is second only to St Bride in height but not in magnificence; the base of the tower is a vestibule to the entrance with a wonderful stone vault. Of the rest of the church only the plain walls, brick with stone trimmings, survived the war and the church was reconstructed to Wren's design by Lawrence King between 1956 and 1964. The barrel-vaulted nave is separated from the aisles by piers with attached half Corinthian columns, while the aisles are vaulted transversely. Below the Wren church are the much-altered remains of an 11th-century Norman crypt with vaulting and columns with crude Norman capitals; it feels much more recent than it ought to.

The criterion for being a proper Cockney is to be born within the sound of Bow Bells and it was these same bells that persuaded Dick Whittington to 'turn again'.

day processional route around the precincts of St Paul's. Paternoster Row was at the beginning of the route, where the first words of the Our Father in Latin would be spoken, and the final 'Amen' would be said by the time the procession reached the corner of the 'U'-shaped court, which houses the canon's living quarters. The gate at the south entrance and Nos. 1–3 date from the 17th century.

The houses have five bays of two storeys over a semi-basement and with dormers. The façades typical of post-fire houses are in red brick with white painted windows and black ironwork. Further houses in a Queen Anne style were added at Nos. 4–9 by Ewan Christian (1878–1880). The massive brick wall to the rear of the houses is said to be a bulky fragment of Newgate Prison; there is reason to doubt this, but if it is not the prison, then what is it?

The College of Arms (49)
1671–1673 and 1682–1688
Queen Victoria Street, EC4;
tube: Blackfriars/Mansion House
Maurice Emmett and Francis Sandford

A most extraordinary, picturesque building for a most extraordinary, picturesque institution. The College of Arms is a branch of the royal household concerned with heraldry and genealogy, and its officers, who rejoice in names such as 'Bluemantle Pursuivant of Arms in Ordinary', are paid miniscule salaries by the state. They earn a living, however, designing and registering coats of arms for individuals and organisations and doing genealogical research. Founded

Amen Court (48)
1671–1673
Amen Court, off Ave Maria Lane, EC4;
tube: St Paul's
Edward Woodruffe

Amen Court, with Amen Corner at one end, takes its name from a Corpus Christi

39

in 1484, they were made homeless by the fire, but, crucially, the records were saved. They built the central block first and the wings ten years later. The building is three storeys over a semi-basement with dormers and lots of chimneys above. The materials are red brick, clay tile and white painted timber window; unlearned attempts to add some classical dignity with Ionic pilasters with garlanded capitals and strange diamond lozenges add to the fun. Originally the building was in the form of an almost complete courtyard but the building of the regrettable Queen Victoria Street swept away the south block necessitating the remodelling of the stumps of the east and west ranges in the 1860s and left the college a little stranded. The wonderful iron gates and screen came from Goodrich House in Hertfordshire and date from the 1870s. The interiors, particularly the Court Room (the entrance hall) and the Victorian Record Room, both double height, are no less picturesque than the exterior.

The Monument to the Great Fire of London (50)
1671–1676
Monument Street, EC3; tube: Monument
Robert Hooke and Christopher Wren

At more than sixty-one metres, the Monument remains the tallest free standing stone column in the world. Erected to commemorate the Great Fire and the rebuilding of the city in its aftermath, it is sited just over sixty metres from the site of the fire's origin in Pudding Lane. Built in Portland stone it is a single fluted Doric column on a raised sculpted base; at the top is a viewing platform crowned

with a domed cylinder, which has a gilt copper flaming urn and a ball at the apex. Inside there is a helical staircase with 311 steps to the viewing platform and a further thirty-four steps up into the urn. The various inscriptions on the pedestal used to include references to the 'treachery and malice of the popish faction' – this was removed in the reign of James II but re-inscribed under William and Mary! It was finally removed in 1830. Hooke and Wren designed the Monument to be of use in various scientific experiments involving gravity and pendulums, while the shaft itself could act as a zenith telescope. A recent refurbishment has seen a 360° panoramic camera installed, which updates every minute.

The Old Deanery (51)
1670–1672
Deans Court, EC4; tube: St Paul's
Edward Woodruffe and John Oliver

There are very few domestic buildings in the city from any period so a very large 17th-century survivor is of great interest. Set behind a brick wall with massive gate piers topped by pineapples, the cobbled entrance yard with its ancient plane trees has a rural feel. It is seven bays wide and two storeys tall over a semi basement with dormers in the tiled roof. The redbrick façade with painted timber windows is plain but handsome with a definite Dutch feel. The building

next door in Carter Lane, the former St Paul's Choir School by Penrose (now a youth hostel), with its sgraffito panels, is also interesting, as are the little courts leading south of Carter Lane.

St Bride, Fleet Street (52)
1671–1678
Bride Lane, off Fleet Street, EC4;
tube: Blackfriars
Christopher Wren

Tightly encircled by commercial buildings St Bride nevertheless makes its presence felt with its slightly odd but charming wedding cake spire, which, at sixty-nine metres, is the tallest of Wren's spires and keeps appearing on the skyline. The stone church is of five bays with round-headed windows, circular in the easternmost bay. Inside, the nave is separated from the aisles by awkward-looking, double Tuscan columns carrying arches, above which is a segmental vault scalloped out for the oval clerestory windows; the aisles are also barrel-vaulted. The galleries were not reinstated in the post-war restoration by Godfrey Allen and, instead, there is a classical timber screen with stalls. St Bride is sometimes known as "the Journalists' Church" because of its proximity to Fleet Street. The journalists, who were well known for their piety, have long since been scattered to the four winds by the newspaper printing revolution of the 1980s.

St Lawrence Jewry (53)
1671–1680
Guildhall Yard, off Gresham Street, EC2;
tube: Bank/St. Paul's
Christopher Wren

A big stone box on an island site, St Lawrence is larger and grander than most of the City churches and closes off the south side of the Guildhall Yard. It was originally a normal parish church, but is now the church of the Corporation of the City of London. A little heavy and lugubrious it fits its new use rather nicely. The highlight is the very grand east façade, Corinthian of five bays with lots of festoonery. The north and south elevations have round arched windows with segmental arched clerestories above. Internally, the church is asymmetrical with an aisle on the north side separated from the nave with a row of Corinthian columns and a timber screen; there are attached pilasters on the opposite wall. The church was badly damaged in 1940 and restored by Cecil Brown in the 1950s.

Inigo Jones
*1573 in London, †1652 in London (54)

Jones was a Londoner, christened in St Bartholomew-the-Less (no. 94) in 1573 and buried at St Benet Paul's Wharf (no. 61) in 1652; his monument there perished in the Great Fire. However, he did leave London for trips abroad which were to be of crucial import for his career and the historical direction of British architecture.

There is some mystery about Jones' early career; he was apprenticed at fourteen to a carpenter, was working as a picture maker by the time he was thirty and two years later was designing a masque for Queen Anne. How did a man with a humble background get himself into such elevated and free spending company? What he offered was unrivalled knowledge of Italian design acquired in a six-year stay at the turn of the century, although how he financed this trip is unknown. We do know that he studied Roman and contemporary Italian architecture and design and read the important Italian authors on these subjects, including Vitruvius, Serlio and Palladio as well as the Frenchman de l'Orme.

With this knowledge he lent an air

of continental sophistication and learning to the elaborate, expensive Court masques. Jones was employed to design sets and costumes and to devise the special effects, set changes and so on. Crucially this brought Jones into close contact with the Royal Family and other powerful members of the court. Two of his earliest architectural designs for a top piece for St Paul's central tower and an Exchange building on the Strand were for the Lord Treasurer, the Earl of Salisbury.

Through this closeness with the Court, Jones was appointed Surveyor of the King's Works to King James I in 1613, a post that varied greatly depending on the reigning monarch. A non-building monarch wanted nothing more than a glorified maintenance manager but a ruler of a building temperament had more ambitious expectations. James I and Charles I were of this temperament. Jones began with a series of minor works on the King's estates, including a stable, a buttery and a brew-house, none of which survive but which were good training for Jones who was still architecturally callow. Between 1616 and 1625 came three larger and higher profile projects which introduced the architectural Renaissance to Britain; the Queen's House (no. 39), Queen's Chapel (no. 41) and the Banqueting House (no. 40).

These three pristine white buildings must have shocked and impressed most observers with their newness and otherness, although they are restrained and rational. Within the broad field of Italian architecture, Jones was not uncritical and favoured the work of the Roman originals and that of neoclassicists, especially Palladio. He thought good architecture was 'solid, proportionable according to the rules, masculine and unaffected', which of course rules out Baroque and Mannerism. This spirit has arguably been part of the British architectural psyche ever since, which has had little appetite for ornate, less masculine continental styles like Roccoco or Art Nouveau.

Such has been the influence and veneration of Jones that the buildings are often overlooked. What remain are perfectly reasonable designs in the restrained sensible manner to which Jones aspired. Although they are enjoyable, it is hard to see where any alleged brilliance in these buildings might lie. Certainly if they had been built in Italy it is hard to imagine them standing out as worthy of special interest. Perhaps enthusiasm for Jones' architecture is more a moral position than an architectural one.

His best surviving building is the Church of St Paul's, Covent Garden (no. 42), built for a private client some years after the more celebrated royal jobs. The Earl of Bedford owned land between the City proper and Westminster and wanted to develop some of it as a speculation. This was the first use of the method that was to be the means of London's development over the coming years. The Earl required a licence from the King who imposed a layout and his architect as a condition of the licence. The plan was for houses and a church arranged around a square or piazza. Jones' sketched designs for the arcaded housing were executed by others and these are now long gone, although the replacements still follow Jones' basic format. The church itself was built to Jones' cheerful and forceful design, which foreshadows 18th-century French neoclassicists in its elemental simplicity. Some evidence, then, that Jones was not of only local significance.

St Paul's Cathedral, Design for West front, 1608.

St Stephen Walbrook (55)
1672–1677
Walbrook, EC4;
tube: Bank/Cannon Street
Christopher Wren

Recognised at the time as the pick of Wren's City churches, St Stephen is modest enough from the outside, squeezed into a cramped site. Its simple stone tower, which is off-centre, was given a steeple in the early 18th century, possibly by Hawksmoor. The glory of the church is its interior where Wren combined a Greek cross plan with domed central crossing and an aisled nave to great effect. The dome is carried on eight Corinthian columns with four more making the corners of the square that contains the octagon beneath the dome; this arrangement is seen as a precursor to that of St Paul's. The overall effect is surprisingly complex but lucid and calm. The altar by Henry Moore, a great lump of a thing, was controversial on installation and understandably so, since, centred under the dome, it interrupts the space horribly. Also in the church is a phone in a glass box commemorating the founding of the Samaritans, which was started in the crypt.

Old Royal Observatory (56)
1675–1676
Blackheath Avenue, Greenwich Park,
SE10; train and DLR: Greenwich
Robert Hooke and Christopher Wren

Built by King Charles II as a space for John Flamsteed, the first Astronomer Royal, in which to live and work, the Observatory was the first building dedicated to research in the British Isles. It is fabulously located – on top of the hill at Greenwich – and is quite small with modest living quarters topped by the Octagon Room. This is where Flamstead worked and received guests; six of its eight sides have large tall windows under a high vaulted ceiling and the views are fabulous. It is surely one of London's most romantic and evocative rooms; Wren understood the romance of the programme and designed accordingly. The turreted octagonal tower attached to little pavilions by screen walls across a terrace is definitely a romantic composition reminiscent of a diminutive Elizabethan prodigy house. The materials are blue and red brick with white painted trimmings and windows, while the exposed roofs are clad in zinc.

There are a number of other interesting buildings at the observatory site, fascinating exhibits and, of course, the meridian line.

George Inn (57)
1676
*George Inn Yard, off Borough High
Street, SE1;*
tube: Borough/London Bridge

Hidden away in one of a series of little
yards off to the east of Borough High
Street is the remains of London's only
surviving galleried coaching inn, built
after the Southwark Fire of 1676. In
fact, only half of the Inn still survives,
as the northern range was demolished
in 1889. However, it still provides a good
idea of what such places were like. Three
storeys, timber framed, and rendered
with open timber galleries, it presents
a suitably ramshackle appearance now.

The long thin plan allows for a rambling
series of pleasant bar interiors. Next-
door was the even older Tabard Inn,
from which the pilgrims set out in the
Canterbury Tales.

St James's, Piccadilly (58)
1676–1684
Piccadilly, SW1; tube: Piccadilly Circus
Christopher Wren

Built to serve the expanding suburb of
St James's, the church was one of Wren's
personal favourites. The exterior is quite
plain in red brick with Portland stone
dressings. Albert Richardson added the
copper spire, which was not built to Wren's

design, along with the copper roof after
war damage (1947–1954). The interior is
very fine in a relaxed and confident way.
The nave is barrel-vaulted with transverse
vaults over the bays of the galleries, which
are supported on square pillars with Corinthian columns above to the ceiling. Wren

thought that a maximum congregation of
2000 could be accommodated, if all were
to see and hear clearly, and that he had
arranged this in the most efficient way
in this church. The virtuoso altarpiece
carvings are by Grinling Gibbons as is
the font.

St James Garlickhythe (59)
1676–1682
Garlick Hill, EC4; tube: Mansion House
Christopher Wren

'Hythe' is an old word for 'landing' and the church is situated by an old Thames landing site that handled garlic amongst other things. There has been a church on the site since the 12th century, presumably a large one, since St James is one of the bigger of Wren's City church rebuildings. Originally, there was a building attached to the south side but this was removed for the hopeless road widening scheme of 1973, which has left the church stranded and exposed. The exterior is plain except for the fancy baroque spire added in the 18th century and, as with St Stephen Walbrook, it is thought Hawksmoor might have had a hand in this. Internally, the church is roomy and lit so well from the many windows that the church is sometimes described as 'Wren's lantern'.

St Martin, Ludgate (60)
"you owe me five farthings"
1677–1687
Ludgate Hill, EC4;
tube: Blackfriars/St Paul's
Christopher Wren

The restrained stone façade of St Martin sits flush with the line of the street terrace, of which it is just one more unit. Its spiky, lead clad spire makes a fine, deliberate, contrast with the bulbous forms of nearby St Paul's at the end of the street. There are references to a church here as early as 677, though references from the 12th century are more reliable. The church is centralised with a cross within a square formed by four Corinthian columns supporting intersecting barrel vaults. To the south on the street side is a narthex with a gallery above, which is formed, like much of the interior, in high quality, dark woodwork.

St Benet Paul's Wharf (61)
1678–1684
Bennets Hill, EC4;
tube: Blackfriars/Mansion House
Robert Hooke

St Benet was infamously treated by 1970s road engineers, who left it isolated and beset. This regrettable stranding has served, very effectively, to hide the church's considerable charm. A simple brick box with stone cornice, quoins, strings and swags, it has a distinctly Dutch and countrified feel. The tower is

topped with a lead-covered dome with urn, and the galleried, flat soffited interior has a similarly simple rural feel to it. Inigo Jones was buried here before the fire in 1652. The church currently serves Welsh-speaking City types as well as the College of Arms (no. 49) located just over the unspeakable road.

St Clement Danes (62)
"oranges and lemons"
1680–1682
The Strand, WC2; tube: Temple
Christopher Wren

St Clement is the patron saint of mariners and this church was reputedly dedicated by 12th-century Danish merchants who settled in the vicinity. Rebuilt by Wren after the fire, the tower was completed in 1670 and the spire added by Gibbs fifty years later. The interior was substantially rebuilt after the war. If the exterior fails to take advantage of its island site, in com-

parison to the nearby St Mary-Le-Strand (no. 90), that may be because the site was not an island at the time of building but tightly constrained; these constraints were also the reason for the odd east end arrangement. The galleried vaulted interior in dark wood, painted plaster and gold is very fine. Since the rebuilding, the church has been closely associated with the Royal Air Force.

St Mary Abchurch   (63)
1681–1686
Abchurch Lane, EC4;
tube: Cannon Street
Christopher Wren

If nearby St Stephen Walbrook is the grandest of Wren's City churches then this must be one of the sweetest. The church and its stony little piazza are crammed atmospherically into the tightest of sites. The building is a simple brick box with limestone dressings and a

hipped tiled roof. The tower in the north-west corner ends in a square-based, lead-clad, ogee domed lantern and spire. Inside, the square volume of the church is covered with a hemispherical dome, pierced with four oval dormers and carried on eight arches spanning between Corinthian brackets with a pilaster and column on the south-west side. There is a tremendous intensity and atmosphere in this small space. The dome was painted with a brown-tinged vision of heaven in 1708 by William Stone. The church contains much 17th-century woodwork of the highest quality, culminating in Grinling Gibbons' super altarpiece.

The Royal Hospital Chelsea   (64)
1682–1691
Royal Hospital Road, SW3;
tube: Sloane Square
Christopher Wren

The Royal Hospital was founded by Charles II for invalided soldiers of the relatively new standing army. Three storeys plus dormers in warm red brick with stone dressings and Tuscan porticos, it is arranged around three courtyards, each open on one side with the central courtyard opening up to the river. The feel is Dutch with a definite whiff of the barrack about it, plain and homely in an institutional sort of way. The Chapel, which is quite grand, and the spartan hall are accessed from the octagonal domed vestibule beneath the cupola in the central, Figure Court. Also on the site are a range of characteristically interesting stables by Soane (1819).

St Paul's Cathedral (65)

1675–1711
Christopher Wren

The cathedral's great dome and west front are visible from all over London and are a wonderful adornment to the city's skyline. These views are now officially protected from many directions and are very often the only obstacle to the maniacal arrogance and greed of the 'development community'. For this alone, the citizens of London are greatly indebted to Wren. Wren received the commission to replace the burnt-out old church (no. 2) when he was thirty-seven, and he was seventy-nine before it was completed – a fantastic feat of endurance in the face of continual interference from the state and the Church.

The plan is that of a traditional Gothic cathedral with nave, chancel, aisles and transepts, although Wren's preference was for a more centralised Greek cross plan with a dominating central dome on the pattern of Renaissance churches he had seen in Paris. Early designs are on this basis but Wren was obliged to strike a compromise with the traditionally minded clergy and the result, like most such compromises, is not entirely satisfactory. The chancel and the nave both have three bays, the latter with an extra wider bay at the west end under the towers. The aisles of the chancel, nave and transepts all have saucer domes at a lower level than the pendentive domes of the main volumes. The crossing is surmounted by the great dome, and to maximise its impact Wren expanded it to the full width of the church, including the aisles. This necessitates the aisles meeting the crossing through arches at 45° to the main axes of the plan, a contrivance that, whether awkward or ingenious, served Wren's ends by creating a centralised focal space and maximising the dominance of the main dome. The dome has triple skins with a ceiling of plastered brickwork under a hidden brick cone, which supports the timberwork of the outer dome and the lantern on top.

Externally, the walls are of Portland stone with Composite columns and pilasters to the upper levels and Corinthian below. The west façade, with its two-storied pedimented porch of paired columns and intricate baroque towers, closes the end of Ludgate Hill wonderfully. Controversy has always surrounded the walling, which consists of two storeys with segmentally arched windows at the lower level and blind pedimented windows above. The whole upper storey is in fact blind and does not therefore express the true nature of the structure. Purists have criticised this arrangement, which detracts from the pleasure of understanding the building. It is hard to believe Wren was truly satisfied but he was no doubt well schooled in the necessity of compromise in resolving such a complex project.

Internally, the sheer scale of the space enclosed cannot fail to impress; it is characteristically cool and restrained, predominately white and grey with much fine carving and many interesting monuments and paintings.

Whatever faults can be found, it is unquestionably the greatest post-Renaissance church constructed in the British Isles. Nothing of comparable ambition was even attempted until Liverpool's pair of cathedrals in the early years of the 20th century, only one of these went the full distance.

View from south east.

St Paul's Cathedral, dome.

Kensington Palace (66)
1689–1695
Kensington Gardens, W8;
tube: High Street Kensington
Christopher Wren

The original house on this site was in the countryside when it was built around 1605, possibly by John Thorpe; nothing of this can now be seen. William and Mary bought the house in 1689 as a place to escape the City. Wren reordered and extended it, and it has been added to and adapted so often that it is difficult to know who did what and when. Overall the appearance is modest for a 'palace', being mostly red brick and slate with white painted sashes and occasional bits of stone dressing. The grandest section is the King's Gallery on the south side, built to house William's collection of pictures; it has eleven bays with giant Doric pilasters in the centre. William Kent was employed by George I to make alterations in the 1720s.

Fenton House (67)
1693
Hampstead Grove, NW3;
tube: Hampstead

In the heart of Hampstead village, Fenton House is a most attractive merchant's house of the late 17th century, its location reflecting that people of wealth in this period wished to and were able to live outside the city in which they made their living. Square on plan and of five bays, the building has two storeys with a basement and attic dormers. It is built

of brown brick with red rubbed brick dressings, steeply pitched clay tile roofs and white painted wooden windows. The entrance was originally on the south side, which has a pediment over three bays and a simple Doric door case. The east side has the central bays recessed; a single-storey Doric loggia was added here in the early 19th century when this became the entry side. The interiors are domestic and pleasant and there is a beautiful walled garden.

Morden College (68)
1695
Morden Road, SE3; tube: Blackheath
Christopher Wren

Not in fact a college but a set of almshouses, Morden College was built for 'decayed Turkey merchants' by John Morden, an 'un-decayed' Turkey merchant. Arranged around a courtyard, the building has two storeys in red brick with rendered quoins and dressings, and steep pitched tile roofs. The

west, entrance, front has projecting end bays and a five-bay pediment; there are statues of the founder and his wife over the door case and a cupola above. The Chapel, opposite the entrance across the courtyard, is a simple and elegant rectangle with a segmental vaulted ceiling. The courtyard has a single-storey Tuscan arcade. The college still serves its original purpose. The Wren attribution is not certain.

St Vedast-alias-Foster (69)
1695–1701
Foster Lane, EC2; tube: St Paul's
Christopher Wren

It turns out that Foster is an absurd Anglicisation of the name of the French Saint Vedast, whose cult spread into England in the 12th century, during which the original church was probably built. The Portland stone facades of the new church with round headed windows under segmental headed upper lights are not entirely easy. The spire, a fantastic Baroque creation, was added later (1709–1712) and is one of the tallest in the City; authorship is seemingly uncertain though it is usually credited to Wren. The interior is plain with a flat ceiling and a Tuscan arcade to a single aisle south of the nave. The colonnaded yard is particularly attractive with a hall from 1691 and a post-war rectory by Dykes Bowyer (1960), making for a charming group.

Bevis Marks Spanish and Portuguese Synagogue (70)
1699–1701
Heneage Lane, off Bevis Marks, EC3;
tube: Liverpool Street/Aldgate
Joseph Avis

Built by a community of Iberian Jews living in the City, Bevis Marks is the oldest extant synagogue in the UK. It replaced an earlier structure of 1656 in Creechurch Lane. The law at the time did not permit the building of a synagogue on a public high road, hence the secluded location. Outside, it is an unassuming brick box with two levels of windows, reflecting the gallery within. They are round-headed on the upper storey, segmental below, and clear glazed. The pleasant airy interior is purportedly based on the Great Synagogue of Amsterdam. There are galleries on three sides

with a lattice-like balustrade supported by wooden Tuscan columns. Seven great brass chandeliers occupy the central space and on the un-galleried wall is a carved two-storey Ark containing the scrolls of the Torah. It is said that the carpenter/designer waived his fee or profit for the job in a demonstration of interfaith goodwill and that Queen Anne donated one of the beams for the roof. Perhaps its most famous worshipper was Benjamin Disraeli, novelist and Prime Minister, who fell out with the congregation over an unpaid fine!

St Andrew Holborn   (71)
1684–1686
Holborn Viaduct, EC1;
tube: Chancery Lane
Christopher Wren

The largest of the Wren City churches sits on an island site, a little isolated. There are records of a church here from the 10th century and although the church actually survived the fire, it was so dilapidated that Wren was set to rebuild it. All that remained of the original structure was the tower, which was refaced by Wren, 1703-1704; some of the detailing of this is sufficiently eccentric for Hawksmoor to get the credit. Otherwise the church consists of a big stone box with seven bays of tall round-headed windows over smaller segmental windows or pedimented doors at the ends, and a large Venetian window in the west wall. Inside, there are gal-

leried aisles with Corinthian arcades; the nave is barrel-vaulted and the aisles groin vaulted. After the war, the interior was rebuilt identical to its former self. The adjacent Victorian Gothic rectory and other buildings are by Samuel Teulon (1868-1871).

Orangery   (72)
1704–1705
The Broad Walk, Kensington Gardens, W8;
tube: Queensway
Nicholas Hawksmoor

An orangery was a fashionable addition to a garden in the early 18th century and was used to protect delicate plants through the winter. This one for Queen Anne is usually ascribed to Hawksmoor working in Wren's office, although Vanburgh allegedly had some input. It is essentially a long, thin, single-storey, redbrick shed with large white painted windows. It is though an exceptionally well-detailed and well-built shed. The central entrance has blocked columns under a stone entablature, while the end rooms, which are expressed as pavilions, have a central window flanked by niches and powerful gables. Internally, the central room has Corinthian columns on the garden side and swags over the openings to the end 'pavilions' with niches either side. The whole is both muscular and refined and now in use as a restaurant.

Bluecoat (or Blewcoat) School (73)
1709
Caxton Street, SW1;
tube: St James's Park

An interesting and evocative little remnant hidden among the ugly giants of Victoria. Bluecoat schools were charitable organizations for the education of poor children and, in this instance, brewer William Greene built a single schoolroom to teach pupils how to 'read, write, cast accounts and the catechism'. The pupils wore blue coats since these were generally the cheapest available. It is a tiny red brick box with white painted windows and has three bays on each side with the middle bays projecting slightly and giant Doric pilasters at the corners. The entrance has a stone surround with a statue of a 'Blewcoat Boy' in a niche above and a clock in a broken pediment above that. The building is now a National Trust shop.

Marlborough House (74)
Pall Mall, SW1; tube: Green Park
Christopher Wren

In gratitude for his victories on the continent, the Duke of Marlborough received two houses from the state: Blenheim Palace in Oxfordshire and this house next to St James's Palace. The Duchess did not approve of architectural grandeur but wanted something 'strong, plain and convenient', and, as far as a palace can be plain, she got what she wanted. Contemporary illustrations show a two-storey, thirteen-bay house with the middle seven bays recessed slightly on both the north and the south sides. The materials are brick with a modest amount of stone dressing; altogether unexceptional but pleasant. Since then, the proportions have been spoilt by a new single-storey north wing added by James Pennethorne (1860–1862) and an extra floor added in 1870 by John Taylor. The interiors have been similarly altered, although the main space of the Wren house, the double-height Saloon, is largely intact. The house reverted to the Royal Family in 1817 and has been used as a residence for various royals, an Art School and, since 1953, it has been the home of the Commonwealth Secretariat.

53

Christopher Wren
*1632 in East Knoyle, Wiltshire, †1723 in London (75)

Reviewing Wren's life must give most people a queasy feeling of inadequacy; even allowing for his ninety years the quantity of achievement is extraordinary. He oversaw the reconstruction of fifty-one City churches, designing the bulk of them; he designed and supervised the construction of St Paul's Cathedral, the Royal Hospitals at Greenwich and Chelsea (no.64), major re-orderings and extensions at Kensington (no. 66) and Hampton Court Palaces, numerous college buildings in Oxford and Cambridge, a library for Lincoln Cathedral, St James, Piccadilly, the Royal Observatory and the Monument (no. 50). This list is not exhaustive and omits masses of minor works done in his role as Surveyor to the King. Beyond architecture he was a respected mathematician and natural scientist, served in Parliament, helped found and led the Royal Society, undertook various business ventures and married three times. Clearly he was a man of exceptional energy.

The sheer quantity of Wren's work has led to speculation about authorship. He was not alone in the office of the King's

Surveyor and some of his assistants were men of talent and energy, most famously Robert Hooke, Nicholas Hawksmoor and latterly John Vanburgh. There were others and much responsibility was divested in a band of trusted craftsmen. Wren's assistants must have contributed much, however the later work of Hawksmoor and Vanburgh is so very individual and characteristic that it is clear any work done by them in Wren's office was strongly directed. Hooke is a more difficult case; St Benet, Paul's Wharf is attributed to him yet it is most Wren-like. It is probable that, to get all the work done, a mode of team working evolved in which all could contribute within an agreed framework, the main points of which were set by Wren.

Wren was born in Wiltshire, 1632, to a comfortable Royalist family, an affinity that impaired his public career until the restoration of 1660. He was educated at Wadham College, Oxford where he attracted notice as a gifted mathematician and natural scientist. In those times the field of enquiry for a natural scientist was wide and included, in Wren's case, an interest in engineering and architectural matters. Wren's first design was the charismatic Chapel at Pembroke College, Cambridge, in 1665. At around the same time he was involved in the design of the Sheldonian Theatre in Oxford. While not entirely successful as a piece of architecture, the theatre is functionally and structurally far more complex than the chapel and marked a real achievement for its young designer.

These buildings and his reputation as a Royalist man of talent were enough for Charles II to appoint Wren King's Surveyor. In normal circumstances this post might present opportunities, particularly under a new regime anxious to make its mark, but the Great Fire brought a tidal wave of opportunity for a man fit to make the most of it. Rebuilding the City churches was an extraordinary undertaking; Wren had to design the same building fifty-one times. That the churches never appear repetitive or tired is a tribute to Wren's inventive resourcefulness. The plans are particularly interesting

since the sites were often very tight or oddly shaped; Wren had to show great ingenuity to achieve lucid and functional spaces. The steeples also demonstrate a sustained creativity. They all serve the same purpose and have a familial resemblance but each one is interesting and different. It is impossible to imagine the City skyline without spires like St Mary-Le-Bow (no. 47) and St Bride, Fleet Street (no. 52). The best of the churches such as St Stephen Walbrook (no. 55) and St Mary Abchurch (no. 63) are very fine indeed; the least of them are still worthwhile. Wren's own favourite was St James's, Piccadilly (no. 58).

Of his other great works, St Paul's Cathedral (no. 65) is the most imposing, the Royal Naval Hospital at Greenwich (no. 44) the most suavely assured and the Royal Observatory (no. 56) the most romantic. Wren's work is cool, rational and lucid but compared, say, to Hawksmoor, it can seem to lack romance and intensity. This is probably a matter of taste as much as anything else and it is surely futile to seek the very qualities an artist lacks in any work of art. Far more sensible is to appreciate what they can offer and few have offered more to London then Wren.

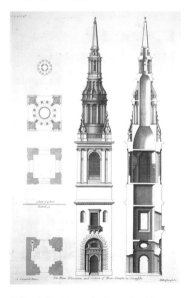

St Mary-le-Bow, Tower elevation and section.

St Alfege, Greenwich (76)
1711–1714
Greenwich High Road, SE10;
train and DLR: Greenwich
Nicholas Hawksmoor

St John's, Smith Square (77)
1613–1628
Smith Square, SW1;
tube: Westminster/St James's Park
Thomas Archer

Reputedly, a church has stood here on the site of St Alfege's martyrdom since that unhappy day in the year 1012. The current church was constructed after its predecessor collapsed in 1710 with money obtained under the Fifty New Churches Act of 1711. The stone exterior is dominated by a full width pediment at the east end, the lower part of which is broken to admit an archway over a porch; this has a powerful Roman feel. The north and south elevations have giant Doric pilasters with two levels of windows that are generally arched, although some are square. All of this weight and force is somewhat diminished by a tower and steeple added by John James at the west end in a much fussier politer style (1730). The interior has a flat soffit that seems to be supported by arches from Corinthian brackets over the north and south galleries; there is a small vaulted chancel.

St John's was the most expensive of the Fifty Churches. Although it is certainly large and, being located in the middle of a square, it has no hidden side where cheaper materials or a simpler treatment could be used, you have to suspect that sheer extravagance played a significant part in its price. Like Archer's other designs, the church is much closer to continental Baroque than any other British work. The form is of a Greek cross with quarter cylinders in the corners; the north and south arms terminate in a broken pediment on a massive Doric arcade between two towers, which terminate with ogee lanterns topped with pineapples. The east and west arms of the cross have giant Doric pilasters and a large Venetian window. The overall effect is rich and wilful and it seems much too big for the square. St John's has always been controversial in Britain, where such architectural extravagance is unusual. The church was burnt out in 1941 and restored as a concert hall by Marshall Sisson in the 1960s. The interior is plainer with galleries behind giant Corinthian columns supporting vaulted ceilings.

St Paul's, Deptford (78)
1713–1730
Deptford High Street, SE8;
train: Deptford, DLR: Deptford Bridge
Thomas Archer

Another of the Fifty New Churches. St Paul's, a full blooded, muscular and very fine exercise in Roman Baroque, seems an extraordinary and moving thing to find in this neglected corner of south-east London. All in stone, there is a circular tower at the west end sitting very neatly on a larger semi-circular Tuscan portico approached by a generous set of radiating steps. The north and south elevations are of five bays with round-headed windows between heavily blocked Doric pilasters; the three centre bays are pedimented with a central doorway and more extravagant but entirely redundant steps. At the west end is a semi-circular apse with a Venetian window. Inside, the plan is highly centralised with only the protruding apse as a concession to east-west liturgical orientation. There are galleries behind Corinthian columns, which form a space within the space. The soffits are flat but heavily modulated.

Christ Church Spitalfields (79)
1714–1729
Commercial Street, E1;
tube: Liverpool Street/Aldgate East
Nicholas Hawksmoor

The mighty tower and stone spire at the west end of Christ Church dominate the low streets of this atmospheric part of the East End and terminate Brushfield Street magnificently. Like much of Hawksmoor's work, it is both original and strange but it is done with such conviction that it seems it must be right. The rest of the exterior is very plain with round and round-headed windows punched starkly into the white stone; the east elevation is especially tough looking. Inside, there are galleries under transverse barrel vaults carried on Composite arcades with clerestories above to a flat soffit over the nave. The church was mutilated in the 19th century and later allowed to decline to the extent that closure was necessary in 1958. Even those who admired its romantic wreckage will have to admit that the recently completed renovations have remade the most gorgeous building. Whitfield and Partners and Purcell Miller Tritton were responsible for these works from 1976 onwards.

St George in the East (80)
1714–1729
Cannon Street Road, E1;
tube and DLR: Shadwell
Nicholas Hawksmoor

No less odd and original than Christ Church (no. 79), St George is not quite

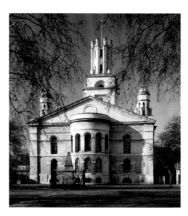

as dominating. There is a rectangular west tower topped with an open octagonal steeple. The stone detailing is plain and angular and the windows on the north and south façades are round-headed. Four stair towers topped with elongated open lanterns with cupolas create a picturesque effect. There is a small semi-circular apse, and the north and south galleries inside were behind giant Corinthian columns. The church was gutted in May 1941 when the roof and interior were entirely ripped out. After the war, the decision was made to build a new, smaller church inside the walls of the old, incorporating all of the aisles and part of the nave and leaving a courtyard space within the walls behind the tower. This very plain and contemporary church by Ansell and Bailey works quite well but, looking at Hawksmoor's surviving churches, it is impossible not to wonder about what is lost.

St Anne's, Limehouse (81)
1714–1730
Commercial Road, E14;
train and DLR: Limehouse
Nicholas Hawksmoor

The third of Hawksmoor's East End churches, St Anne's is the least strange. The rectangular west tower has an octagonal spire formed with stone piers; the tower's clocks were intended to be visible from the river. The entrance is an apsidal projection with Doric pilasters and a half dome roof. The tower bay stands proud

on the north and south sides and has an attic storey as does the last bay in the east. The north and south façades are very plain with round-headed above square windows with segmental-headed windows to the high crypt. There is a small rectangular chancel projection to the east. The interior was restored in the 19th century by Philip Hardwick, who was reputedly faithful to the original. There are galleries on three sides supported on Corinthian columns and pillars.

St Mary Woolnoth (82)
1716–1727
King William Street, EC3; tube: Bank
Nicholas Hawksmoor

Crammed onto a very tight corner site, St Mary Woolnoth broods over the City's most important junction like some mythical armoured beast, eternally ready to strike. The west tower is nearly the full width of the church and quite shallow. Its lower section with the entrance and window above has Tuscan columns in the corners and the whole is very heavily and frequently rusticated. Above are three bays with attached composite columns with two turrets on top. The north façade is blind, in order to block out noise from Threadneedle Street, and has three heavily modelled and rusticated Baroque niches. The south side has five bays with round-headed windows, only four of which light the hall of the church.

The façades are so different because there was only a narrow alley to the south at the time of construction. At the end of the 19th century a ticket hall was constructed underneath the church and partially in its crypt. The railway company had had permission to demolish the church but retreated after protests. The lower screen wall on King William Street was also built at this time. The interior is square with an inner square defined by twelve Corinthian columns, bunched into the corners, supporting a clerestorey with four large lunettes. The narrow galleries were removed in the 1870s and must surely be reinstated. Even mutilated it is a very powerful and intense space.

St George's Bloomsbury (83)
1716–1731
Bloomsbury Way, WC1;
tube: Tottenham Court Road/Holborn
Nicholas Hawksmoor

Like Christ Church (no. 79), St George's has just seen the completion of a triumphant restoration, by Molyneux Kerr (2002–2008). The site is very cramped and the main street frontage is to the south while the liturgical constraints demanded an altar at the east end. Hawksmoor overcame these difficulties by making a giant five-bay Corinthian portico to the street at the top of a great flight of steps; this was only a ceremo-

nial entrance and today serves as the finest bus stop seating in the city. The real entrance is at the base of the tower, which is placed to the west of the body of the church. On entering, the altar is

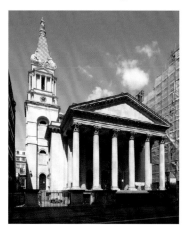

clearly visible in its arched apsidal niche in the east. The tower is a fabulous creation capped with a stepped pyramidal spire sporting a statue of George I and pairs of lions and unicorns, the whole supposedly based on Pliny's description of the mausoleum of Halicarnassus. The north elevation is five bays under a pediment with round-headed windows between Corinthian plasters at the lower level and attached columns above, solid and serene. The interior has galleries behind arched Corinthian screens and Hawksmoor's trademark flat panelled soffit over a high clerestory. The little passage to the west of the church is a delightful, grimy short cut.

Royal Arsenal, Woolwich (84)
1717–1720
No.1 Street, off Beresford Street, SE18;
train: Woolwich Arsenal
John Vanburgh

Woolwich was the army's equivalent in London of the navy's Greenwich, the difference in their grandeur reflecting the difference in standing of the two arms of the Empire's military. The Arsenal, which was in use by the army from the 16th century until 1994, is a vast site cur-

rently being redeveloped in a multitude of ways. A number of buildings on the site are attributed to Vanburgh, mainly because no one else is known who could have designed such things. The very tough, two-storey, brick Boardroom with its heavily modelled centrepiece and the remains of Dial Court with its piles of cannonball pinnacles are surely by Vanburgh; the Royal Brass Foundry may be. The Arsenal was the birthplace of cordite and a renowned but little loved football team.

Vanburgh Castle (85)
1718–1726
Westcombe Park Road, SE3;
train: Maze Hill/Blackheath
John Vanburgh

Vanburgh's own house, an awkward attempt at a baronial castle in brick, is fascinating for what it foreshadows. It was part of a whole development of houses in

twelve acres for various members of his family; unfortunately, the other houses of this very early garden suburb have all been demolished. Vanburgh's interest in the picturesque, clearly evident in his famous country houses, returned him to the Gothic (however superficially) a good fifty years before Georgian Gothic made its appearance. To begin with, the house comprised only of the slightly absurd central block with its stair tower. Vanburgh later extended this, however, in a very casual asymmetrical way that anticipates architectural developments even further in the future.

Christ Church Rectory (86)
1726–1729
Fournier Street, E1;
tube: Liverpool Street/Aldgate East
Nicholas Hawksmoor

Fournier and the surrounding streets are lined with many fine houses developed at the beginning of the 18th century. The rectory, sitting immediately behind the church, is the finest and consists of four bays over three floors with a half basement. The walls are in brown brick with red rubbed brick dressings and the white painted timber sash windows with segmental heads are set deep into the wall. There is a simple door case and, at the top, a projecting stone cornice under a parapet. To the rear are full height canted bay windows. Internally, the rooms are panelled on the lower floor and the main feature is the full height stair.

Most of the Fournier Street houses are of interest; many have fully glazed attics where their Huguenot silk-weaving inhabitants practiced their trade.

St Luke Old Street (87)
1727–1733
Helmet Row, off Old Street, EC1;
tube: Old Street
Nicholas Hawksmoor

This was a fine stone church with a tower to the east end surmounted by a obelisk spire; the nave is five bays long with round headed above square windows and a large Venetian east window. The Church of England declared it redundant in 1960 and took the roof off! It was left deteriorating as no buyer could be found. Finally, the shell was converted into a rehearsal hall for the London Symphony Orchestra by Levitt Bernstein (1999–2004). The new roof, lined with plywood, was constructed on the line of the old and is supported on steel trusses, themselves supported on unusual tree-like steel columns in lieu of Hawksmoor's Ionic stone columns. There are lightweight narrow galleries on three sides. Hawksmoor's domed entrance vestibules have been preserved. The crypt contains cloakroom facilities and a café. The churchyard is most atmospheric with lovely old plane trees. Buried there are George Dance (elder), who was at one time a member of the vestry, and, in a chest tomb, father and son type founders, William Caslon.

"When a man is tired of London, he is tired of life." (88)

Samuel Johnson, Lexicographer (*1709, †1784)

Delineating the Georgian period is not straightforward; there is no clear cut off but a gradual shifting away from the more Baroque tendencies of Wren and Hawksmoor back to the Palladianism of Jones. James Gibbs, for example, completed the distinctly Wren-like St Mary le Strand (no. 90) in 1717 before producing a prototypically Georgian exterior to St Martin in the Fields (no. 92) only seven years later. The great architectural historian John Summerson considered that the period from 1714 to 1830 made sense in both architectural and historical terms; if it was good enough for him then it will surely do for the rest of us.

It is in this period that the extensive grounds of the houses scattered between the City and Westminster were divided up and developed as tree lined terraces and squares of mostly housing. The buildings are generally in a restrained classical style between two and six storeys and built in thin strips by individual developers who leased plots from the landowner. They are mostly of brick sometimes with stone or cast stone trimmings and the windows are rectangular multi-pane sashes regularly arranged. It is a sober, sensible scheme of building most successful as ensembles of modest parts. Much remains and forms the bulk of what might be thought of as central London. As this fabric has aged, it has proved both lovely and very adaptable. Amongst the mass of housing was a scattering of mansions (nos. 100, 102), shops (nos. 134, 139), markets (no. 157) and churches (no. 132).

This housing was needed to accommodate a rapidly growing population. In 1700, the city had around 550,000 residents, which grew to 1.6 million by 1831, making London the world's largest city. There was also a great deal of Georgian development in the London 'villages' of Richmond, Greenwich, Hampstead and especially Islington. These urban developments culminated in John Nash's extravagant 'Metropolitan Improvements' with their vast terraces at Regent's Park and St James's Park, connected by the grand route up Regent Street and Portland Place. In 1807 Pall Mall became the first gas lit street.

The population increase was driven by the Agricultural Revolution, which

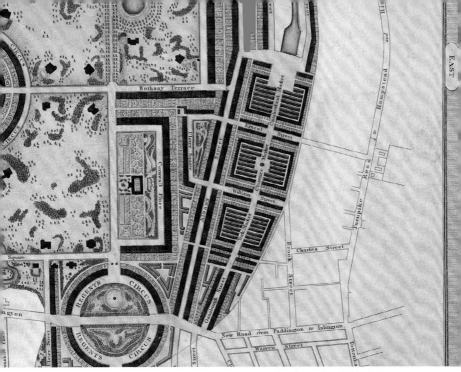

Plan of Regent's Park, John Nash.

increased food production but forced people from the land. It was also a period of relative stability and peace. Britain, as it had become, seemed eternally at war with France but these wars were largely fought at sea. Despite losing America, London was becoming the capital of an expanding global empire. Few great state buildings of the period were built however and most of those have gone, the most galling losses being John Soane's Courts of Chancery and Bank of England. The only significant extant state building of the period is Horse Guards (no. 99). The Georgians renewed London Bridge and built nine new bridges, all since replaced. Mark Brunel's Thames Tunnel (1825–1843), the first tunnel under a navigable river, is the only Georgian crossing still in use.

Rising prosperity was also supported by the beginnings of the technological age and the embryonic Industrial Revolution; an early factory can be seen at Three Mills (no. 118) and renewed dock facilities and warehouses at Wapping (no. 129). The docks were linked to the new canal network; the Grand Union Canal (1793–1820) and the River Lee Navigation (1765–1777) can be seen but the rest of the London network has been filled in. The increased importance of the arts and sciences is evident in the many learned societies established in the period. Somerset House (no. 117) was built for the Royal Society and others including the London Zoological Society, the British Museum (no. 143), the Royal Institution and others were all founded in the period. Related developments were the appearance of gentleman's clubs for men with particular intellectual interests (nos. 152, 155) and renewed theatre building (nos. 128, 136). This was Enlightenment London, the London of Humphry Davy and Michael Faraday, William Blake, Joseph Turner and Thomas Gainsborough, Jane Austen and Percy Shelley, Thomas Paine and Mary Wollstonecraft, William Hogarth and George Handel. Truly a city of wonders was now located on the banks of the Thames: an intellectual, financial, military and technological powerhouse.

Geffrye Almshouses (Museum) (89)
1712–1714
Kingsland Road, E2;
tube: Old Street, train: Hoxton
Robert Burford

The structure consists of three two-storey blocks arranged around a 'C'-shaped courtyard that is open to the road on the west side. The Ironmongers' Company built the almshouses using a bequest from Robert Geffrye, a wealthy merchant and former mayor. Burford was both designer and builder. It is built of a browny-red brick with white painted windows and red tiled roof, and the rooms are arranged in fourteen groups of four around a stair. The scale and feel is very domestic. The centre of the east block houses a chapel with bigger arched windows, some stone quoins, a clock and a little bell tower. A recreation room was added to the south wing in the 1890s by Richard Roberts and the whole was converted to a museum of Domestic and Garden Design by London County Council in the early 20th century. The witless extension of the museum to the rear is by Branson Coates and Sheppard Robson (1994–1997). The gardens, shaded by lime and plane trees, are a real pleasure.

St Mary le Strand (90)
1714–1717
Strand, WC2; tube: Temple
James Gibbs

Situated on an island in Strand the church is visible on all sides and, with its finely worked and proportioned stone façades, it is admirably suited to the exposure, looking for all the world like some beautiful highly wrought casket you could slip under your coat. The general arrangement is seven bays with Corinthian over Composite attached columns. The even numbered bays all have pediments set into the parapet balustrade, a detail echoed in the central bay of the west front. The bays have niches at ground level and Venetian windows above. The tower rises from the west pediment and diminishes most elegantly in stages to a domed lan-

tern; at the bottom is a lead roofed, semi-circular porch. The east end is apsidal with round-headed windows behind the altar. Gibbs was evidently influenced by Wren as well as by the churches he had seen in Rome. The inside has neither aisles nor galleries but is a simple box with a coffered segmental vault, while the apse is framed under a pediment like those outside. The walls are divided with pilasters corresponding with the external columns.

St George's, Hanover Square (91)
1721–1725
St George Street, W1;
tube: Oxford Circus
John James

One of the Fifty Churches and built to serve the expanding and fashionable district of Mayfair, this was the first of what was to become a characteristic London church type – essentially a large classical temple with a full width, full height portico to the west end. However a church requires a bell tower which is absent in the language of classical temples. One solution, used here, was to place the tower centrally just behind the portico. The drawback with this, apart

from the lack of precedent, is that it is visually weak with the roof apparently supporting the tower. St Georges has this visual problem. The portico is Corinthian and sits over the pavement, and the north and south elevations each have five bays, with the bay under the tower given a pedimented attic; otherwise, they are rusticated and pedimented. At the east end, there is a large Venetian window. Inside are galleries on piers, topped with Corinthian columns supporting the vaulted ceiling. The overall impression is watery and thin compared to, say, Hawkmoor's churches.

St Martin in the Fields　　　(92)
1721–1726
St Martin's Place, WC2;
tube: Charing Cross
James Gibbs

Facing onto Trafalgar Square, St Martin is now on one of the most prominent sites in London. It was built 100 years before the Square and was far less exposed but it nevertheless became highly influential

and was repeatedly copied throughout the UK, Ireland, the USA, and beyond. It takes the form, like St George's, Hanover Square (no. 91), of a Roman temple with an almost full width giant Corinthian portico to the west end with the most elegant but still highly problematic tower perched on the roof. The flanks of seven bays are delineated with giant Corinthian pilasters with round-headed above segmental windows; the two end bays, facing stairways, are given further emphasis with a pair of attached columns in addition to the pilasters. There is a large Venetian window to the east end with newly created glass by Shirazeh Housiary. The interior is on the pattern of St James's, Piccadilly (no. 58), though more ornate – galleries on three sides with a vault over the nave on Corinthian columns and saucer domes over the isles. The altar/chancel is expressed as a niche with a vaulted ceiling lower than that of the nave, although this is not expressed externally.

Because of its location and having been blessed with a succession of very active clergy, St Martin has long played an important role in London life: musically, socially, charitably and even just as a catering operation. To better facilitate these roles, a substantial redevelopment of the underground spaces was undertaken by Eric Parry Associates (2006–2008). On the outside you see a freestanding glass entrance kiosk in the passage north of the church and, to the east of that, a sunken all glass lightwell. The adaption is surely ingenious if nothing else.

Chiswick House (93)
1727–1729
Burlington Lane, W4;
tube: Turnham Green
Richard Boyle

Richard Boyle was the third Earl of Burlington and he built for himself a 'pavilion' in the grounds of the family's Jacobean house, which has since been demolished. The new house is heavily influenced by Palladio's Villa Rotunda and itself became very influential on the neo-Palladianism that was soon to become the fashion. It is essentially a series of rooms around a central octagonal that rises through the roof to form a rotunda with half round clerestory windows. The lower storey is vermiculated stone, while the upper is rendered and the slate roof is low pitched behind a parapet. The south side has two stone dressed pedimented windows either side of a five-bay Corinthian raised portico with elaborate steps. The other façades have Venetian windows in the centre. In contrast to this chaste exterior, the inside was lavishly decorated by William Kent in the Roman style. Kent also worked on the extensive grounds, which are now a public park.

St Bartholomew's Hospital (94)
1730–1768
Giltspur Street, EC1;
tube: Barbican/Farringdon
James Gibbs

London's early hospitals had been attached to religious houses and when Henry VIII dissolved these in 1536, the hospitals generally disappeared with them. The City of London persuaded the King to re-found Bart's, as it is known, eight years later, and hence, with an original start date of 1123, Bart's is the oldest hospital in the UK. In architectural terms the interest lies mostly with the rebuilding in the middle of the 18th century. Gibbs was on the board of the hospital and did the work free of charge. His hospital looks very much like an Oxbridge college quadrangle of the period. Three blocks remain of the original four; they are each three storeys above a basement, eleven bays wide and all in stone. It is plain but dignified and obviously serviceable. The north block housing the entrance has some interesting interiors, including the imposing and lavish Great Hall and the Staircase Hall, home to two large paintings by Hogarth and donated by the artist.

Also of note on the rambling site are the Henry VIII gatehouse, an unusually proportioned Ionic aedicule by Edward Strong of 1702, and St Bartholomew-the-Less, the Hospital Chapel, originally by George Dance (younger) and later rebuilt to the same design by Thomas Hardwick. It is in the Gothick style but there is an original 15th-century tower and vestry. Inigo Jones was baptized here.

Mansion House (95)
1739–1752
Mansion House Place, EC4; tube: Bank
George Dance (elder)

The home, offices and 'state rooms' of the Lord Mayor of London, Mansion

House, sits on the main intersection of the City in conversation with St Mary Woolnoth, the Bank of England, the Royal Exchange and No.1 Poultry and by and large gets the worst of it. All in limestone it was originally of two storeys above a rusticated semi basement. The main frontage has nine bays with a giant five-bay Corinthian portico. Various alterations and additions in the quest of more space in the 18th and 19th centuries culminated in an additional attic storey by Sydneys Perk and Tatchell (1930–1931). The most important interiors are the Saloon, the Long Parlour and the very grand Vitruvian/Palladian Egyptian Hall with its giant Corinthian arcades and vaulted ceiling, haunted by countless turgid City banquets past.

Berkeley Square (96)
1742–1747
Berkeley Square, W1; tube: Green Park

ENSEMBLE In the heart of Mayfair Berkeley Square was developed piecemeal, with no masterplan as such, by the Lords Berkeley of Stratton who granted leases to various entrepreneurial builders and carpenters. It is best known for its 220-year-old plane trees and a group of houses on the west side of the square. Nos. 45–46 by Henry Flitcroft (1744–1745) are handsome, stone faced, four-bay residences but the most impressive is No. 44 by William Kent of the same time. The front – three storeys above a basement and three bays in brick with stone dressings – betrays very little and only the elegant first floor window cases hint at what lies inside. The interiors are sumptuous and intense, particularly the central staircase.

It would be fair to say that the square has not always been this lucky with its architects and developers in succeeding eras.

Brick Lane Jamme Masjid (97)
1743–1744
Fournier Street, E1;
tube: Aldgate East/Liverpool Street
Thomas Stibbs

69

The mosque (as it is now) was originally built as a protestant chapel by Huguenot weavers, who had fled to this part of London from the religious conflicts in 17th-century France. It later served as a Methodist chapel and then became the Great Synagogue of the east London Jewish community, who arrived in Spitalfields in the 19th century. It changed to its current use in 1975 and it is interesting to wonder what might come next. It was a reduced version of the Georgian city churches suited to the budget and the temperament of the French Calvanists. The walls are brick with minimal stone trimmings under a slate roof. There are six bays facing Fournier Street, of which the middle four lie under a pediment housing a sundial, with round-headed above segmental-headed windows. There is also a gable pediment facing Brick Lane. The galleried interior now contains little of the original fabric.

Fetter Lane Moravian Chapel (98) and God's Acre
circa 1752
Moravian Close, off King's Road, SW3; tube: West Brompton

Moravian missionaries used Britain as a stepping-stone on their way to their missions in the West Indies. They discovered that, as they put it, there was work for them on these godless islands as well. Their principle church was in the City's Fetter Lane but the headquarters and burial ground were located in then rural Chelsea. Attached to the burial ground is a small and very simple chapel, built in brown brick with red rubber brick dressings, slender, round arched windows and a steep, slated, hipped roof. The chapel was used as a boys' school after 1812 and artists' studios from 1906. It is much altered but the gist and spirit of the simple original structure remain. The Fetter Lane chapel was destroyed in 1941 and the Moravians decided to reoccupy the Chelsea chapel after the war. The burial ground with its many mature trees is lovely.

Horse Guards (99)
1750–1759
Whitehall, SW1; tube: Charing Cross
William Kent and Stephen Wright

The buildings originally here were to guard the entrance to the Palace of Whitehall and provide accommodation for the horses and men. The Palace was of course demolished, so they now seem to be guarding a large empty car park. The 18th-century rebuilding incorporated features of the earlier structure, such as the arch and clock tower, although not the actual fabric. The new building also housed the army high command and a divisional command is still in-situ. It is generally of three storeys in cream stone, rusticated at ground floor level but otherwise quite plain. The central seven-bay block has a picturesque quality; it is strongly modelled with a central pediment, corner attic pavilions and a central clock tower with a lantern. The five-bay recessed wings are plainer and finish at projecting gabled three-bay end blocks. The principle interiors are an octagonal room, which rises through three storeys up into the clock tower, the General's office, and the conference room, which are all quite plain as befits their martial purpose.

Dover House (Scotland Office) (100)
1754–1758
Whitehall, SW1; tube: Charing Cross
James Paine and Henry Holland

Originally built as a private dwelling by Paine for a wealthy politician, Dover House was substantially altered after 1787 by Holland for occupation by the Duke of York. It subsequently had a series of private owners, the last being Baron Dover who lent the house its name. It was taken over by the government in 1885 to become the Scottish Office.

Holland filled the entrance court to Paine's house with a single-storey entrance hall crowned with a glazed rotunda, twelve metres in diameter, from which steps lead to the upper hall on the piano nobile of the main house. This is faced to Whitehall with a very chaste, lightly rusticated screen wall with an Ionic portico and some attached columns. The House is in a pure Greek style and much influenced by French neoclassicism. The elevation to Horse Guards is dignified and simple, if less striking than the Whitehall side.

Cambridge House (101)
1756–1758
Piccadilly, W1; tube: Green Park
Matthew Brettingham

A fine Palladian aristocrat's house with a forecourt overlooking Green Park, Cambridge House was built for the Earl of Egremont and had a succession of private owners, including Lord Palmerston, until it was purchased by the Naval and Military Club in 1878. In 2001 it was sold for conversion to a luxury hotel, although the status of this plan is now unclear and there are fears for the building's future. Three storeys tall and with seven bays,

the building is in pale stone and has a pediment over the central three bays. The first-floor windows are pedimented with a long balcony, but otherwise the detail is minimal. The Doric portico and single-storey wing were added by John Macvicar Anderson in the 1870s. The interiors are also mostly from the 19th century although they are still arranged around a central top-lit stair.

Spencer House (102)
1756–1758
St James's Place, SW1; tube: Green Park
John Vardy and James Stuart

The grandest of the 18th-century aristocratic houses, Spencer House has a fantastic location looking westwards over Green Park. The park façade is in stone and prototypically Palladian with its two storeys over a rusticated and vermiculated basement. The ground floor is rusticated with rectangular windows in arched openings. Above this, the middle five of the seven bays are under a shallow single-storey pediment with attached Doric columns to all bays; the first floor windows are pedimented. In 1758, Vardy was replaced by James 'Athenian' Stuart, who completed the decoration of the upper floor rooms in a historically 'accurate' Greek style, highly coloured and ornate, extravagantly displayed in the Great Room and the Painted Room. Vardy nearly surpassed Stuart's lavishness with his flamboyant ground floor Palm Room while there are contributions from both of them in the stairway.

71

Sir John Soane
*1753 in Goring-on-Thames, †1837 in London (103)

Soane was born the son of a builder in Goring-on-Thames, a pleasant rural part of the world near Reading. Although Soane had received some education, when his father died in 1768 he and his brother were poorly provided for and Soane worked as a hod carrier for his bricklayer brother; not many successful architects had as far to go as the young Soane. Through some connections in the building industry a place was found for him as an assistant to the younger George Dance in 1769, a fortunate placing as Dance was one of the most talented and professional architects of his generation. Beyond what he picked up in the course of his work for Dance and later Henry Holland, Soane attended the evening architecture lectures at the newly founded Royal Academy of Arts. This pattern of pupillage in an office and attendance at evening classes became the standard training for an architect. Soane, ambitious and hard working, won the Academy's silver and gold medals and, in 1777, its travelling scholarship allowing him to tour Italy studying its Roman and Renaissance architecture.

On returning to England in 1780, Soane moonlighted for his old employers and took up a few small projects on his own before his practice began to gradually expand with a number of country houses, few of which survive. Striving to expand his practice further Soane applied for surveyorship posts with various public institutions and finally succeeded with the Bank of England. Between 1788 and 1827 Soane rebuilt the Bank's premises in Threadneedle Street (no. 122). Inevitably, the role of the Bank changed and expanded and the whole site was extensively redeveloped in the 20th century, leaving very little of Soane's work. This is perhaps the biggest single loss ever suffered in British architectural history; what is left is a set of stunning perspective drawings by Soane's favourite draughtsman Joseph Gandy and some wonderfully atmospheric black and white photos.

Similar fates awaited a long list of buildings Soane designed for the State, including the Chancery Courts and Royal Hospital Chelsea, although some interesting stables survive at the latter. All have fallen victim to fire, Blitz or feckless governments. His principle surviving monument is the wonderful Dulwich Picture Gallery and Mausoleum (no. 130). His own houses also survive and the Soane Museum (no. 121) at Lincoln's Inn Fields is now one of the City's most interesting small museums. Pitzhanger Manor was Soane's country house but can now be found at the west end of the District and Central lines. His tiny, moving tomb (no. 133) for his wife is in St Pancras Churchyard, where Soane was also buried. The survivors make the losses harder to take.

More equivocal monuments are his Commissioners' Churches. The 1818 Church Building Act set aside £1 million for the building of 600 churches in areas lacking them. They were to be built expressly 'with a view to accommodating the greatest number of persons at the smallest expense within the compass of an ordinary voice'. There are no prizes for guessing what kind of legacy this sort of thinking would leave behind: some very cheap, stark and mostly unloved churches. Soane was stubborn and never could do anything uninteresting; his three buildings are all charismatic although marked by their budgets. The centrally located Holy Trinity, Marylebone (no. 153) received additional funding and reveals what Soane would surely have wanted to do with St Peter's Walworth (no. 144) and St John's, Bethnal Green (no. 151).

'Soanian' is a much used word in the architectural world and is used to mean many things. First and foremost it is shorthand for a quality of spatial complexity where defined and implied spaces interweave and richly interconnect. Next would be notions about subtle and often hidden lighting effects from above or from the side. More superficially, 'Soanian' might refer to the shallow saucer and handkerchief vaults he was so fond of employing. Most superficially of all, it might refer to the strange stylistic language he developed; although a convinced classicist he applied classical motifs in a manner entirely his own. This and the eccentric, spidery decorative markings he employed provoked contemporary mockery. What is clear now is that he was by far the most original architect of a not very architecturally inventive era and that the less superficial things about his work will be studied and wondered at for as long as people do wonder about such things.

73

Bank of England, 3% Consols Office Perspective by Joseph Gandy.

built on the foundations of the wall and a small section of the wall survives here. A subtitle was necessary to differentiate it from no less than seven other All Hallows churches in the medieval city, although only one other remains today. The church is a very simple brick box with a high crypt and only semi-circular clerestory windows. There is a small and undemonstrative but charming stone tower at the west end and an apsidal chancel attached in the east. The interior is unprecedented, for the time, in its simplicity, consisting of an aisle-less box with attached Ionic columns under a minimal entablature supporting a barrel vault scalloped out for the clerestories, and a semi dome over the apse. It must

Lichfield House (104)
1764–1766
St James's Square, W1; tube: Piccadilly
James Stuart

Although only three bays wide and three storeys tall, this house makes a powerful impact with its finely chiselled stone façade. There is a full width pediment on two-storey Ionic attached columns over a rusticated ground floor. The ground floor windows are arched and the first floor pedimented with simple squares above and it is all most elegant and refined. The well-designed interiors are in the highly decorated and authentic 'Athenian' style. The Square, begun immediately after the fire of 1666, was one of the first new West End squares. There is nothing of that date remaining but plenty of interest from later dates and good big trees. No. 20 is by Robert Adam (1771–1774), No. 7 by Edwin Luytens (1911–1912) and No. 14 is the London Library, a very interesting institution if not a fantastic piece of architecture.

All Hallows-on-the-Wall (105)
1765–1767
London Wall, EC2;
tube: Liverpool Street/Moorgate
George Dance (younger)

The church gets its suffix from its proximity to the London Wall; part of it is

have seemed extraordinary at the time and certainly had an impact on Soane; even today it feels fresh and pure.

Kenwood House (106)
1764–1774
Hampstead Lane, NW3; tube: Highgate
James and Robert Adam

74

The Lord Chief Justice, William Murray, bought a modest brick country house in grounds overlooking Hampstead Heath and commissioned the Adam brothers to make something of it. The seven-bay house was given an extra storey and finished in ornate stucco work with pilasters and a small pediment. An existing orangery to the east was given an Ionic arcade and matched to the west with a library block, and the north entrance was adorned with an Ionic portico. While still not much more than a rendered box, it certainly sits impressively in the landscape. There are some fine interiors and one splendid one in the library. The grounds are mature and picturesque and were probably designed by Humphry Repton. Further extensions to the north and east were added by George Saunders in the 1790s. In 1927 the House, together with an important collection of paintings, was bequeathed to the public by the Earl of Iveagh. Since then a small collection of modern sculpture has been sited in the grounds.

Adelphi (107)
1768–1772
Adelphi Terrace, WC2;
tube: Charing Cross
James, Robert and William Adam

DEMOLITION Built as a speculation by the Adam Brothers, the Adelphi district, whose name derives from the Greek word for 'brothers', never quite went to

plan and later became a much-lamented victim of passing fashion and a high value site, lying between the Strand and the river, just east of Somerset House. The central block, Adelphi Terrace, was four storeys high and forty-one bays wide. This was at the Strand level with a terrace overlooking the Thames supported on an arcade of warehouses at river level, an arrangement that had been suggested to Robert by the Roman Palace of Diocletian in Split. There were side ranges and streets running up to the Strand. It was constructed in brick with the thin but pretty stucco decoration of pilasters and so on that we now think of as being typically 'Adamesque'. Money was not made and the Victorians savaged it; demolition came in 1932. Some scraps of the larger development remain at Nos. 6–10 Adam Street and at the Royal Society of Arts in John Adam Street (no.112).

Cavendish Square (108)
1769–1772
Cavendish Square, W1;
tube: Oxford Circus
John Price

ENSEMBLE The Square, which was originally designed by Price for Edward Harley in 1717, was intended as the centrepiece of the whole district. Development proved much slower than Harley had hoped and it never became as grand as intended. The best remaining sections are Nos. 11 and 14, a pair of dignified stone Palladian houses with rusticated ground floors and attached Corinthian columns under pediments on the floors above. The authorship of these is unclear, although James Stuart is mentioned, and they surely bear some familial resemblance to John Vardy's Spencer House (no. 102). The linking bridge was added in 1953 by Louis Osman. The Harley/Cavendish development allowed for both a market and a chapel; Oxford Market is long gone but Gibbs' charming little church of St Peter can be seen in Vere Street off the southwest corner of the square, a miniature of one of his West End churches in a simple brick box.

Newgate Prison (109)
1769–1778
Newgate Street, EC4; tube: St Paul's
George Dance (younger)

DEMOLITION New Gate was the fifth of the City's gates and was used from the 12th century to house prisoners. Through the following centuries, it expanded into a full-scale prison and underwent frequent extensions, alterations and re-buildings. The younger Dance offered the final iteration, which was replaced by the Old Bailey criminal court in 1904. The prison was arranged around three courtyards, one each for debtors, male felons and female felons. The philosophy of criminal justice in the 18th century was extremely primitive and did not extend much beyond punishment and deterrence. Dance's building was the stony embodiment of these crude and cruel ideas: a massive pile of super rusticated, mostly blank masonry, heavily influenced by Piranesi's Carceri etchings. It was a rare thing for a building to be designed to arouse fear and to achieve its aim, but it is in-

deed the fear, misery and degradation of Newgate that haunts the 19th-century London of Charles Dickens' novels and Gustave Doré's illustrations. A fragment of the brute may remain to the rear of Amen Court (no. 48).

Stratford House (110)
1771–1776
Stratford Place, off Oxford Street, W1;
tube: Bond Street
Richard Edwin

The House forms the centrepiece of a development undertaken by Edward Stratford on land bought from the City. A short close lined with terraces of houses ends in a small square, of which Stratford's own house is the main feature terminating the vista. With its serene architecture and trees it seems that only an enchantment could keep it so calm and quiet just steps away from the bedlam of Oxford Street. The house was originally of five bays with a rusticated ground floor and four two-storey Ionic pilasters above to a three-bay pediment. It is very much in the style of Adam. The wings have been rebuilt many times up until the early 20th century. The interior too has been much altered, most recently when the House was taken over by the Oriental Club in 1963. Some fine interiors remain however, especially the panelled library. Some of the brick and stucco terraces to the south of the House have been lost but enough remains to form an impression of how it must have been.

Apsley House (111)
1771–1778
Hyde Park Corner, W1;
tube: Hyde Park Corner
Robert Adam

The house that Robert Adam built for Henry Bathurst (Lord Apsley) was more modest than the one now occupying the address Number One, London. It was only five bays wide and in brick. The two extra bays, the Bath stone facings and the Corinthian portico were added at the behest of a new owner, the Duke of Wellington, by Phillip and Benjamin Dean Wyatt (1826-1830). Some of the interiors remain from the Adam house, including the Portico Drawing Room and the Stairway. The Wyatts' principle interior is the giant Waterloo Gallery built to house Wellington's picture collection and decorated in a lavish Louis XV style. Unfortunately, the building has been terribly isolated by various traffic schemes. A curse also suffered by the Wellington Memorial opposite the house by Decimus Burton, 1826-1829. It consists of a very Roman Corinthian Arch with chariot atop; Mussolini would surely have approved. Burton was also responsible for the Ionic screen to the west of the House, which is now the Wellington Museum.

The Society for the Encouragement of the Arts, Manufactures and Commerce (112)
1772–1774
John Adam Street, W2;
tube: Charing Cross
James and Robert Adam

The largest surviving fragment of the Adam brothers' Adelphi, the Royal Society of Arts (RSA) was originally housed in No. 8, and Nos. 2–6 were only later incorporated. No. 8 is to the south and of brick with stone dressings. The very simple ground floor has a small portico, above which are four two-storey attached Ionic columns under a pediment with a large Venetian window in the centre of the first floor, all of which is in the distinctive Adam style. To the north, the

first and second storeys are blank with an attached pediment with Ionic pilasters; below this is an off-centre archway. The archway is now glazed over but was originally a passage under the building down to the river. There are a number of excellent Adams interiors, the most impressive of which is the Great Room used for discussions and lectures and lined with James Barry's series of paintings, 'The Progress of Human Culture' (1777–1783); also of interest are the Adelphi and Tavern Rooms, originally part of an inn in No. 2, the Benjamin Franklin Room and the entrance hall. In 1990, one of the courts to the rear was glazed in and a staircase inserted for access to the impressive brick vaults of the basement, which served originally as warehousing. The architects were Green Lloyd.

Home House   (113)
1773–1776
Portman Square, W1;
tube: Marble Arch/Bond Street
James Wyatt, Robert Adam

Built for Elizabeth Home, dowager countess and Jamaican heiress (also known as the 'Queen of Hell'), the house was started by James Wyatt who was replaced by Adam in 1775. Most of the exterior is the work of the former and very plain, comprised of five bays over three storeys, nearly all of brick with some string courses, garlanded inset panels and a modest portico at the entrance as the only relief. The proportions, however, are very satisfying. This scarcely prepares you for the interior, which represents Adam at his most gorgeous with a series of lavishly decorated

interlocking spaces of different shapes and character, of which the highlight is the circular top-lit stair. Some idea of how Wyatt might have finished No. 21 can be gleaned from No. 20 next door, which he was allowed to finish. It too is a very fine 18th-century house but not such a tour de force. Both houses are now a private club; No. 20 has lately been embellished with a bar unit and other furnishings by Zaha Hadid in her trademark seamless organo-futurist style, managing to look expensive and ludicrous at the same time.

Portland Place   (114)
1773–1781
Portland Place, W1;
tube: Regent's Park/Portland Place
James and Robert Adam

ENSEMBLE Apparently undaunted by their Adelphi experience, the Adam brothers embarked on another ambitious development: a street of houses running north from Foley House up to Marylebone Fields. They were obliged by the owner of Foley House to maintain a clear vista from the House and it is this that explains the, for London, extraordinary width of the street – it is one of the few in the city with the feel of a continental boulevard, even if most of the 'extra' space is now occupied by parked cars. James designed the houses between each pair of traversing streets as single architectural units in the thin, decorative, classical Adam style. Much of this has now gone and although the replacements are generally not very distinguished, the street retains a decided air. The only reasonably intact section of the original Adam development is at Nos. 27–47. The street became a through road only in the first quarter of the 19th century when it was incorporated into John Nash's plans for 'Metropolitan Improvements'.

Bedford Square   (115)
1775–1786
Bedford Square, WC1; tube: Tottenham Court Road/Russell Square
Thomas Leverton

ENSEMBLE Bedford is the most intact of London's squares with very little missing. Each side of the Square is designed as a single symmetrical architectural composition although the modulation is slight. Generally of three storeys over a basement, the houses are mostly in brick with sparing use of Coade stone dressings, while the central elements are in stucco, project slightly and have a pediment with Ionic pilasters over a rusticated ground floor, all with Adamesque decorations. The end elements, which again project slightly, have only a balustraded parapet to mark them out. The Square amply demonstrates what a delightful effect can be achieved using minimal architectural means and some good trees. Only No. 1 is marked out from the general run of houses; this was built for a specific client and has an unusual plan and particularly fine interiors.

Hertford House   (116)
1771–1788
Manchester Square, W1;
tube: Bond Street
Samuel Adams and Joshua Brown

It is hard to recognise the 18th-century Palladian House that is at the core of the current building. Constructed by the builder Adams and architect Brown for the Duke of Manchester, it had five bays over three storeys with a rusticated ground floor with pilasters to a cornice above. It was a little awkward but did not deserve the makeover to which the Victorians subjected it. Thomas Ambler added further bays and a portico to the front of the house with extensions to the rear around a new courtyard, as well as rich Victorian interiors. The House became a museum in 1900 displaying the Wallace Collection, bequeathed to the nation by Richard and Julie Wallace, the last owners of the house. During the late 1990s, Rick Mather Architects reordered the galleries and glazed in the courtyard.

Somerset House (117)

1776–1801
William Chambers

In 1775 an act of parliament was passed for the construction of a building to house various academic societies and government departments on a site by the Thames that was home to a collection of old palace structures. This represented an overdue triumph of shame at the lack of noble public buildings as compared to the continent over the traditional suspicion of expensive government self-aggrandisement. The architect was the academic establishment man par excellence and a bitter rival of Adam whose work and character Chambers thought vulgar.

The building is arranged around a courtyard with an entrance through a brilliant Doric loggia from the Strand. The blocks are three storeys over basements and all in stone with much rustication; the Strand block is divided by composite columns and pilasters while the others have central and end features with recessed pediments. The south block, which has a small dome, faces a terrace overlooking the river; it is below the terrace that Chambers really goes all out with a powerful expressive Piranesian arcade, which at the time had its feet in the river. The materials and workmanship are consistently of the very best quality. The Palladian language of the building is a little stiff and fussy but overall the sheer weight of it all does convince.

Either side of the main courtyard block are two further blocks envisaged in Chambers' plan and designed in complete sympathy with his central block; to the east a building for King's College of 1829 partly to Chambers' design, to the west offices for the Inland Revenue by James Pennethorne (1851–1856).

In recent times the Government has acted to clear out its remaining departments and to reintroduce cultural uses. The Strand block now accommodates the Courtauld Institute of Art with its marvellous collection of art; this has allowed public access to the principle interiors of which the Royal Academy Meeting Room is the centrepiece. The south block, which was originally occupied by the Admiralty, has the Gilbert Collection and an outpost of the Hermitage Museum of St Petersburg; the most interesting interiors here are the Seamen's Hall in the middle at ground level and the Navy Stair at the west end. In 2000 Dixon Jones redesigned the central courtyard with new paving, lighting and water feature; it has been a great popular success.

Vaulted entrance area.

Somerset House, South façade to Thames, detail.

81

Three Mills (118)
1776
Three Mill Lane, E3;
tube: Bromley-by-Bow

London has always had a great appetite
for both bread and strong drink and, on
the eastern boundary of the city abutting Essex and Kent where the grain was
grown, the Three Mills were an important provider of both. The motive power
was the tidal channels of the River Lea,
which were retained in millponds and
released over time to drive undershot
waterwheels. The buildings accommodating the wheels on the ground floor
had to be built over the channels, and
the wheels drove both grinding wheels
and hoists. The Domesday Book recorded
eight mills here in the 11th century. The
current surviving pair, the Clock Mill and
the House Mill, date from the second half
of the 18th century and were in use at
that time in association with a gin distillery. The massive timber frames are
clad in brick and timber weather boarding with small windows under steeply
pitched tiled roofs. Set by the water they
have a picturesque bucolic air, especially
Clock Mill with its clock tower and pair
of drying kilns.

Skinners' Hall (119)
1770–1779
Dowgate Hill, EC4; tube: Cannon Street
William Jupp

The Worshipful Company of Skinners, who
obviously do not think there is anything in
a name, were a guild of furriers and allied
trades. They were founded in 1327 and
have been on this site since 1409. The core
of the current premises is a post-fire hall

of 1670, though it has been worked over
so many times that it is hard to see it. The
street façade of three storeys and five bays
of painted stone has a rusticated ground
floor with Ionic pilasters above, and there
is a pediment over the three central bays
with some decoration on the entablature.
It is all very flat and very pretty. Inside is
a delightful tiny cloistered stone courtyard

onto the east wall of the hall, by William
Campbell-Jones (1902–1916). The hall itself is double height with a minstrel's gallery on the north side, all panelled in dark
wood with luscious, early 20th-century
murals at the upper level by Frank Brang-
wyn. The rest of the interiors are certainly
fine if not of great interest.

Watermen's Hall (120)
1778–1780
St Mary-at-Hill, EC3; tube: Monument
William Blackburn

The Watermen's Company differs from the other City Livery Companies in that it was founded by Parliament, in 1555, with the aim of regulating and training the men who worked on the Thames, in which it still has a part. It also organizes the annual Doggett's Coat and Badge rowing race, held on the Thames since 1715. The present Hall is small but with architectural pretension. The ground floor has three bays and is rusticated, above which there is a single pedimented bay with paired Ionic pilasters and a large tripartite window with a semi-circular fan light. This window serves the Court Room, which, with its vaulted ceiling and delicate decorations, is the principle interior.

Soane Museum (121)
1792–1824
Lincoln's Inn Fields, WC2; tube: Holborn
John Soane

Like many an architect since, Soane was happy to live in a building site, in his case for a mere thirty-two years. It began with No. 12 which he rebuilt for use as his home and office. As the latter expanded alongside his collection of art, castings, architectural fragments and general bric-a-brac it was necessary to buy and rebuild No. 13 and finally he bought No. 14 and incorporated the rear part of that into the larger house while letting out the front part. The houses are three bays and four storeys over a basement facing the square, while the rear yard

spaces are built over at basement and ground levels. The two outer houses appear as standard brick Georgian to match their neighbours. The central one has a projecting stone screen, full width with round headed windows at ground and first floor level and a single bay on the floor above; it is articulated with Soane's trademark linear incisions. The screen was originally open but Soane gradually glazed it in. There are flat pilasters and a perforated balustrade/parapet above the bay. The interior is extraordinarily intense, cranky and complex with many dense, highly decorated but muted spaces, the most celebrated of which is the dining room with its floating handkerchief domed ceiling. The rear parts, all lit from above via atria, roof lights and a tiny lightwell, are a fabulous warren of fantasy spaces. Soane bequeathed the house to the nation 'for the study of Architecture and the Allied Arts' as well he might!

Bank of England (122)
1788–1827
Threadneedle Street, EC2; tube: Bank
John Soane

The Bank or 'Old Lady' was established in 1694 and constructed their first premises in the 1730s with the aid of George Sampson, who continued to make additions (along with Robert Taylor) throughout the 18th century. These established a pattern on which Soane was to build: a blank perimeter screen wall with the accommodation top-lit or lit via internal court-

yards, this is a secure system but only works for fairly low level development. This is precisely what Soane designed when he was called upon to rebuild the expanding Bank. The glory of his design was a series of salons lit from clerestories under pendentive domes detailed and decorated in the Soanian antique manner. These are only to be seen now in the perspectives produced by Soane's office. The Bank continued to expand and a further rebuilding was undertaken by Herbert Baker (1923–1942). Despite promises to the contrary, none of Soane's major interiors survived the rebuilding. Soane's screen wall is still there, a bit of tinkering aside, but it is now dominated by Baker's unattractive lump. A museum in the Bank has, apparently faithful, reconstructions of a couple of the Soane rooms.

Fitzroy Square (123)
1793–1798
Fitzroy Square, W1; tube: Warren Street/Great Portland Street
Robert Adam

ENSEMBLE The Square is the focal point of a development by the Fitzroy family and comprises a good part of what is now referred to as Fitzrovia, a famously bohemian district in the middle years of the last century. The south and east blocks were one of Adam's last designs before he died in1792. All of Portland stone, they are a handsome pair of three-storey buildings with a basement and an attic storey. The centrepieces

protrude but are recessed in the middle with attached Ionic columns and large semi-circular tripartite windows above, a motif that is echoed in the end blocks. The north and west blocks – stucco with Ionic columns and pilasters – were only completed in 1935 and neither are very good.

The Paragon (124)
1794–1807
The Paragon, SE3; train: Blackheath
Michael Searles

Searles was a local architect/developer who was responsible for various schemes in south-east London, of which the Paragon is the grandest by far. Six pairs of semi-detached houses and a single detached house in the centre are joined, forming an enormous crescent, by single-storey Tuscan arcades, which contain the entrances and some ancillary accommodation. The houses themselves are quite plain, three-storey brick boxes with basements and attics. Desirable as they are, overlooking the heath, it still took Searles thirteen years to sell off such large houses. They were converted into flats by Charles Brown in the 1950s.

Stationers' Hall (125)
1800–1801
Stationers Hall Court, off Ave Maria Lane, EC4; tube: St Paul's
Robert Mylne

The Stationers' Company was re-founded in 1403 and came to this site in 1611. The hall itself is of 1670 and was refaced in the 19th-century rebuilding. The principle block containing the hall is a high single-storey structure over a

raised basement; it has six bays all in stone to the entrance court with five tall thin round-headed windows to the hall and an entrance in the easternmost bay. Beyond that is a passage through to the inner courtyard with its big old plane tree. A wing was added to the south in the 1880s by Robert Mylne with a bay window under a conical roof. The wing to the north facing the inner courtyard was rebuilt in brickwork for the last time in 1957 by Dawson and Son. Some of the interiors are excellent, particularly the hall with its fine carved screen of 1670.

West India Warehouses (126)
1800–1803
Hertsmere Road, E14; tube: Canary
Wharf, DLR: West India Quay
George Gwilt and Son

Built to store sugar, the warehouses consist of nine great brick boxes, which are mostly five storeys with an

attic and basement. The windows are generally semi-circular at the top and segmental below with circular windows lighting the stairs. The pitched roofs are in slate. Inside, the massive timber floors are supported on the walls and cruciform cast iron columns, which replaced earlier oak posts. Some blocks were originally lower but were extended seamlessly upwards by John Rennie in 1827. Identified for reuse rather than demolition, No. 1 Warehouse is now the well-regarded Museum of London's Docklands. The rest are in mixed domestic and commercial use.

Royal Hospital School, Greenwich (127)
1807–1816
Romney Road, Greenwich Park, SE10;
train and DLR: Greenwich
Daniel Alexander

The Royal Navy had established an 'asylum' or school for orphans in Paddington in 1798, with the idea that all these orphans would choose a career at sea. It was decided to amalgamate this school with the one for pensioners at the Naval Hospital (no. 44) and, to this end, wings were bravely built flanking the Queen's House and connected to it via Tuscan colonnades. The new wings are unexceptional but unexceptionable, consisting of two storeys over a rusticated basement with attached Doric columns to the end elevations. Additional buildings for the school were built further to the west as the century progressed, including a gym or school hall with an unfortunate florid frenchified north elevation. The school moved out in 1933 and after some years the buildings were designated the National Maritime Museum. The gym was demolished in the 1990s while retaining its façade, and the space behind, between the other school buildings, was covered in a giant glass roof to provide a central space for the refurbished museum. The architect was Rick Mather.

Theatre Royal Drury Lane (128)
1810–1812
Catherine Street, WC2;
tube: Covent Garden
Benjamin Dean Wyatt

There have been theatres on this site since 1635, including one designed by Wren and refurbished by Adam and one designed by Henry Holland in 1794, which burnt down after only sixteen years. After the fire a competition to design a new theatre was won by Benjamin Wyatt. At thirty-six he was young for such a large project, although he came from a dynasty of successful architects. The exterior facing onto tight little streets off Drury is very basic, with stucco to the entrance front and brickwork down the sides. A crude stucco porch with square Doric piers was added to the front in 1820 and an iron Ionic colonnade down the side a decade later. The contrast between the positively rough exterior and the inside could not be greater; the foyers and associated spaces are sumptuous, especially the double height rotunda. The auditorium, which seats 2,300, was renovated in the 1920s by Emblin Walker, Edward

Jones and Robert Cromie. It does not match the standard of the foyers but it is an impressive space

Tobacco Warehouse (129)
1811–1814
Wapping Lane, E1;
tube: Shadwell/Wapping
Daniel Alexander

The warehouse was built as a bonded store with spaces on the ground floor level for tobacco and later furs, and vaults below for wines and spirits. What remain of an originally larger complex are six parallel halls, each 112 metres long and sixteen metres wide. They are spanned by composite timber and cast iron trusses of great elegance carried in turn on strange tree-like cast iron columns. The large brick vaults below have an organic Gaudi-esque quality. The 1980s saw a heroic attempt to re-use these wonderful but redundant and remote halls as a shopping destination, the architect was Terry Farrell. The gamble was a spectacular failure and the fate of the Warehouse is still uncertain.

Dulwich Picture Gallery (130)
1811–1814
Gallery Road, SE21;
train: North Dulwich
John Soane

Noel Desenfans and Francis Bourgeois, two London art dealers, had been charged by the King of Poland to assemble a collection of painting for his nation, and when that was temporarily indisposed in 1795 the paintings were in need of a home. On his death Bourgeois bequeathed the paintings to Dulwich College, along with money for a building to house them as well as for some almshouses and a mausoleum for Desenfans, who had died ear-

lier. This was Soane's unusual composite brief, often described as the first purpose built art gallery in the world. He designed a string of rooms, each opening onto the rooms adjacent and, in order to maximise hanging space, entirely without windows. The rooms are lit indirectly from above. This has been the template for many subsequent galleries. The mausoleum is a freestanding structure to the west, although connected to the main building. The almshouses were also on the west side, disposed symmetrically about the mausoleum. Later in the 19th century the almshouses were converted into additional gallery space. Although the arrangement is simple and the materials humble – brick with stone trimmings – the building is highly wrought in Soane's individualistic intense classicism. The mausoleum is particularly sombre and moving. In the late 1990s Rick Mather was commissioned to add a temporary exhibitions gallery, café and other amenities, which he did in the shape of a very elegant steel, glass and brick pavilion off to one side of the entrance court.

Park Crescent (131)
1812–1822
Park Crescent, NW1; tube: Regent's Park/Great Portland Street
John Nash

ENSEMBLE In Nash's great plan for 'Metropolitan Improvements', Park Crescent was the northern end of his route from the new Regent's Park to Whitehall. Nash had intended a circus at this point but his builder went bankrupt. Nash decided to make do with the crescent he had, adding terraces to the north to cre-

ate Park Square. In terms of its relationship to the park this was surely a better solution. Bisected by Portland Place the crescent is almost devoid of detail. There is a grid of windows regularly punched into the stucco, a recessed colonnade

of paired Ionic columns at ground level and excuses for pediments at the ends of the two blocks. If it feels a bit like a stage set then at least it is a grand sweeping one.

St Marylebone (132)
1813–1817
Marylebone Road, W1; tube: Baker Street/Regent's Park
Thomas Hardwick

A church has been hereabouts since the early 15th century and one of its incarnations appears in Hogarth's 'A Rake's Progress'. As civilization spread northwards the congregation grew and something larger and grander was required. The new church has a large, five-bay Corinthian stone portico the width of the

nave under a circular tower topped with a cupola carried splendidly by golden caryatids. The first bay, containing stairs to the galleries, has attached columns and projects beyond the nave. The last bay, also with columns, projects at 45°, the north side having once been an entrance from Marylebone High Street. Behind the west front, the church is stucco with stone dressings. The interior originally had two levels of galleries on three sides supported by slender iron columns under a flat ceiling. The upper galleries on the north and south sides were removed in the late 19th century by Thomas Harris, who added the apse at the east end. The small churchyard is lovely.

Funerary Monument (133)
1815
St Pancras Old Church Yard, Pancras Road, NW1; tube: Mornington Crescent/ Kings Cross St Pancras
John Soane

The church here has fragments dating back to the 7th century, but it is now mostly Victorian and quite dreadful. The architectural interest is all in the monument that Soane designed for his wife and under which he was later buried. The marble monument itself is sheltered under a square pendentive dome carried on four square 'Ionic' pillars and topped with a pineapple. There is much of the distinctive Soanian inscribed decoration and his treasured acroteria. The churchyard itself has been sundered from the world by excessive infrastructure and is wonderfully atmospheric. Near to Soane are memorials to two other English greats, the feminist, Mary Wollstonecraft, and her anarchist husband, William Godwin.

Burlington Arcade (134)
1818–1819
Between Piccadilly and Burlington Gardens, W1;
tube: Green Park/Piccadilly Circus
Samuel Ware

The arcade was developed as a speculation by George Cavendish (Lord Burlington) on a strip of land running down the west side of his house. It is London's first, longest (178 metres) and most consistently successful and glamorous arcade. The shops have delicately detailed protruding wooden fronts with curved glass at the corners, above which are white painted oriel windows. The length is divided by Ionic pilasters under arched timber portals supporting the glazed pitched roof. In three places the arcade steps up to three storeys. The south façade was reworked by Arthur Beresford Pite in 1911 and the north by Bates and Sinning in 1937; neither is a great success.

St Pancras New Church   (135)
1819–1822
Upper Woburn Place, NW1; tube: Euston
Henry and William Inwood

On account of its prominent location and its large ladies, St Pancras is probably one of the best known and best loved buildings in London. In response to population growth the decision was made to subdivide the parish of St Pancras and a competition for a new church was held. It was won by a local father and son, the latter of whom had recently returned from a trip to Greece and it certainly shows. The full width six-column Ionic portico to the west front is topped awkwardly by a three stage octagonal tower based on the Tower of the Winds in Athens. The flanks have simple rectangular windows with an array of acroteria at the roof edge and the east end is apsidal. Two porticos, north and south, form an unusual feature at the east end and serve as entrances to the burial vaults under the church, each with four large terracotta caryatids modelled by John Charles Felix Rossi. The porticos are replicas of those at the Erechtheum, a Greek temple on the acropolis. The interior is fairly simple with the galleries supported by columns with lotus leaf capitals, a flat soffit and giant Ionic columns around the apse.

Theatre Royal Haymarket   (136)
1820–1821
Haymarket, SW1; tube: Piccadilly Circus
John Nash

Nash was keen to rebuild the old Haymarket theatre to serve as a suitable termination to his extension of Charles II Street. His design at least accomplishes this. A big stucco box with an imposing five-bay Corinthian portico with gilded capitals stuck on the front, it does look impressive coming down Haymarket from Piccadilly Circus. Over the portico are nine pretty little round cast iron windows with a few more scattered about the elevation; that is about the extent of Nash's contribution. The interior has been rebuilt more than once. The 888-seat auditorium was remodelled at the start of the 20th century by Stanley Adshead; it is intimate and nicely proportioned with two levels of balconies in an ornate French neoclassical style, with lots of gilt.

John Nash (137)
*1752 in London, †1835 in Cowes, Isle of Wight (137)

Nash is an intriguing figure, seemingly a man looking to make money and get ahead rather than perfect his art. Yet it is he, beyond any other architect, who has had the greatest impact on London. The young Nash was apprenticed to Robert Taylor, a reasonably eminent Palladian architect working mostly on large houses for the wealthy. Nash's own practice followed similar lines though he was flexible about style and showed an early interest in romantic 'picturesque' compositions; his Blaise Hamlet of 1811 for instance takes the form of nine exaggeratedly 'rustic' cottages.

Even talent is scarcely more useful for an architect's career than a rich and powerful patron and Nash was lucky to fall in with the Carlton House set centred on the Prince Regent, the future King George IV. It was for the Prince Regent that Nash created the extraordinary, absurd, Hindoo confection that is the Brighton Pavilion. In 1806 Nash was appointed Surveyor to the Office of Woods and Forests. The post ordinarily yielded few opportunities but in 1810 the farm leases of Marylebone Park, then on the northern fringe of the growing city, were to revert to the Crown, giving the Prince the chance to beautify his capital and make a great deal of money. Instead of a continuation of London's pattern of streets and squares, Nash proposed the radical creation of a Great Park dotted with free-standing mansions and ringed with imposing terraces.

To provide access to this, then outlandish, suburb a new processional route was devised. Starting at Carlton House on the north side of St James's Park, Regent Street heads north to Piccadilly Circus, bends around the Quadrant and continues north across Oxford Circus to Langham Place where it executes its famous shimmy around Nash's All Souls Church (no. 141) to join Portland Place. At the top of Portland Place, Nash devised Park Crescent (no. 131) as a suitably imposing introduction to the new park with its colossal terraces. These are all stuccoed residences aggregated into neoclassical compositions on the grandest scale. East of the park, north of the terraces is Park Village (no. 145), one of the earliest picturesque suburbs with villas scattered about in sylvan disarray. South of Park Village were a series of squares and markets of which little survives. Regent Street itself was developed for commercial uses, again behind unified neoclassical façades; these were redeveloped but the plan of the original street remains. In a related development to Carlton House Terrace (no. 156) at the end of Regent Street, Trafalgar Square (no. 138) was laid out and the west Strand terraces were constructed. St James's Park was remodelled and the Mall was set out to focus on a refaced Buckingham Palace (no. 147).

All of this represents an extraordinary burst of activity unparalleled in London's history and never repeated. In fifteen years the face of the West End was transformed with new public spaces of unprecedented formality and grandeur. Most importantly, London and its citizens had gained a wonderful new park bounded by fairytale, wedding cake architecture.

Despite his contributions Nash has been the subject of much criticism. He is charged with being interested in the picturesque aspects of architecture to the exclusion of all else. The quality of construction of his big set pieces was found to be poor and his designs lack a sense of materiality – it is all just painted 'stuff'. His buildings are also internally uninteresting, lacking the spatial ingenuity and complexity of Soane's contemporary work. Famously, the backs of his buildings are messy and ill-considered as if Nash only ever gave thought to the show fronts. In summary, it seems he was more a designer or even painter of stage flats than a proper architect. Some of the fault no doubt lies in the nature and quantity of the works he was responsible for: generally speculative housing done on a large scale to a tight budget. His stone-built church, All Souls (no. 141), would suggest that he was capable of better things when circumstances permitted.

Whatever deficiencies have to be admitted, Nash must be credited with his virtues which, when strolling around Regent's Park of a summers evening, are both obvious and considerable; he had a great eye for the picturesque and a very un-British gift for ambitious large scale urban design. If it is only scene painting then it is a very fine scene.

Cumberland Terrace, Regent's Park

Trafalgar Square (138)
1820–1845
Trafalgar Square, WC2;
tube: Charing Cross
John Nash

ENSEMBLE This is the only square in central London with a hard surface and, as such, has become the focal point for many gatherings of the populace, both happy and unhappy. It lies at the junction between two important axes through the city, The Strand running east to west and Whitehall and Charing Cross Road north to south. It was presumably this strategic location that prompted Nash to propose a public square at this point and it became possible after the Royal Mews (no. 142), which occupied the site, were moved to Buckingham Palace in 1820. The terrace and steps on the north side that negotiate the fall across the site were designed by Charles Barry (1840-1845). The principle monument is Nelson's Column; standing at just over fifty-seven metres, it was designed by William Railton and Nelson was sculpted by Edward Baily. Edwin Landseer's much-loved lions at the base were added in 1865 and the fountains by Edwin Luytens date from 1939. Despite its prominence in national life it is not entirely successful as an external space; of the buildings around it only St Martin and the Admiralty Arch have the

presence to address such a big space and it is much plagued by traffic. Foster and Partners' recent overhaul improved the site, particularly the pedestrianisation of the north side.

Woburn Walk (139)
1822
Woburn Walk, between Upper Woburn Place and Duke's Road, WC1;
tube: Euston
Thomas Cubitt

A delightful little bosky pedestrian cut through, Woburn Walk was built on the edge of the Bedford estate. The ground floor of the three storeys has timber doors and bayed shop fronts, while the upper floors are rendered with large tripartite windows with paterae on a raised surround. There are pretty ironwork balcony railings at first floor level and Greek-looking scrolled parapet decoration. The fabric carries on around the

corner into Duke's Road. It is so simple but works so well you have to wonder why we have been unable to do more like this in our cities.

Sussex Place (140)
1822
Outer Circle, Regent's Park, NW1;
tube: Baker Street
John Nash

Nash's intention was to surround the newly laid out Regent's Park with a series of grand terraces that would have enough presence to match the scale of the park and would be a lucrative development

leried on three sides and supported by piers, while Corinthian columns standing on the balcony walls support a coved ceiling. A basement was installed in the

opportunity for his client, the Prince Regent. Of all of these, Sussex Place is the most picturesque and the oddest. It is four storeys high with the top storey expressed as an attic behind the parapet balustrade, and seventy-seven bays long, nearly 200 metres, with a long tri-partite central section and curved wings to the end. Most of the stucco façade to the park is behind a screen wall with giant Corinthian columns on an arched arcade and there is an insignificant pediment in the centre. The most striking feature consists of ten octagonal bays, which push through the screen wall and are terminated with tall octagonal domes with spikes – it all has a slightly odd, Indian feel. Sussex Place is now home to the London Business School.

All Souls Langham Place (141)
1822–1824
Langham Place, W1; tube: Oxford Circus
John Nash

This is Nash's only extant church and he used it cleverly to help him with a little problem he had – his grand ceremonial north-south route had a kink in it where Regents Street met Portman Place. By designing the church with a circular portico and tower and locating it at the kink, it acts as a pivot around the corner and significantly improves the route. The portico has Ionic columns and radiating steps up and the tower above has a drum of Corinthian columns and a steep spire. Otherwise, the church is a plain Bath stone box with two levels of punched stone windows. The entrance in the base of the tower leads to a nave gal-

1960s when it was discovered that the outer walls continued below the ground for nearly four metres.

Royal Mews (142)
1822–1825
Buckingham Palace Road, SW1;
tube: Victoria
John Nash

Relocated adjacent to the Palace from Charing Cross, the Mews proper are in the form of a brick and stucco quadrangle with stone dressings. The arched entry has paired, heavily blocked Doric columns and a stubby little square clock

93

tower, a design that repeats around the tree-planted courtyard. The ground floor is used for stabling and coach houses and is lit by large semi-circular high level windows. The first floor is accommodation for staff and is accessed from external balconies. Adjacent is the Riding House, a thirteen-bay shed with large semi-circular windows and a central pediment housing a frieze. It certainly seems strange that the stables have some of the simple architectural dignity and quality that the Palace sorely lacks.

British Museum (143)
1823–1852
Great Russell Street, WC1;
tube: Tottenham Court Road/Holborn
Robert Smirke

The Museum came together in an ad-hoc way as various disparate collections came into the ownership of the state. Montague House in Holborn was purchased for the display of these and opened in 1759. Once established, the Museum grew rapidly through bequests and it became clear that the old house would have to be replaced. Smirke's pure neo-Greek design in Portland stone is based around a two-storey courtyard. The massive Ionic portico

and colonnade on the south elevation has become iconic and is a popular meeting place. Once started, the collection never stopped growing and, despite launching daughter institutions like the British Library (no. 403) and the Natural History Museum (no. 202), there was always a need for extra space. Smirke's brother Sydney filled in the courtyard with the celebrated Reading Room and stacks in the 1850s. The north wing was added between 1907 and 1914 by Burnet Tait and Partners, and the Duveen Gallery to the west by John Russell Pope between 1938 and 1962; both are in a neoclassical style. There was a small extension westwards in 1980 and one into the roof space a few years later.

In 1994, Foster and Partners won a major competition for the rearrangement of the courtyard. The stacks were demolished, the Reading Room was retained as a free standing object, the original courtyard elevations restored and the remainder of the courtyard was covered with a geometrically complex fully glazed roof. It is a most extraordinary room. Further developments are underway in the north-west corner of the site scheduled for completion in 2012.

94

St Peter's Walworth (144)
1823–1825
Liverpool Grove, SE17; tube: Kennington
John Soane

St Peter's displays all of Soane's originality and, while having the same basic elements of countless such churches, it manages to be very different. The main structure is a big yellow brick box unusually wide and low, the entrance to which is a recess in the front containing giant Ionic columns supporting a Greek key frieze and an emphatic flat entablature. The eight bays of the nave itself have single round-headed windows in stepped recesses with a stone transom marking the level of the gallery inside. The rear, where there is a setback at the upper level, uses the same elements but has a distinctly Egyptian feel to it. The stone tower is very slender in contrast to the horizontality of the façade and its square base with a circular drum of Composite columns supports a dome. Inside, the galleries are supported on Doric columns, which rise to support an arcade of semi-circular arches under a flat panelled ceiling. There are corresponding segmental arches across the nave at the altar and the west gallery; together they define a space within the space. There is an impressive series of brick vaulted crypts beneath the church.

Park Village West and East (145)
1824–1828
Park Village West and East, NW1;
tube: Camden Town
John Nash

ENSEMBLE Tucked away behind the great terraces at the north end of Nash's

developments to the east of Regents is a pioneering picturesque garden suburb. It is by no means the first, but one of the earliest and most influential of such developments. A series of detached middle sized stucco villas are arranged apparently casually along narrow winding roads lined with trees. Each house is stylistically different, with Gothick and Italianate styles predominating. Most have some picturesque 'feature' such as a balcony or a tower. No. 12, with its octagonal tower, wizard's hat roof and inset painted relief panel, is

the most striking. Many dreary suburbs may have been formed in their wake but the Park Villages themselves are most charming and remain to this day highly sought after places to live.

St Mark's (146)
1824–1828
North Audley Street, W1;
tube: Marble Arch/Bond Street
John Gandy-Deering

The church front sits in a Mayfair terrace and is scarcely wider than the adjacent housing blocks. Built of stone, it is in a very convincing neo-Greek style. The three-bay Ionic portico, which is the full width of the plot, has no pediment. There is no tower as such and instead the bell is housed in a pretty little latticed lantern. This front leads into a large three-bay anteroom with square

piers and stairs to the balconies at the end. The church proper is deep within the site; unfortunately this was reconstructed by Arthur Blomfield in 1878 in an entirely uninteresting Gothic style. The church was declared redundant in 1974 and has led a precarious existence ever since.

Buckingham Palace (147)
1825–1837
The Mall, SW1;
tube: Victoria/St James Park
John Nash

The construction history of the Palace is extremely muddled and the resultant fabric bears the marks of it. Buckingham House was built at the beginning of the 18th century by the Duke of that county and designed by William Winde, but none of this house

is visible externally. William Chambers encased it and added wings for Queen Charlotte (1762–1780). When George IV decided to make the place his principle residence he hired his good friend Nash to do what was required with the £250,000 voted for the purpose by Parliament. Between George and Nash, they managed to spend £600,000 and still be nowhere near completion before George died and Nash was sacked in 1830. Edward Blore was summoned to finish the Palace, and did so during the following two decades. The well-known east façade is a necessary re-facing of Blore's work by Aston Webb in 1913. After this long history, we are left with a very large house arranged around a central courtyard with some grand rooms inside; externally it is dull and uneven, with a touch of dignity if no great delight bestowed by Webb.

Lancaster House (148)
1825–1827
Stable Yard Road off Cleveland Row, SW1;
tube: Green Park
Benjamin Dean and Philip Wyatt

The House was meant for the heir to the throne, the Duke of York, but he died in a welter of debt in 1827 with the House partially completed. The site was taken over by George Leveson-Gower, by repute the richest man in England, who retained the Wyatts but added Robert Smirke and later Charles Barry – a lot of architects working on one building. The House is huge, freestanding and in Bath stone. Originally two storeys tall with eleven by nine bays, Smirke added a further storey, which spoiled the proportions. The ground floor is rusticated and there are Corinthian porticos on three sides, all of which are single-storey, flat to the west and the south and pedimented to the north. The colossal rooms are arranged around an impossibly grand central stair and the décor is in a colourful French Renaissance style known, in England, as Louis XIV. The house eventually came into the hands of William Lever who renamed it and left it to the state. The Foreign and Commonwealth Office use it for conferences and suchlike.

Custom House (149)
1825–1828
Lower Thames Street, EC3;
tube: Monument/Tower Hill
Robert Smirke

There has been a series of Custom Houses in this vicinity, regulating the business of the port and levying taxes since the 14th century. It is a line of business subject to fires. After yet another fire in 1812, David Laing completed the construction of the outline of the current building, the central part of which collapsed into the storage vaults underneath. Smirke rebuilt the central sections to a revised design. The long – too long – Portland stone façade has a central Ionic portico with attached groups of Ionic columns to either side. Behind the portico at first floor level is the severe and aptly named Long Room with Tuscan pilasters and an elliptical vaulted ceiling, which combine to create a severe room. It is still in use by HM Revenue and Customs.

Cumberland Terrace (150)
1826
Cumberland Terrace, NW1; tube: Great Portland Street/Camden Town
John Nash

Cumberland is the most grandiloquent and enjoyable of Nash's Regent's Park terraces. Stucco like the rest, it has four storeys with a rusticated ground floor, two intermediate floors between giant

Ionic columns or pilasters, and an attic storey over the entablature. The central unit sits forward and has eleven bays, of which nine are pedimented over detached columns. The pediment's tympanium is full of figures and topped with statues. Recessed sections with pilasters lead to pairs of three-bay pavilions with attached columns, between which are great arches which provide access to service mews behind the terrace. Further recessed sections terminate in a single pavilion block. The terrace has proved adaptable to all manner of uses and remains a very popular place to live.

St John's, Bethnal Green (151)
1826–1828
Cambridge Heath Road, E2;
tube: Bethnal Green
John Soane

This has the same basic elements as Soane's other commissioner's churches but it has suffered far more during its history. The structure is a brick box with double height windows to the nave and pilasters of indeterminate order to the front and marking the end bays of the flanks. The horribly clumsy window tracery is not original. The tower has a square base, which Soane had intended to top with a thin round domed stage, similar to St Peter's, Walworth (no. 144), but this was cut down for cost reasons and the tower still looks somewhat

sawn off. The church suffered a fire and the interior was remodelled in 1871 by William Mundy. The galleries are supported on Doric columns, according to the Soane design, above which Mundy installed Gothic timber arcades and a lame hammerbeam roof; he was also responsible for the window tracery. Soane was luckier with Bodley, who added a sympathetic two-bay chancel in 1888.

United Services Club (152)
1826–1828
Pall Mall, SW1; tube: Charing Cross
John Nash

The Club is a decorated stucco box of seven bays by seven and two storeys, although a mansard was added later. The ground floor is rusticated and all of the windows are pedimented with round heads at the ground floor level and triangular above. There is a two-storey portico on the north side with ground floor paired Doric columns and Corinthian columns on the upper storey. Beneath the pediment is a highly decorated frieze, which runs around the whole of the building, and there is similar sculptural ornament in the pediment. Much of this is credited to Decimus Burton, who carried out alterations in the 1850s. The London gentlemen's clubs were closely modelled on country houses so that their members would feel at home when they visited the capital. In this case, there are a

series of large-scale rooms, of which the library is the grandest, arranged around a theatrical central stair hall.

Holy Trinity, Marylebone (153)
1826–1828
Marylebone Road, NW1; tube: Great Portland Street/Regent's Park
John Soane

This, the last of Soane's commissioner's churches, appears very much like a more expensive and elaborate version of St Peter's, Walworth (no. 144). It is in stone and the budget extended to rows of attached Ionic columns between the double height windows down the flanks. The front has a projecting Ionic portico with no pediment and an external pulpit, although the vicar would find it hard to be heard in Marylebone Road now. The etiolated tower has a square base under a drum of columns carrying a small dome. Inside, there are Tuscan columns carrying the balconies with piers above carrying rounded arches under a flat ceiling. As at St Peter's, there are segmental transverse arches but also additional arches one bay from the end of the nave, which further complicate an understanding of where spaces begin and end.

Belgrave Square (154)
1826–1837
Belgrave Square, SW1;
tube: Knightsbridge/Hyde Park Corner
George Basevi

ENSEMBLE The establishment of the royal family at Buckingham Palace only served to confirm the gradual westward drift of the centre of gravity of money and fashion in the city. This shift, away from Bloomsbury towards Belgravia, persists to this day. It was with this in mind that Thomas Cubitt, the great builder and developer of his age, leased fields a little south of the Palace and set out the mightiest of London's squares. He contrived the roads to enter the square at the corners a little apart, so that there is not only space for four huge terraces, but also for a large mansion in each corner, three of which are occupied. The terraces were designed by Basevi, a pupil of Soane, and are four storeys tall in stucco with the centre and end blocks embellished with attached Corinthian columns. The south mansion was built by Henry Kendall (1826), the west by Robert Smirke (1830–1833), and the east by Philip Hardwick (1842–1845). It is all impressive and grand but not exactly beautiful or loveable, though seemingly well-liked by diplomats.

99

The Athenæum   (155)
1827–1830
Waterloo Place, SW1;
tube: Charing Cross
Decimus Burton

The founders of the Athenæum believed that the growth in private clubs had caused the demise of many of the old coffee houses, where men of artistic and literary inclination used to meet. They founded this new club as a meeting place for such men. On the advice of fully occupied club member Nash, they appointed the twenty-four-year-old Burton, who designed for them an absolute beauty of a building – a simple, very classical, beautifully proportioned two-storey stucco rectangular box, seven bays long and five bays wide. The ground floor is rusticated and the windows are rectangular throughout, with voussoirs at ground level and flat topped projecting surrounds above. A continuous balcony runs around at the upper floor level on masonry brackets with iron railings. The entrance has a single-storey portico with paired Doric columns. A carved frieze runs around the tops of the walls copied by John Henning from the Parthenon, the background of which is painted Wedgewood blue. A regrettable second storey was added at the end of the 18th century by Thomas Collcutt, which he at least kept well back from the balustered parapet. Like other such clubs, the rooms are arranged around a central stair hall. The interiors are finely judged and tasteful rather than grand, and much space is given over to libraries; the double height south library is especially atmospheric. Despite its age and its emphasis on the antique, the Athenæum still looks wonderfully clean and fresh.

Carlton House Terrace   (156)
1827–1833
Carlton House Terrace, SW1;
tube: Charing Cross
John Nash

The Terrace is a suitably grandiose southern termination to Nash's triumphal route through the city. In the centre is the Duke of York's column by Benjamin Dean Wyatt, commemorating the Prince Regent's military brother. This stands at the head of a ceremonial flight of steps down to The Mall and St James's Park. To either side of the steps are the east and west terraces, each of which contain nine vast houses. The central part of the blocks have a giant Corinthian colonnade running between five-bay end blocks, which protrude and are a storey higher. Above the colonnade is an attic storey with a limp pediment in the middle. On the south (park) side there is a broad terrace under which is the service accommodation for the houses, expressed with a bulky-looking Doric attached colonnade. The Crown Estates' policy has been to let the terrace to professional, cultural and scientific institutions. One such is the Institute of Contemporary Arts, whose section below the terrace was converted by Fry, Drew and Partners in the 1960s.

Covent Garden Market   (157)
1828–1830
Covent Garden, WC2;
tube: Covent Garden
Charles Fowler

Covent Garden Piazza had been laid out by Inigo Jones for Francis Russell between 1629 and 1637, and various developers had built uniform arcaded houses around the square as required by the leases. It was the first such London square and, for a time, the most exclusive. This ended with the introduction of a formal market for fruit, flowers and vegetables in 1670, the enclosures for which were repeatedly rebuilt, more elaborately each time. The final form has three parallel wings running east to west, of which the outer two are two-storied with Tuscan arcades to the street, pyramid roofed lodges at the ends and a central pedimented archway leading to a passage. The central block has two banks of shops facing onto a central walkway with a glazed roof. At the east end is a sheltered outdoor area with a flat terrace roof and the west end is open with a portico across the middle block. To provide more sheltered space the gaps between the wings were roofed over in the 1870s and 1880s by W. Cubitt and Co.

In 1974 the market was moved to a more convenient location and the old buildings refurbished as an exclusive shopping destination by Greater London Council; this has been an unqualified success and something of a victim of that very success.

101

"London: a nation not a city." (158)

Benjamin Disraeli, Novelist and Prime Minister (1804, 1881)

Victorian London began as Georgian London ended, with modest residential development and some cultural institutions, such as the National Gallery (no. 163) and Kew Gardens (no. 168). The pace of change soon picked up however. From 1831 to 1901 the city's population grew from 1.6 million to 6.5 million and the world's first super city came into being, not entirely smoothly, against the backdrop of the Industrial Revolution. As if to compensate for the internal upheavals, most of the period was spent at peace abroad. Britain was the world's leading financial, industrial and military power, all of which was flamboyantly celebrated at the 1851 Great Exhibition (no. 175).

The first great change was the arrival of the railways cutting brutal swathes through the fabric of the city and headed by massive terminals (nos. 176, 177, 191). Where trains could not be run on the surface they were put in tunnels; the world's first underground line was built between Paddington and Farringdon (1860–1863). Scarcely less disruptive than the railways were slum clearance/road widening schemes. Road widening was often

related to new or renewed crossings of the Thames; there were four new bridges in this period including Albert Bridge (no. 198), Tower Bridge (no. 220) and Joseph Bazalgette's suspension bridge at Hammersmith. In all the Victorians built nine road and eight rail bridges and four tunnels crossing the Thames. A related development was Bazalgette's Victoria Embankment providing a pleasant and useful thoroughfare for vehicles and an essential link in the network of life-saving sewers built between 1859 and 1865.

The Victorians' infrastructure transformations were the glory of the era. Of the terror and the pity of it Charles Dickens and French engraver Gustave Doré still speak most eloquently; many Londoners lived in appalling poverty and squalor. Without work you might die on the street; with work you might yet die young, undernourished and exhausted. The city struggled to keep pace with its growing population and in many crucial respects it made no effort until near the end of the period. Legislation was passed in 1870 for the universal provision of education (see nos. 204, 236) and for the provision of

Sectional View of Thames Embankment at Charing Cross.

working class housing in 1890 (see nos. 238, 245).

Noted for its commerce, it is easy to forget that London was a major industrial city in the 19th century with important shipbuilding, food processing, metalworking and watchmaking industries. Much of this took place on the edges of the city and has left scant architectural traces. More visible, in its ruin, is London's role as the world's largest port for much of the 19th century.

For those who could afford it, house building continued at a furious pace, moving further from the centre and from the Georgian model as the century wore on. The new West End suburbs like Kensington and Brompton deviated early on from Georgian brickwork and adopted a rendered white classical wedding cake style. Georgian architecture, characterised as 'boring', was replaced by a range of different styles, including neo-Greek, Roman, Gothic of all descriptions, Byzantine and Tudor. Much of this looks ill-conceived and anti-rational in hindsight, even when executed with skill, conviction and panache.

As the century drew to a close, a more rationalist style focused on functionality and the logic of building began to develop. The Arts and Crafts Movement tried to dispense with overt stylistic references, though an attachment to English Vernacular buildings is apparent in its early phases. The Victorian design age was enormously improved by the Arts and Crafts sensibility, which could be brought to bear on any building or style.

Many important government institutions were housed in the period, most notably the Houses of Parliament (no. 169), but also the Royal Courts of Justice (no. 200) and the Metropolitan Police (no. 225) among others. Important cultural buildings include the Tate Gallery (no. 237), the Natural History Museum (no. 202) and the Royal Opera House (no. 179). Catholic emancipation prompted a mighty new cathedral at Westminster (no. 243). The rising professional classes were building headquarters for their associations (nos. 160, 229). Retail was also on the rise; London got its first department store, Harrods (no. 239), at the end of the century.

Goldsmiths' Hall (159)
1829–1835
Foster Lane, EC2; tube: St Paul's
Philip Hardwick

Founded in 1327, the Worshipful Company of Goldsmiths had their first Hall on this site twelve years later. A duty of the Company was to ascertain and mark ('hallmark') the quality of precious metals. They retain this function and one of the UK's four Assay Offices is at the Hall. The Goldsmiths are one of the richest of the Livery Companies and seemed set on underlining the point when they rebuilt their Hall as an imposing stone Renaissance palace. The central feature of the three-storey façades consists of six attached giant Corinthian columns with corner pilasters, creating an atmosphere of early 18th-century England. The interiors are vast and lavish particularly the marble lined, domed stair hall and the Livery Hall, which has attached Corinthian pilasters, a heavily coffered ceiling and awful a lot of gilding.

Law Society (160)
1829–1857
Chancery Lane, WC2;
tube: Chancery Lane
Louis Vulliamy

The building was constructed in phases: the central block was built first and was followed by three bays to the north and

then to the south. The latter was by Philip Charles Hardwick, who maintained strict symmetry and also remodelled some of the interior. The elevation to Chancery Lane is chaste stony neo-Greek with a giant recessed pedimented Ionic portico and simple forceful detailing. The inside has been much altered and is not of great interest. Much more so is the extension by a young Charles Holden (1902–1904). Standing on the corner, it has two identical façades with a central section emphasized by cutting away the upper storey of the ends. It is a very successful and inventive Neo-Mannerist reading of the classical and could easily be mistaken for high-quality work of the 1930s. The ground floor has great arched windows whose mullions are topped by sculpted figures of various ill clad legal ladies, above which are large Venetian windows.

The stone vaulted stair hall is spatially inventive and has eau de nil tiling inset with floral panels by William de Morgan; they feel like an anachronism in this building but a very pretty one.

Eaton Square and Eaton Place (161)
1830–1855
Eaton Square and Eaton Place, SW1;
tube: Sloane Square
Thomas Cubitt

ENSEMBLE Cubitt's scheme is the apotheosis of the West End developments, in grandeur and ambition if in nothing else. The 'Square' is 500 metres long and 120 metres wide. Usually of four storeys, some is in brick with stucco dressings but most is entirely in stucco with giant Corinthian pilasters turning to columns where emphasis is required. There are generally individual entrance porticos, but Nos. 83-102 have a continuous Doric colonnade at ground floor

level, which is more satisfactory. It is interesting to see how a few variations on the very successful Georgian system results in its downfall and instead of the unassuming charm of Bedford Square, for example, this is typical of overweight, pompous and monotonous west London wedding cake architecture. Eaton Place is equally 'grand'.

Fishmongers' Hall (162)
1831–1835
King William Street, EC4;
tube: Monument
Henry Roberts

Perhaps surprisingly, the Fishmongers' Company is one of the older, grander and richer of the City Livery Companies. Certainly, if Fish Hall is second to the near

contemporary Goldsmiths' in point of architectural ambition, it is second to none in terms of its location at the north end of London Bridge. The rusticated and arcaded ground floor is at river level and was let out to commercial enterprises related to the river. The entrance faces the bridge approach with a recessed three-bay Ionic portico set in eleven bays; the south facing river elevation of seven bays has two-storey attached Ionic columns under a pediment, all on top of a riverside terrace. The material is Portland stone and the style a restrained and refined neo-Greek; the stair and livery hall are the most impressive spaces. The Hall has Corinthian pilasters and an elliptical coffered vaulted ceiling. The Fishmongers retain wide-ranging powers regarding the quality of fish for sale in the capital, salmon fisheries throughout the country and the import of shellfish.

National Gallery (163)
1833–1838
Trafalgar Square, WC2;
tube: Charing Cross
William Wilkins

While the collection is undoubtedly a national treasure, the buildings have been a long-running saga of national embarrassment and controversy. The site on the north side of Trafalgar Square is perhaps the most prominent in the whole city, but unfortunately the façade does not do justice to its location. In stone and with thirteen different sections it lacks coherence, and at only two storeys over a raised basement it lacks presence. The central Corinthian portico with its thin pediment attempts something grander, but it is topped by the feeblest of domes matched with equally feeble lanterns stuck on the ends. The interiors, while not so disappointing, are by no means memorable. As the collection expanded so did the building, and in 1866 Charles Barry won a competition to redevelop the whole site. In the end he was only able to complete a large extension on the northeast side of the Wilkins' building that is scarcely visible externally. It is large and

axially planned about a central octagon with four arms creating four lightwells. It has been loathed by generations of curators for its massive scale, pomposity and overbearing décor. Between 1907 and 1911 the government Office of Works created a similarly planned mirror image of the Barry block to the west with a little less bombast but no great charm. In the 1970s, the Department of the Environment's architects created the north extension, seemingly in response to a road that was never built. It is in the unpopular 1970s bunker style with small slit windows in mostly blank walls.

A further site for expansion to the west had long been identified, but unlike the previous extensions, it was a prominent site highly visible from the square. This naturally engendered a very protracted procurement and it was only in 1981 that an official competition was held, which had to be abandoned after the Prince of Wales criticised the winner. At this point, retail magnates, the Sainsbury brothers, stepped in and offered to fund the extension with a slightly altered brief, thereby necessitating another competition. The eventual winner of this were the American post-modern theorists, Venturi, Rauch and Scott Brown, and the Sainsbury wing was finally completed in 1991. The new wing is slightly detached from the Wilkins' building and takes the form of a nearly blank stone box with a dribble of Corinthian pilasters scattered about it, supposedly a very clever play with the language of classicism for the modern age. It is very hard to see where the cleverness lies or to like the build-

ing's exterior. The intimate top lit gallery rooms, however, are the nicest in the building. More recently, Dixon Jones have been refurbishing and altering the east wing, most notably creating a street level entrance hall in one of Barry's courtyards. Against the run of play this isn't all bad.

Giraffe House (164)
1836–1837
Regent's Park, Prince Albert Road, NW1;
tube: Regent's Park/Camden Town
Decimus Burton

The Zoological Gardens as a whole were laid out by Burton, but all that remains of his work are the entrance tunnels, Clock Tower and the Giraffe House. This is a simple three-bay brick box with large round arched openings to the front and high-level windows on the other sides. The slate roof overhangs at the eaves and at the verge forming vestigial pediments. Effectively, the building is a typically robust and straightforward Victorian stable block, which gains extra charm from the necessity of being scaled up in only one direction, the vertical, to accommodate its unusual inhabitants. In response to criticism the Zoo has been reviewing its accommodation with respect to animal welfare in recent years and it seems that the Giraffe House works well enough to remain in its original use.

Euston Arch   (165)
1837–1838
Euston Road, NW1; tube: Euston Square
Philip Hardwick

DEMOLITION Euston Arch was a huge Doric propylaeum in sandstone built as a celebratory entrance to Euston station. Two flank walls supported a pediment roof with a pair of gigantic columns at each end, there was never an arch as such. The structure was never really necessary but it stood as a concrete symbol of the confidence and panache of the golden age of railway development. By the 1960s the decision had been made to 'modernise', that is, demolish and rebuild, the station, and the Arch was to be destroyed along with it. The Arch attracted much support, becoming a cause célèbre for conservationists. The controversy crystallised the arguments surrounding London's development, seeing the conservationists line up against the modernisers. Eventually, after some unsavoury politicking, the Arch was demolished along with the station, which was the work of Hardwick's son. The losers of the conflict have never reconciled themselves to their defeat, mainly because the demolition was entirely unnecessary. Large as it was for a gateway, the Arch occupied very little space and any redevelopment could have accommodated it if the will had been there. Alternatively it could have been moved.

The fight for the rebuilding of the Arch goes on.

Reform Club   (166)
1838–1941
Pall Mall, SW1; tube: Charing Cross
Charles Barry

The Reform Club was established for liberal-minded politicians who had supported the Reform Acts and who, on this account, were unwelcome in some of the older Whig clubs. The exterior resembles an Italian Renaissance palace, the Farnese Palace in Rome is a likely source. This was a new idea in London and became immensely influential. The structure consists of a large Portland stone box, three storeys over a raised basement and nine by eight bays with an additional recessed and lower bay abutting Barry's Travellers Club to the

east. The stone is very plain with only minimal quoins at the corners, string courses, window surrounds and an ornamented cornice breaking up the ashlar face. It is, however, elegantly proportioned. The interior is cleverly planned around a central atrium with a glazed roof and the staircase over at one side is less dominant than in earlier clubs, though neatly elaborated with some mirror trickery. The principle rooms, the Library, Coffee Room and so on, are certainly rich and elegant but quite sombre. The Club is usually described as Barry's masterpiece.

Highgate Cemetery (167)
1839
Swains Lane, N6; tube: Highgate
Stephen Geary

Amongst all its other troubles, the growing city had a problem disposing of its dead, as all the cramped little central churchyards were full and unsanitary. Parliament passed a bill permitting the founding of modern private cemeteries on the then fringes of the city. This gave rise to the so-called 'Magnificent Seven', of which there is no doubt that Highgate is the most magnificent. The older part is to the west of the lane and is maintained in a state of 'managed neglect' by the Friends of Highgate Cemetery. The highpoint is the tomb-lined Egyptian Avenue leading to the Circle, where the tombs are in a basement level circle around a fine Cedar of Lebanon. Elsewhere there is a profusion of rotting tombs and monuments in rampant vegetation, it is certainly heavy on the Gothic atmosphere. The more interesting internees are probably in the extension of 1859 on the east side of Swains Lane, though it is all a little more municipal over there.

Kew Gardens (168)
1840
Kew Road, TW9; tube: Kew Gardens
William Chambers, Capability Brown,
Decimus Burton et al.

Kew was designated the National Botanic Garden in 1840. Its constituent parts were Princess Augusta's Kew Park gardens by Chambers, and Queen Charlotte's Ormonde Lodge gardens by Brown, both of the mid 18th century. Totalling over 120 hectares it is probably unrivalled among such gardens for botanical and landscape interest and there is also much of architectural note. The Palm House (1844–1848), which is entirely of glass and wrought iron and entirely curved, was by Burton along with engineer and iron founder Richard Turner. The much bigger Temperate House (1859–1862) is also by Burton and it too has a wrought iron structure but, with rendered masonry walls and straightforward pitched roofs, it is not nearly as exciting as its predecessor. Its glazing, which was originally in timber, was renewed in aluminium between 1978 and 1982. Less exciting still is the Princess Diana Conservatory of the 1980s by Gordon Wilson Architects. The accommodation is sunk into the ground with an agglomeration of simple glazed pitched roofs visible on the surface. The much smaller and much more recent Alpine House takes the form of frameless glass clad steel arches leaning together, which are reminiscent of the bridges for which its architects, Wilkinson Eyre, are best known. Of the incidental buildings the Pagoda by Chambers is the most famous – it is picturesque, if not at all authentic. Recent interesting additions are an eighteen-metre high treetop walkway with corten steel structure (Marks Barfield) and the Sackler Crossing, a sinuous bridge in granite and bronze (John Pawson).

Palace of Westminster (169)
1840–1870
Parliament Square, SW1;
tube: Westminster
Charles Barry and Augustus Pugin

The Royal Palace at Westminster had been used for meetings of Parliament since 1295. Most of this building was consumed by fire in 1834 and what survives is described in the pre-Renaissance section (no. 15). A competition was held for the design of a replacement, with the stipulation that the design must be in either Gothic or Elizabethan style, on the basis that these were properly English styles and therefore appropriate for the English Parliament. This was an interesting choice since, although there had been increasing artistic and academic interest in the Gothic as the 17th century had progressed, in 1834 no significant Gothic styled building had been built for a century or more. The competition winner, Barry, was well known for his skills as a planner and constructor, yet he had no better idea how to design a Gothic building than any of the other leading architects of the day. He overcame this disability by employing Pugin, a young and energetic Gothic propagandist and designer. Arguments surrounding who was responsible for what are ongoing, but they certainly worked closely together on the project, which may have eventually killed them both.

The building is a huge rectangle of generally four storeys with a chunk removed for Westminster Hall; around this perimeter block are offices, libraries, dining rooms and bars. The parliament itself is arranged symmetrically around the octagonal Central Lobby with a corridor and lobby leading to each of the Houses of Commons and Lords. It is fairly certain that this formal arrangement was Barry's, since Pugin is known to have disliked it. The regularity of the scheme is relieved by asymmetric Gothic elements, primarily the Victoria Tower, the Clock Tower and the spire over the Central Lobby. The styling cue is the Perpendicular Gothic of the Lady Chapel of the Abbey just to the north, and it is in comparison to this that the Palace suffers. The exterior seems stiff, pernickety and repetitive when set against any true Gothic building and the lavish interiors terribly fussy and crotchety compared to the organic wonders of the Perpendicular. Nonetheless, it is an extraordinary building and has become an icon of London.

After suffering bomb damage, the House of Commons and its lobby were rebuilt by Giles Gilbert Scott in a much simpler Gothic style (1941–1950).

Royal Exchange (170)
1841–1844
Threadneedle Street/Cornhill, EC3;
tube: Bank
William Tite

The Royal Exchange was founded on this site in 1566 and based on that of Amsterdam. The current building is the third, the earlier two having succumbed to fire. Two-storey shops were arranged around the perimeter of an open courtyard with arcades of Doric columns. Although the site tapers, the court is rectangular, and there is an impressive giant Corinthian portico at the west end facing Mansion House. The flanks and the internal courtyard elevations are in a mannered muscular Italianate style with large rusticated round-headed arched openings between the columns and pilasters, there is a little baroque spire on top of the east elevation. The courtyard was glazed over in 1884 by Charles Barry (younger). In 1939 trading came to an end. Fitzroy Robinson Partnership added an additional storey and a new glass roof in a historical style in the 1980s, which, since it is recessed and the streets are narrow, has little impact externally but does not sit entirely happily inside the courtyard. The Exchange is now a 'luxury shopping' destination.

Lincoln's Inn New Hall and Library (171)

1842–1845
New Square, Lincolns Inn, WC2;
tube: Holborn
Philip and Philip Charles Hardwick

When Lincoln's Inn built their chapel at the beginning of the 17th century, they had built one of the last convincingly Gothic buildings in the city, so it is perhaps no surprise that they were early adopters of the new old Gothic for their new Hall and Library. The buildings are in diapered red brick with buff stone dressings and, although their spikiness prevents them being mistaken for Tudor buildings, they are a reasonably convincing group. The Hall itself follows the exact pattern of mediaeval halls, with five bays

of high level mullioned windows and a pair of double height bay windows to the north end. There is a pair of towers at the south end, which have no obvious purpose, and a flèche on the roof. Inside, the Hall is panelled below the windows and there is what appears to be a hammerbeam roof, though the pendants are in fact suspended with iron rods. There is a true fresco on the north wall of 'The Lawgivers', by George Frederick Watt (1852–1859). The Library, which was extended in the 1870s by George Gilbert Scott, lies to the north and east of the Hall.

Wilkins Building, University College (172)

1827–1829
Gower Street, WC1; tube: Euston Square
William Wilkins

University College was founded in 1828 as an institution of higher education that was free from the influence of Anglicanism, which was the ruling ethos at Oxford and Cambridge. Wilkins won the competition with a design for a quadrangle in a neo-Greek style, which was at the time a style beginning to be associated with religious non-conformism. Financial restrictions meant that only one side of the quadrangle could be built initially, what is now known as the Wilkins Building. It follows the template of his National Gallery building with a large raised pedimented Corinthian portico with a dome above. It is far more effective in a more confined space and with shorter wings. The quadrangle was gradually extended through the 19th and 20th centuries by various hands and the buildings by the entrance were only completed in 1985 by Hugh Casson and Partners. It makes for an attractive escape from the monotony of Gower Street.

The Roundhouse (173)

1847
Chalk Farm Road, NW1;
tube: Chalk Farm
Robert Dockray

Built as an engine shed for the London
and North West Railway, the Roundhouse
is a brick drum, forty-nine metres in diameter, with a shallow conical slate roof
with glazing at the apex and in a ring
about halfway up. The brick walls are
seventy centimetres thick and have some
surface modulation by way of piers, but
no decoration. The circle is divided into
twenty-four equal segments. The trains
entered at the west and moved onto the
central turntable, which rotated to locate
an empty berth among the twenty-three,
while a series of vaulted basements allowed access to their underbellies. Between the turntable and the outer berths
is a ring of delicate cast iron columns
supporting the roof. By only 1869, the
engines had outgrown their shed and
the building was used as warehousing
until the 1960s, when it became a famous, if barely converted, music and
arts venue. This closed in 1983 and the
building languished until the funds were
finally found to convert it, ingeniously,
into a proper venue. The work was done
by John McAslan and Partners and completed in 2006. The auditorium is still
pretty and is still plagued by problems,
the facilities are minimal but improved
and crucially it is still pretty rough
around the edges.

All Saints, Margaret Street (174)

1848–1859
Margaret Street, W1; tube: Oxford Circus
William Butterfield

All Saints was built for one of the highest factions in the Church of England's
liturgical civil war that was raging at this
time, as it is again today under a different
guise. That the church was a broadside in
this war may explain its extraordinary
intensity. The client wanted a church, a
choir school and a clergy house on a very
tight, enclosed urban site. The church occupies the full width of the back of the
site, with the school and the housing
either side of a small courtyard off the
street. The whole structure is constructed
of red brick with various patterns formed
in bricks of other colours and stone, a
structural polychromy that follows from
the critic John Ruskin's theories regarding colour in architecture. The subsidiary
buildings are built as simply as possible
with varied windows loosely positioned
under steep gables. This relaxed kind of
design foreshadows the English freestyle
of twenty years later. Not much can be
seen of the church externally, apart from
the towering steeple and broached slated
spire. Inside, the tiny nave and choir are
aisled under a high timber roof. Almost
every surface is painted or patterned in
some way – it is dazzling and harsh and
mysterious all at once.

Crystal Palace (175)

1850–1851
Joseph Paxton

DEMOLITION The plans for the Great Exhibition in Hyde Park were not going well. By 1850 a competition had been held but none of the entries seemed likely to be realisable in time. Enter Paxton, 'the busiest man in England' and the Duke of Devonshire's head gardener, who had been experimenting with modular prefabricated iron and glass constructions for his employer's greenhouses. He produced a design which was published and built within nine months. It was 563 metres long and 138 metres wide, and at thirty-three metres to the top of the barrel-vaulted transept, it was large enough to enclose mature elm trees on the site. Made entirely of glass and iron, such a building had never been seen before and it was more exciting than any of the exhibits. It was as much a technical revelation as it was an aesthetic one; the logic of industrialised production of building components had never previously been taken to these lengths. Brunel, who was on the original building committee, immediately applied the lessons learnt to his Paddington Station and they have been applied the world over ever since.

After the exhibition, the building was taken down and re-erected in a park in the South London suburb of Sydenham Hill, where it served as a tourist attraction, exhibition and concert venue and later as a museum until it burnt down one night in 1936. By then it had lent its name to the park, the suburb and a hapless professional football club. The building itself had been christened by 'Punch', a 'humorous' magazine.

The legacy of the Palace was greater still in Kensington. The exhibition had succeeded beyond even the most optimistic forecast. The money this generated was used to buy eighty-seven acres of land immediately south of Hyde Park and to establish on it a series of institutions which have all played important roles in national life. The impetus for the project came from Prince Albert and Henry Cole, both great proselytisers of design, technology and education. The area is sometimes called 'Albertopolis' after the Prince. Institutions housed there include Imperial College, the Royal Colleges of Art, Music and Organists, the Natural History, Victoria and Albert and Science Museums (nos. 202, 250, 281) and the Royal Albert Hall (no. 190). Buildings originally in Albertopolis were later re-erected in Bethnal Green to eventually become the Museum of Childhood (no. 195).

115

Crystal Palace, Great Exhibition.

Albertopolis.

Paddington Station (176)
1850–1854
Eastbourne Terrace, W2;
tube: Paddington
Isambard Kingdom Brunel and
Matthew Wyatt

The station was built as the London Terminal for the Great Western Railway by Britain's most celebrated engineer, with the assistance of the architect Wyatt. The three sheds are amongst the earliest and largest (between twenty-one and thirty-one metres) of the Victorian stations. At the time, Brunel was on the building committee for Crystal Palace and the station's design is much influenced by the ideas of modularity and prefabrication evolved for the Exhibition Hall (no. 175). The sheds have segmental curved wrought iron arches carried on steel columns, the top half of the arch is glazed. There are two 'transepts' connecting the three spans, the purpose of which is no longer understood, but they certainly enhance the spatial richness of the concourse. The glazed screens at the ends of the arches are overlaid with curved iron tracery that has a distinctly Art Nouveau feel, lending this part of west London an unexpected Parisian air. The fourth shed to the east was added between 1913 and 1915. In 1868, Paddington became the western terminal of the world's first underground railway and the platforms of the Metropolitan and Circle lines do feel authentically ancient. The eponymous bear can still be found on the station concourse.

King's Cross Station (177)
1851–1852
Euston Road, N1; tube: King's Cross
Saint Pancras
Lewis Cubitt

In many ways the most architecturally satisfying of the new railway terminals, King's Cross was built for the Great Northern Railway. There are two parallel sheds with slender wrought iron ribs spanning thirty-two metres, which are supported on robust brickwork arcades. The top halves of the semi-circular roofs are glazed. The yellow brick façade, which used to be close to the street, directly expresses the internal arrangement with two great arched openings between a central clock tower and two end piers. The design could not be sim-

pler and scarcely better. Unfortunately, a realignment of the road allowed the notorious British Rail architects department to erect a set of poorly designed 'temporary' sheds in front of the station in 1974. At long last work is underway to remove these and reinstate the dignity of the station by transferring the retail elements to the west of the platforms.

Public Record Office (Maughan Library, Kings College) (178)
1851–1896
Chancery Lane, WC2;
tube: Chancery Lane
James Pennethorne

This was a repository for government and court records dating back to the 11th century. Built after Westminster Palace, it was the second major public building

only became home to the Royal Opera and Ballet companies as they were formed in the post-war period. This is the third theatre on the site, its predecessors having succumbed to fire, but it is nonetheless the oldest auditorium in London. Beyond the auditorium, the façades and the foyer, little remains of the original building, which was subject to an extensive redevelopment in the late 1990s by Dixon Jones BDP. The façades are in stucco with a two-storey Corinthian portico above a rusticated arcade to Bow Street, while the second visible façade to Floral Street has a series of giant pilasters with blind window openings over four storeys and a rusticated ground floor. The auditorium itself is horseshoe-shaped and has three galleries with bowed gilded fronts and a shallow saucer dome on pendentives that floats over the space. There are seats for 2,268 and, while it does not match some of the grander continental halls, it is certainly the finest in London.

The auditorium apart, the building was not large enough to house two national companies, and land had been made available by the government for expansion, when Covent Garden Market closed in 1974. Gollind Melville and Ward built a bland extension to the rear in the following decade, housing some rehearsal spaces behind windowed versions of Barry's Floral Street elevation. A competition was held in 1984 and won

in the Gothic style, though it is clear that its author was not comfortable with the essence of it. The building was erected in a series of stages to Pennethorne's design, although the original plan of a block to the south was never realised. The joins are still visible in some places. The basic unit is a three-storey bay of mullioned windows with a pointed arch at the top between projecting stone piers and it is only at parapet height that Gothic details like corner towers and finials start to appear. In the centre of the symmetrical, north façade is a rather clumsy 'Gothic' tower. Inside were a series of storage cells, which were constructed, as far as possible, to be fireproof – even the shelving was made of slate. The galleried octagonal Reading Room, with its glazed roof, and the stair halls are interesting spaces. The records were moved out in 1997 and the building was cleverly converted into a library for the nearby King's College, University of London, by Gaunt Francis, completed in 2001.

Royal Opera House (179)
1857–1858
Bow Street, WC2; tube: Covent Garden
Edward Barry

Originally a general private theatre known as the Italian Opera House, it soon began to specialise in opera, but

by Dixon Jones BDP. The redevelopment is quite an achievement – all of the missing back and front of stage facilities, a ballet school and two studio theatres have been fitted onto a tight, super-sensitive site. In the process, the complex urban design requirements have been smoothly met and some admirable new spaces created. A masterstroke was to reuse Floral Hall, a decaying glass and iron market hall located close to the theatre. Four bays of this were reconstructed on a plinth immediately to the south of the theatre and it now houses a fantastically glamorous bar. To the south of that is a modern stone block in a style highly reminiscent of the Italian, Carlo Scarpa. Around the corner facing into the Market Piazza, a re-creation of the old classical arcades was inevitable but it is coolly done. The restaurant at high level overlooking the market, the ballet studio, and the 420-seat studio theatre in the basement are all excellent spaces.

Wilton's Music Hall (180)
1858–1859
Graces Alley, off Ensign Street, E1;
tube: Tower Hill
Joseph Maggs

Music hall or variety theatre began in rooms attached to pubs where the entertainment cost a small fee or where the drinks were more expensive. As time passed, the rooms became more

and more elaborate. By the latter half of the 19th century there were hundreds of such places, but Wilton's is almost the only survivor. The Hall was attached to the Prince of Denmark, or the Mahogany Bar, as it was known. The pub consisted of four early 19th-century houses knocked together, behind which the Hall is located. There is little to see externally, although the carving around the door is more elaborate than is usual in the area. Inside, all that remains is the auditorium, which has a balcony on three sides with a bowed decorative papier mâché front supported on the thinnest cast iron, gold-painted, barley sugar columns. The walls are panelled with pilasters and arches below a ribbed barrel-vaulted ceiling. The apse at the back of the space is covered with a semi dome. It is most pretty, very dilapidated and really quite moving. After it closed as a theatre, it was used as a chapel and a warehouse. A trust has been formed that will try to ensure its repair and survival.

Royal Academy (181)
1866–1876
Piccadilly, W1;
tube: Green Park/Piccadilly Circus
Colen Campbell, James Gibbs,
William Kent, Sydney Smirke

The Royal Academy was founded in 1768 to 'promote the arts of design'. Its numerous critics have suggested that it is just a club for establishment artists, but it does hold important exhibitions. The core of the existing building is a house of 1668, which came into the hands of Robert Boyle who had it substantially remodelled by Colen Campbell, James Gibbs and William Kent (1716–1720). The stone Palladian principle façade to the courtyard is by Campbell, although he would scarcely recognise it, and some of the imposing first floor interiors are also from this period. The House came into government ownership and eventually given over to the Academy and various other learned societies. Campbell's elevation was spoiled by Smirke's addition of a very high floor of mostly top lit exhibition space. Smirke was also responsible for the rusticated ground floor arcade between the slightly projecting end bays; all in all it's not a pretty sight. Smirke also added an extensive range of top lit galleries behind the house arranged around a central octagon; these are pleasant and by no means as overbearing as Barry's National Gallery rooms. There are some discrete interventions from Norman Shaw (1882–1885) to the sides of the house.

Foster and Partners were appointed to design the Sackler Galleries in the late 1980s, the exhibition spaces are reworkings of Smirke's second floor galleries. Access to them was greatly improved by means of a lift and stairs inserted into old light wells at the back of the original house under a slickly detailed glass roof. There is no doubt that the contrast between the warm masonry and the new glass and steel is most striking, but what benefits most from the exchange is a matter for reflection.

Other buildings around the courtyard are still occupied by the various learned societies. They are three storeys, stone and in an inoffensive Italian Renaissance style facing the courtyard. The elevation to Piccadilly is more ambitious and less successful. The architects were Banks and Barry.

Shops and Flats (182)
1862–1863
Worship Street, EC2;
tube: Liverpool Street
Philip Webb

This little terrace was built by a Colonel Gillum as a charitable venture to provide affordable accommodation and workspace. Gillum was an associate of Morris and the pre-Raphaelites, which was presumably the connection to Webb. There are shops on the ground floor with wide canted asymmetric timber fronts and tiled roofs between brick piers; the semi basement below houses workshops. Above are two storeys of flats behind a simple brick wall with a minimal cornice; the windows are square headed under the roofs and with pointed arches in the brickwork. The steep tiled roofs have dormer windows. It is all handled in a free, informal way, for which there was very little precedent. What 'style' there is, is Gothic but it is only vestigial and marks the start of the English free-style and a step along the road to the Bauhaus.

Foreign and Commonwealth Office (183)
1862–1875
Whitehall, SW1; tube: Westminster
George Gilbert Scott

In the 19th-century 'battle of the styles', as it was called, Scott was one of the principal figures of the Gothic party. It was in this capacity that he achieved third place in the competition for a new Foreign Office building. In the confused

way of things at the time, this secured him the job. A change of government later and Scott was instructed that the building must be Italian and Renaissance. Seemingly without a qualm, principles were laid aside, books were consulted and a perfectly reasonable set of Italianate offices were produced; the result is a little dull and the building rather too large but that must be expected in government buildings. It is mostly three storeys tall with a basement and attics and arranged around an enormous quadrangle and four smaller courtyards. There is an escape into picturesque Gothic to the west where a curved façade and tower are employed to some effect. The inclusion of the newly formed India Office meant the involvement of Matthew Wyatt, whose Durbar Courtyard, which was given a glazed roof in 1868, adds a welcome element of fantasy. Scott's Grand Reception Rooms and State Stair for the Foreign Office are exactly what their names suggest.

Albert Memorial (184)
1863–1872
Kensington Gore, SW7;
tube: South Kensington/Knightsbridge
George Gilbert Scott

In the aftermath of the Victorian era, Britain experienced a severe and long-lived backlash against Victorian taste. During this phase, the Albert Memorial was seen as the epitome of the excess, bombast and visual illiteracy that characterized the period at its worst. More recent reassessments have focused on the monument's craftsmanship, earnest-

ness and confidence, but a reassessment of the reassessment is surely overdue. There is a gilded bronze statue of Albert looking out over Albertopolis and seated on a great throne at the top of tiers of stairs; overhead is a multi-tiered spiky Gothic canopy on granite columns – what

Scott called a ciborium. There is sculpture, allegorical and representational, encrusting every surface. It is all perfectly ghastly and silly.

National Provincial Bank (Gibson Hall) (185)
1864–1865
Bishopsgate, EC2; tube: Liverpool Street
John Gibson

This single-storey Banking Hall is one of the most attractive of the City's Victorian survivors. In comparison to the buildings that have sprung up in the vicinity, it is very low and small, but neverthelss manages to project the aura of dignity and solidity requisite of a bank. The entrance is on the corner with Threadneedle Street, where the façade is curved. Otherwise, there are large round-headed windows beneath sculpted relief panels

between large attached Corinthian columns, while the parapet is adorned with various allegorical figures. The Banking Hall is lit by three shallow glass saucer domes in a ribbed soffit over columns and pilasters with gilded Corinthian capitals. It is all quite splendid and now used as a function room by the National Westminster Bank, which took over the National Provincial before being consumed in its turn.

Holly Village (186)
1865
Swains Lane, N6; tube: Highgate
Henry Darbishire

The 'Village' was a speculative development for persons 'on considerable incomes' by the very wealthy philanthropist Angela Burdett-Coutts and was built in the grounds of her own house, Holly Lodge, which was demolished in the 1920s. Darbishire was Burdett-Coutts' favoured architect for many of her charitable works, where he wouldn't normally have had the budget for the intensive fussy Gothic detailing of the Village. It consists of no more than eight fairly small domestic buildings arranged around a green, mostly of brick and steep pitched roofs with elaborate timber and stone trimmings. With its towers, chimneys and endless pinnacles, it represents some sort of fantasy Gothic idyll, and one must be grateful that not everyone has the resources of Burdett-Coutts to do with as they will.

Abbey Mills Pumping Station (187)
1865–1868
Abbey Lane, E15; tube: West Ham
Charles Driver and Joseph Bazalgette

Joseph Bazalgette was one of the most important men in Victorian London. It was he who had built the sewage system that would save countless lives from the scourge of cholera and raise the standard of civilised life in the city. The pumping station still running today was an essential part of the complex mechanism that he created. The building is cruciform and two storeys with a slate mansard roof, and there are little towers in each of the inner corners of the cross, topped with cupolas and a large domed central lantern. It is mostly built in yellow brick with red dressings in a kind of Byzantine Rundbogenstil with hints of a French chateau about the roof and a Russian church about the lantern. The interior is gorgeous with cast iron arcades and galleries in a unique and impressive style that combines elements of the Gothic, the classical and the Romanesque. There is an equally splendid station in the south-east at Crossness beyond Thamesmead.

Smithfield Market (188)
1866–1867
Charterhouse Street, EC1;
tube: Farringdon
Horace Jones

Meat has been sold on this site for more than 800 years, driven in on the hoof in earlier times. It was the scene of even more ghastly butchery having been a

place of public execution for over 400 years. The building is a large two-storey rectangle with octagonal copper domed towers at each corner. It is built in red brick with Portland stone dressings in a very vaguely classical style. The Grand Avenue divides it on its long side, heralded by slightly weak pediments. Internally, it has decorative cast iron trusses supporting an exposed timber roof with glazed lower portions. A recent redecoration in the original colours shows the roof off to its best advantage. Unlike the other central London markets, Smithfield has avoided being dispatched to some sheds in the suburbs and was upgraded to modern standards by HLM (1992–1995), who added the glass canopies and filled the upper levels with office spaces. The interior of the Poultry Market with its very large elliptical concrete dome, by Thomas Bennett in the early 1960s, is worth viewing.

Drapers' Hall (189)
1866–1870
Throgmorton Street, EC2; tube: Bank
Herbert Williams

Although externally modest, the Drapers' Hall has some lavish Victorian interiors. The exterior is a little chaotic, having been reworked at the end of the 19th century by Thomas Jackson to maximise the commercial opportunities at ground floor level. In red brick with Portland stone dressings, the principle feature is the entrance portico to the Livery Hall, heavily rusticated with turbaned atlantes taking the strain. Through this entrance the accommodation is arranged around a pleasant classical courtyard and the principal rooms, on the first floor, are approached via Jackson's Italianate stair. The Livery Hall is double height with a very narrow gallery supported on marble columns with gilded Corinthian capitals. It has an apsidal south end and a painted panelled flat soffit. While the other interiors are not as grand, they are impressive enough to be used for the Buckingham Palace scenes in a recent film.

Royal Albert Hall (190)
1866–1871
Kensington Gore, SW7;
tube: South Kensington/Knightsbridge
Francis Fowke

Yet another memorial to the late Prince, the Hall was financed partly by subscription and partly from the profits of the Great Exhibition. It takes the form of a huge oval drum mostly of brick with the ground floor and dressings in buff terracotta. There is a projecting arched porch at each cardinal point. The ground floor is low and mostly consists of entrances, while the first and second floors have high windows, the latter with round heads between terracotta pilasters. Above that is a projecting balcony to a mostly blind storey topped with a mosaic frieze representing 'The Triumph of Arts and Sciences'. The

auditorium has accommodated 9,000, although 5,500 is the current capacity arranged around a circular stalls area with three tiers of boxes and a gallery above. The roof, which is obscured, is glazed on a wrought iron structure. The acoustics of the hall have been problematic from the start and, while they have been greatly improved, they are still far from perfect.

St Pancras Station (191)
1895-1901
Euston Road, NW1;
tube: Kings Cross St Pancras
William Barlow, Rowland Ordish and
George Gilbert Scott

The station was built by the Midland Railway, who very much wanted their station in the capital to exceed, or at least match, all of the others. The shed, designed by Barlow and Ordish, spans seventy-four metres, which was the largest single span in the world at the time. It is in the form of a slightly pointed arch made from wrought iron lattice trusses, which spring directly from the base of the side walls, while the upper half of the roof is glazed. It is not as complex as Paddington Station, for example, but straightforwardly impressive.

The Midland Hotel on the front of the shed does not bear much relationship to it. It is a huge, vaguely Italian Gothic structure with four very large storeys plus two levels of attics in the steeply sloping roof. It is made of red brick with buff stone dressings and granite column shafts. The massing is most romantic with two large towers and a forest of smaller pinnacles and chimneys – as the Midland Railway had hoped, the structure's imposing presence dominates for miles around. The interiors were no less imposing, especially the iron and concrete vaulted stair and the huge dining rooms.

The hotel had become offices by the 1930s, and by the 1970s it was verging on dereliction; the shed too was shabby as National Rail downgraded its use in favour of Euston and Kings Cross. There were moves, strongly resisted by conservationists, to have the building demolished. It was saved, however, by the Eurostar cross-channel rail link, which now occupies the old shed, with other services terminating in a new shed to the north by Foster and Partners. This latter structure has a sawtooth roof and is appropriately self-effacing. In the old shed, large areas of the undercroft have been opened up for use as passenger facilities, the lead architect was Alistair Lansley. The station reopened in 2007 after more than a decade of planning and construction. The hotel is currently being refurbished for its old use.

Leighton House (192)
1866–1896
Holland Park Road, W14;
tube: High Street Kensington
George Aitchison

The home and studio of Frederic Leighton are representative of another phenomenon new to the Victorian age – the wealthy and highly respected establishment artist. From the outside, the House is modest enough with its three storeys in an undecorated classical style in deep red brick with a stone door case and projecting eaves; only the domed octagon at the end of the two-storey west wing gives any hint that there might be anything unusual about the place. The dome is over the double height Arab Hall, which was built to display Leighton's collection of Middle Eastern artefacts including many tiles, a carved wooden mashrabiya window from Cairo and coloured Damascene glass. With a small marble pool in the middle it seems as if a scene from the Arabian Nights has been unaccountably transferred to West London. Elsewhere, the House is richly coloured with contributions from Leighton's artist friends including tiles by William de Morgan. The upstairs is dominated by the large studio where Leighton worked and entertained the great and the good and the artistic. The Perrin Gallery was added to the east in 1929, designed by Halsey Ricardo.

Shops and Offices, Eastcheap (193)
1868
Eastcheap, EC3; tube: Monument
Robert Roumieu

Built as the London outpost for a Worcester manufacturer of vinegar, Nos. 33–35 represent an extreme of Victorian neo-Gothic and it is indeed most frightening. The façade is predominately red brick with blue brick stripes, stone dressings and marble columns. The five-bay ground floor has a pointed arch arcade and, above this, at first and second floor levels the central wider bay is flanked either side by three very narrow bays, which culminate in a frenzy of little projecting Gothic hoods carried on tiny marble columns. Above this, each side narrows to a pointed gable at fourth floor level with a little pavilion between. Eve-

rything is hard and everywhere is spiky. The critic Ian Nairn described the building as 'the scream that you wake on at the end of a nightmare'. Astonishingly, this building was to be the inspiration for a 1980s 'modern' office building.

Studio House, Glebe Place (194)
1868–1871
Glebe Place, SW3;
tube: South Kensington
Philip Webb

The house was built for George Boyce, one of the lesser known, but admired, pre-Raphaelite painters. The three-bay, three-storey main façade sits back from road with a two-storey porch, which projects forward to the pavement. The building is, entirely in deep red brick with a slate roof and white painted rectangular sash windows in arched openings. Webb's skill as a designer was such that these simple elements combine to produce a building that is quite beautiful as well as being eminently practical and rational. It is one of the first Queen Anne revival buildings, although Webb would not have described it in that way. A slightly more picturesque extension was added by Webb to the west in 1876. Inside, the double height studio with gallery of the original design has been floored over. A little to the east of

this house at No. 49 is the only London building by Charles Rennie Mackintosh, a very modest studio house for his own use, but which has been somewhat spoilt by the addition of an upper storey.

Museum of Childhood (195)
1868–1872
Cambridge Heath Road, E2;
tube: Bethnal Green
James Wild

The structure of the building was originally erected in Kensington, where it formed the temporary Exhibition Halls of the Victoria and Albert Museum. Clad in corrugated iron, they were known as the Brompton Boilers and were relegated to the less prestigious Bethnal Green. Relocated, they became a sort of East End annex of the Victoria and Albert Museum and were officially designated its childhood wing in 1974. After the move, the structures were clad in red brick in the South Kensington style with mosaic panels over large windows between pilasters to the flanks. At the front and back, the three parallel sheds are expressed as

three gables, each with a large semi-circular tripartite window. The internal structure is very light with slender cast iron columns supporting wrought iron, bow shaped trusses, which, with a glazed roof above, make the spaces light and airy. The central nave has no intermediate floor and the ground floor is sunk, creating the effect of two gallery levels around it. The beautiful marble mosaic floor of the nave was laid by female convicts. Caruso St. John added a cheerful extension to the front providing much needed entrance facilities, 2001-2003.

Princelet Street Synagogue (196)
1869–1870
Princelet Street (No.19), E1;
tube: Aldgate East/Liverpool Street
Mr Hudson

This synagogue is a haunting emblem of the tides of peoples that have flowed through London, who move on just as mysteriously as they arrive. The house facing the street is from the early 18th century and not untypical of the Huguenot houses in this part of town – four storeys in a Georgian style with the characteristic continuous attic windows at the top. Hidden in the house's back yard, however, is a synagogue built for the Eastern European 'Loyal United Friends

spire, located on the north side of the west front. The entrance is through the tower into a generous narthex. The originality of the church only becomes apparent as you enter the nave. As in the famous cathedral at Albi, the buttresses for the roof are inside the church and pierced at ground and first floor level to form narrow aisles and galleries; here there is an additional aisle under lean-to roofs outside the volume of the nave. This unusual arrangement of double aisles and gallery lends great rich-

Friendly Society'. It is of necessity long and thin, with a thin gallery on three sides with timber and iron balustrades supported on tiny barley sugar columns. The roof is pitched with a lay light under a central glazed section. There is an arch to a niche for the Ark on the north un-galleried side. By 1970, the congregation had moved on or passed away. It is now badly dilapidated, although serves nominally as a Museum of Immigration and Diversity.

ness, complexity and a sense of mystery to the worship space. All the interiors are vaulted with brick in stone ribs and Early English detailing. Over the arches of the arcades are a series of panels painted by Clayton and Bell.

St. Augustine's (197)
1870–1877
Kilburn Park Road, NW6;
tube: Kilburn Park
John Pearson

Sometimes called the 'Cathedral of North London' on account of its grandeur, it is in fact just a parish church, but a most impressive one. London was lucky to acquire a church by Pearson, who was by far the most convincing and gifted of the Victorian church architects working in the Gothic style. Within and without, the church is predominately in red brick with stone trimming. The exterior is square-cut with large solid volumes pierced by tall thin lancet windows in an early French style. The whole is dominated by the seventy-seven metre high tower and stone

Albert Bridge (198)
1871–1873
Chelsea Embankment, SW3;
tube: South Kensington
Rowland Ordish

While it is certainly the prettiest of London's bridges, it is also perhaps the

least successful. Built as a toll bridge, its design, a modified cable stay, is now unique but it had a tendency to wobble from the start and was known as 'The Trembling Lady'. Joseph Bazalgette introduced some suspension elements in 1875 and, in the 1970s, its 120 metre main span was halved by the introduction of a pier in the river. There are many reasons why it should be demolished, but with its spidery delicacy, its beautiful colour and its lighting schemes no one can bear to lose it.

Criterion Theatre (199)
1871–1874
Piccadilly Circus, W1;
tube: Piccadilly Circus
Thomas Verity

The theatre was built on the site of the White Bear Coaching Inn as a multi-purpose entertainment centre, by caterers Spiers and Pond. Various eating and drinking venues were arranged over the basement theatre. The façade is painted stone in a florid-free French Renaissance style with steep mansards.

Most of the complex has been taken over by Lillywhites and converted to retail use after a complex reordering by Renton Howard Wood Levin (1989–1992). What remains is the gorgeous neo-Byzantine long bar, now called the Criterion Grill, and the theatre. The auditorium, which seats 598, has two levels of iron fronted undulating balconies under a flat soffit. The ground floor entrance spaces are elaborately decorated with mirrors, paintings and tiled panels.

Royal Courts of Justice (200)
1871–1882
Strand, WC2; tube: Temple
George Street

The façade to the Strand must be the most filmed façade in the country, as people are interviewed after their day in court on the wide pavement outside. It is very long at 140 metres, mostly three storeys, and changeful in the extreme. Built in Portland stone with steep slate roofs, the style is lancet windowed Early English with hints of France. In some ways, as it changes along its length, it is more successful than some of the long and low classical elevations in the city. The problem then, as now, is convincing oneself that a modern court building has need of so many towers and pinnacles and fleches, or that the clothes of the 12th century are appropriate wear for a 21st-century legal system. There are some impressive stony interiors, most obviously the Central Hall with its vaulted ceiling and marvellously patterned floor.

Leopold Buildings (201)
1872
Columbia Road, E2; tube: Old Street,
train: Shoreditch High Street
Matthew Allen

The state and living conditions of the urban working and non working classes became an increasingly problematic question as the 19th century progressed and London's population grew. Nowhere was the problem worse than in the rookeries

127

of Bethnal Green. The Improved Industrial Dwelling Company were founded to provide basic but decent housing for working families. The Leopold Buildings

are typical of their early developments. They consist of alternating four and five-storey blocks in grey brick with crude dressings in painted stone and the flats are accessed via open balconies with iron balustrades. They are pretty grim and have suffered periods of appalling neglect under various London Boroughs charged with their care, but they still survive and continue to serve, long after many schemes that followed have been demolished. Floyd Slaski added new lifts, stairs and other amenities to the rear in the late 1990s.

Natural History Museum　　　**(202)**
1872–1881
Cromwell Road, SW7;
tube: South Kensington
Alfred Waterhouse

Hans Sloane's bequest, which formed the nucleus of the British Museum collection, had contained much natural history material. This had been neglected by successive directors of the museum, and the natural history section had become a badly run backwater. The appointment of Richard Owen as superintendent of the Natural History Department at the Museum changed all of this. Aided by the interest and controversy surrounding the publication of Darwin's 'On the Origin of Species', he was able to persuade the Government that a separate museum was essential. The initial scheme was drawn

up by Francis Fowke, and Waterhouse took on the project after Fowke's death. The building has a long thin block facing south in a German Romanesque style; the centrepiece could be the west front of a cathedral of the period. Either side are long wings, two storeys with a half basement and a dormered roof terminating in higher end pavilions. Running at right angles behind this range are a series of top lit halls disposed symmetrically about the Central Hall; they alternate wide and narrow for the public and scholars respectively, although this distinction was never adhered to in actual use. The universal material is buff and blue terracotta panels on an iron frame, the steep roof are slate. Waterhouse was considered greatly skilled in the Gothic style, but his buildings are rigid and mechanistic in a very un-Gothic way. Even so, there is much to like at the Museum: the fantastic castings of animals that festoon the building inside and out, extinct to the east and extant to the west, the painted ceiling panels depicting the natural world, and the Central Hall with its iron roof structure is a wonderful room, one of the best in the city.

To the east of the Waterhouse building is a dullish 1970s extension by Department of the Environment architects. To the west is the Darwin Centre, completed in 2009 by Danish practice, C. F. Møller. It takes the form of a huge eight-storey sprayed concrete cocoon contained inside a glass box, with public galleries at the top and specimen storage and laboratories below.

VICTORIAN

Christchurch CE Primary School (203)
1873–1874
Brick Lane, E1;
tube: Aldgate East/Liverpool Street
James Tolley and D. Robert Dale

Before the 1870 Education Act, London's poor children were educated, if at all, in charitable schools, whose coverage was patchy. Christchurch is one such school, built at the east end of the churchyard attached to Hawksmoor's structure. The central gabled four-bay classroom block is set back from the street and was constructed on arches at first floor level to provide a sheltered play area under the classrooms and to keep clear of grave

sites. The undercroft was filled in over succeeding years. The projecting end blocks housed the school's mistress and master. The walls are in red brick with stone trimmings and indecisive outbursts of blue brick diapering. There is a plaque showing an earlier school that stood on the site and a large stone drinking fountain facing the street. The little school on its terribly cramped site is still in use.

Bowling Green Lane School (204)
1873–1875
Bowling Green Lane, EC1;
tube: Farringdon
Edward Robson

The 1870 Elementary Education Act was one of the single most important pieces of legislation that ever went before Parliament. Envisaged in it were the establishment of School Boards to oversee the provision of schools for the educa-

tion of all children aged between five and twelve. To this day, London is full of what Conan Doyle had Sherlock Holmes describe as 'lighthouses', built as a consequence of this act. Bowling Green Lane is a very early and simple school, designed by the London Board's architect. At two

storeys, it is casually, asymmetrically massed and built in yellow brick with red brick dressings below slate roofs. The styling, wherever the budget could stretch to any detailing, is vaguely Queen Anne. It is now in use as offices, but still interesting to compare with the nearby Hugh Myddelton School (no. 236).

Liverpool Street Station (205)
1874–1875
Liverpool Street, EC2;
tube: Liverpool Street
Edward Wilson

The Great Eastern Railway had a terminus in Shoreditch but wanted to be a step closer to the City. The cost of the land and of bringing the tracks down to the level of the subsurface Metropolitan line, however, meant that there was little money left for the ancillary buildings. This is evident in the surviving fabric, which is in an undemonstrative brick Gothic style. The actual train sheds themselves, however, do not appear to have suffered in the same way and are quite lovely. There are two principle naves divided by twinned columns with smaller side aisles. The wrought iron trusses, triangular on top and arched below, are very slight and supported by cantilevering filigree cast iron brackets on top of thin

129

Old Billingsgate Market (206)

1874–1878
Lower Thames Street, EC3;
tube: Monument
Horace Jones

The market received its charter in 1699 and was originally no more than an open area where fish were unloaded from boats in the river. Today's building has at least four predecessors. It is in yellow brick with Portland stone dressings and there is a two-storey, eleven-bay arcade facing the river with circular dormer windows in ornate stone gablets. Flanking this are four-storey, three-bay end pavilions, which housed pubs, fishmongering being notoriously thirsty work. The lead roof is curved, which lends the building a decidedly French look, and is adorned with dolphins and distinctly fishy weather vanes. Inside, the market hall is divided by a central gallery and roofed in glass on a timber structure. Crustaceans were sold in the beautiful brick vaulted basement. In 1982, the market suffered the same melancholy fate as many other ancient London markets and was dispatched to an obscure suburban location. The old building was converted into a dealing room, but

cast iron columns. As at Paddington, there is a transept which adds some spatial complexity and the effect is of a forest of iron trees. The whole station was drastically overhauled in the late 1980s by British Rail's architects, who extended the naves south and created the current concourse transept, all exactly as the original structure. In theory, this was a fairly controversial decision, but it proved so successful that there has been little complaint. Four additional radial braces in the north-south brackets are all that betrays the new structure. The fake Victorian clock towers at the entrances are less successful.

no tenant was ever found for this use and the building now serves as a party venue! An ignominious end for a handsome building.

Swan House (207)
1875–1877
Chelsea Embankment, SW3;
tube: West Brompton/South Kensington
Richard Norman Shaw

Perhaps following on from Webb, whom he admired, Shaw made much use of the Queen Anne style for urban buildings, but whereas Webb was interested in its potential simplicity and directness, Shaw transformed the raw materials into something lush and sophisticated. This is amply demonstrated in Swan House. It is in red brick with white painted woodwork and there are three lavish curved oriel windows carved with swans over the simple ground floor. The second floor jetties out over the oriels with tall thin windows alternately projecting and lying flush with the wall. The upper floor is straightforward under a projecting brick cornice. There are three pedimented dormers in the tiled roof. The building served as offices for many years but has now reverted to domestic use. The interiors are as suave as the exterior. Chelsea Embankment is also home to other Shaw houses at Nos. 8, 9, 11 and 15, while Nos. 4–6 are by Edward Godwin (1877–1878) and No. 13 has a fine interior by Charles Voysey (1906).

Bedford Park (208)
1875–1883
Woodstock Road, W4;
tube: Turnham Green
Edward Godwin, Coe and Robinson,
Richard Norman Shaw

ENSEMBLE Bedford Park has often been described as the first garden suburb, which might give Vanburgh and Nash cause to feel aggrieved although there is some justice in it; it was the first large-scale speculative suburb planned informally around existing trees with so much private and communal green space and, as such, it was to be tremendously influential. The development came in the wake of Turnham Green underground station in 1869. The developer was Jonathan Carr and his first architects Edward Godwin and Coe & Robinson. Carr was not entirely satisfied with their efforts and, in 1877, Shaw was appointed. It was Shaw who set the tone for the rest of the development – red brick predominates with tiled roofs, some tile hanging, render and some weather boarding. The style is

an amalgam of English vernacular, Queen Anne and Dutch, and something of this style was maintained after Shaw left the project. The estate was a tremendous success, particularly among artistic and left-wing pioneers. Today it is a tremendous success with bourgeois suburban families.

Richard Norman Shaw
*1831 in Edinburgh, †1912 in London (209)

Shaw began his career in 1849 poor, unknown and unconnected and finished around 1910 as the undisputed 'Grand Old Man' of the profession. Generally not an originator, he was a serial early adopter, ever quick to see potential and brilliantly inventive in maximising it. He was articled to William Burn and later Anthony Salvin, both respectable but uninspiring country house architects, and attended the Royal Academy architecture school in the evenings. Like Soane, he won the silver and gold medals and finally the travelling scholarship. In contrast to ear-

lier generations, however, Shaw spent his two years looking at the northern Gothic styles, reflecting his interest in the coming Gothic Revival.

When he returned in 1859 Shaw worked as first assistant to George Street, one of the leading Gothicist church architects of his day. After setting up his own practice in 1862, his first commissions were artists' country houses. The railways were opening up the countryside around London and cheap printing technologies had given rise to a class of genre painters who could afford to build there. Richer clients and bigger houses followed. Shaw and other 'Goths' were committed to the free non-symmetrical planning and truth to construction of the Gothic as they saw it. No other style was to be considered for churches, but there was less certainty about other building types. Britain has few examples of secular Gothic buildings to serve as models and what there is did not lend itself well to residential or institutional purposes. Like George Devey, Shaw saw the solution to this (in the country at least) in what came to be known as the 'Old English' style. This involved free planning and seemingly casual picturesque massing with prominent many gabled roofs all constructed with local materials and vernacular methods. Shaw exploited the 'wealden' vernacular of the South East in his country houses for decades.

An inherently rural style however could not be brought to the city and for this Shaw turned to Philip Webb. Webb had been Shaw's predecessor at Street's office and was greatly admired by Shaw. The little that Webb built was of the highest quality and greatly influential; he had started to adapt the Old English style with a little more formality, much red brick and some elements of early Renaissance detailing. This style came to be known rather oddly as 'Queen Anne', of which Shaw became a master and with which he is most closely associated. His early work in the city was still overwhelmingly domestic and included two fine houses on Melbury Road, Kensington (no. 210), a romantic house at 39 Frognal built for children's illustrator Kate Greenaway and Shaw's own house nearby at 6 Ellerdale Road. On the Chelsea embankment are a whole string of Shaw houses, the best of which are Cheyne House, Clock House and Swan House (no. 207). In contrast to these urban residences, Lowther Lodge, on a large site at Kensington Gore, is almost as sprawling as some of Shaw's country houses.

Perhaps the most interesting of Shaw's residential projects was his involvement with the Bedford Park suburb (no. 208), a developer's idea of how a new progressive and artistic residential enclave should be.

The estate is a landmark in the history of the suburb. Shaw was not responsible for the overall plan but his early houses set the tone for many that followed and he designed the suburb's centrepiece. St Michaels and All Angels Church (no. 215) and the Tabard Inn and stores (no. 216) are wonderfully fresh and inventive.

Although most famous for his houses Shaw did design other building types. Lost to us now, New Zealand Chambers, a Queen Anne office building, was highly influential. Equally influential was his only major public building, New Scotland Yard, headquarters of the Metropolitan Police (no. 225). It is almost impossible to categorise the style of this highly charismatic building; there are elements of French and Hanseatic Gothic, Scottish Baronial and Baroque all mixed up together in a new and entirely convincing way. The splendid White Star Building in Liverpool, 1896-1898, is in a similar vein but more romantic. At the very end of his career Shaw developed an interest in classical and Baroque forms. The troubled Piccadilly Hotel and Regent Street Quadrant project is the most prominent example in London of this phase. The problems Shaw encountered were not of his making and he was ingenious in their resolution, but it feels a little disappointing after what had gone before. Such work might have been done by any number of architects lacking, as it does, the splendid originality, inventiveness and zest characteristic of Shaw's early and middle years.

Perspective of Marcus Stone's house and studio, 8 Melbury Road, Kensington, London.

Melbury Road (210)
1875–1880s
Melbury Road, W8;
tube: High Street Kensington
Norman Shaw, Halsey Ricardo,
William Burges, John Belcher

ENSEMBLE   A perhaps not altogether surprising instance of like-minded individuals gravitating towards each other, a large proportion of the art aristocracy of the 1870s and 1880s decided to settle in the same little corner of Kensington, building for themselves an impressive bunch of studio houses. The land was previously attached to Little Holland House, which had been demolished in 1871. The overtly Gothic brick Tower House at No. 29 is by Burges, and Nos. 8 and 31 are by Shaw in his favoured Queen Anne style, of which the latter is a particularly good example. Nos. 55–57 are by Ricardo in his beloved tiles but are otherwise conventional. Nos. 2–4 were created by Belcher and the sculptor Hamo Thornycroft for his own use. Around the corner in Holland Park Road is Leighton House (no. 192) with a large Philip Webb house at No. 14.

St. Christopher's Chapel,
Great Ormond Street Hospital (211)
1876
Powis Place, WC1; tube: Russell Square
Edward Barry

The children's hospital's Old Building had, by the mid 1980s, become a liability, with an uninhabitable top floor and a collapsed stone stair and nor did it make effective use of the cramped site. The decision to demolish and redevelop was therefore easily made and only complicated by the fate of its exquisite neo-Byzantine chapel. The choice of the

Hospital and their architects Powell and Moya was to unstitch the chapel from the rest of the building, build a slab underneath it and remove it out of the way on jacks into a new waterproof box. It was surely worth the trouble. With its marbled columns supporting a central dome, mosaics and gold leaf, it is a jewel. No-one, when they consider the scenes this place has witnessed, can fail to be moved by it.

Union Chapel (212)
1876–1877
Compton Terrace, N1;
tube: Highbury and Islington
James Cubitt

The chapel's location in the midst of a terrace hides the form of the building and provides no hint of anything out of the ordinary. The street façade has three bays, the middle of which is the wide and tall tower housing the entrance. Behind the tower is a cruciform roof with gables to each side and topped by a lantern. The materials throughout are red brick with buff stone dressings and the style is early French Gothic with lancet windows. The surprise inside is a huge octagonal volume, defined by massive pointed arches carrying the timber roof, around which are galleries on segmental arched arcades. There is a rich interplay between the main octagonal volume and those arraigned around it beyond the giant arches. The basic spatial arrangements are reminiscent of a large Ottoman mosque, as are the lighting and lancet windows in the gables. The building still

functions as a chapel, but it has also become one of London's most charismatic music venues.

New West End Synagogue   (213)
1877–1879
St Petersburgh Place, W2;
tube: Bayswater/Queensway
Audsley and Joseph

A large basilica with aisles, the synagogue is built of red brick with early Gothic details that have a distinctly eastern feel, particularly the little towers that flank the rose window and entrance at the west end. The aisle windows are paired lancets while the clerestory lights are circular. Inside, there are timber fronted galleries on three sides and the central nave has a vaulted ceiling supported on arcades of octagonal columns with Moorish capitals. The aisles have straightforward lean-to panelled timber soffits. The niche at the

east end holding the Ark under a rose window is framed by a large saracenic arch.

Church of the Immaculate Heart of Mary (Brompton Oratory)   (214)
1878–1884
Brompton Road, SW3;
tube: South Kensington
Herbert Gribble

The Oratory is an association of lay worshippers with a particular interest in music and singing. The Oratory in London was founded in the 1850s, and by 1874 they were organising funds for the building of a dedicated church. Many English Catholics of this period were converts with all of the zeal that implies. They wanted their church to convey the sense of passion and *romanità* that they associated with the church in Rome. They certainly succeeded in building a very

Roman-looking Italian Baroque church. It is in Portland stone and the west front has a pediment over an Ionic porch or narthex. The flank walls are mostly blank and modulated with pilasters with small windows at clerestory level. The nave is groin-vaulted in concrete with small occuli at the apexes and there are a series of side chapels rather than aisles. The dome over the central crossing was rebuilt in a larger form in 1896 by George Sherrin. The choir terminates in a half domed apse.

St Michael and All Angels (215)
1879–1880
Bath Road, W4; tube: Turnham Green
Richard Norman Shaw

The little church has great charm and originality in a typical Shavian manner. The four-bay nave is in red brick with small, perpendicular, rectangular stone windows with a cornice at their heads and a very low eave above that. The steeply pitched tiled roof has a series of 18th-century slightly Dutch gabled dormer windows serving as clerestory windows into the nave. Trees permitting, the west front with the Parish Hall next door is particularly picturesque. The tiled roof has a white timber railing to the eaves and is topped by a delightful little lantern. The entrance porch is at the west end of the south side. Inside, the church is light and airy and highly coloured; the nave is roofed with open timber trusses while the aisles have timber boarded lean-to soffits. Maurice Adams added the Parish

Hall and north aisle in 1887, and later the little Chapel of All Souls to the south of the chancel.

Tabard Inn and Stores (216)
1880
Bath Road, W4; tube: Turnham Green
Richard Norman Shaw

Facing his church over Bath Road, the pub is in an 'old English' style, which sounds fusty but the reality is fresh and lively.

The ground floor is in brick and the jettied first floor in render with very shallow bay windows. The gabled second floor, also jettied, is tile hung and the steep roofs are tiled. Inside, the bars have upper panels of tiles by William de Morgan and tiled fireplace surrounds by Walter Crane. The upstairs has been converted, a little awkwardly, into a studio theatre. The stores next door to the pub are similarly lively.

Showroom and Offices, 20–24 Old Street (217)
1880
Old Street, EC1; tube: Barbican
Ford and Hesketh

Although common in New York and Glasgow, the use of prefabricated cast iron panels on façades is almost unknown in London. These were built for a blind and shutter manufacturer. The structures are five storeys arranged into two groups, one of seven and one of six bays, the latter of which was added in the late 1890s. The upper floors have identical arched units with thin Composite columns carrying round arches with filigree spandrels, while the ground floor units have a central door and wide shop fronts to either side. There is something similar but less convincing just to the west at Nos. 1–5, Clerkenwell Road.

Leadenhall Market (218)
1880–1881
Gracechurch Street, EC3;
tube: Monument/Bank
Horace Jones

The nicest and much the most lavish of Jones' city markets, Leadenhall was originally for food wholesalers but is now dominated by retail and the food element is much diluted. The site has been that of a market since at least 1321 and has been occupied by a variety of buildings. The irregularity of the current set suggest a series of streets that have been roofed over; the basic form is a crossing of two streets. The roofs are glass on open timber trusses, supported on cast iron shop fronts. At the crossing point the corners are chamfered to create an

irregular octagon and Ionic over Tuscan pilasters give way to giant gryphonated Composite columns. Some subsidiary alleys to the south were roofed over in 1885. The early 1990s refurbishment of the market reinstated a lovely rich colour scheme that highlights much of the intricate detail.

Peabody Buildings (219)
1883
Pear Tree Court, EC1; tube: Farringdon
Henry Darbishire

George Peabody was a very rich American financier and serial philanthropist, who came to live in London in 1837 and was appalled at the squalid living conditions of the majority of London's lower classes. He established the Peabody Trust to build clean and healthy housing at relatively low rents. There are dozens of Peabody schemes throughout the city, amongst which the Pear Tree Court estate is typical of the early estates, which were built on a template. Blocks of five and six storeys with slate roofs are arranged around a courtyard; they are built in yellow brick with white brick trimmings and painted stone door cases. Grim and prison-like as they are,

they provided facilities far in excess of what else was available although not, for instance, private toilets or baths. Facilities have been improved over the years but what preserved the Peabody Estates has been good management and maintenance.

Tower Bridge (220)
1886–1894
Tower Bridge, E1/SE1; tube: Tower Hill
Horace Jones, George Stevenson and
John Wolfe-Barry

London's most absurd bridge, it has become one of the city's most recognizable icons. The need was for a bridge that could be configured to leave a clear navigation of sixty-one metres wide and forty-one metres high. Barry's solution is a bascule bridge where the central span, in two parts, can hinge up; the towers were needed to accommodate high level pedestrian walkways. The two side spans are suspension bridges with spans of eighty-two metres. The steel frames of the four towers were clad in stone and detailed in a Gothic manner by Stevenson, as a gesture to the nearby tower, although no one could ever mistake the strange cranky Gothic on display here for anything remotely medieval. Some of the original hydraulic machinery has been retained, although the leaves are now lifted by electricity.

Old Spitalfields Market (221)
1883–1893
Commercial Street, E1;
tube: Liverpool Street
Henry Lovegrove and George Sherrin

The market received a license for this site in 1682. Lovegrove demolished the pre-existing building and constructed the current glazed roof on a series of flat lattice trusses on tall iron columns. Around this, Sherrin constructed a series of Queen Anne style buildings, generally of three storeys with lots of gables and dormers in the steeply pitched tiled roof. In brick, with decorative render (some of which is in relief) and half timbering to the gables, it is a lively if unexceptional ensemble. On the east side is the single-storey flower market, which has vast semi-circular brick arches under a pyramidal glazed roof. The market was expanded to the west in the 1920s and 1930s but progress was halted in 1991 when it was moved to Leyton. After protracted disputation, the western parts of the market were demolished and

replaced by an office and retail development by Foster and Partners – too big,
too corporate, too ugly.

Church Of Our Most Holy Redeemer (222)
1887–1888
Exmouth Market, EC1; tube: Farringdon
John Sedding

Rebelling against the prevailing trend of
building churches in the Gothic manner,
Holy Redeemer is Italian Renaissance,
albeit reduced to the basics. The nave
is expressed as a vast striped brick box
in brown and red, which looms mightily
when viewed from the south. The west
front has an arched entrance, above
which is a round window in a panel where
the brown brick stripes are replaced by
a buff stone. The roof projects strongly
to form a pediment, beneath which is a
lettered frieze. To the right of the front is
a tall campanile and priests' house and to
the left, a church hall, all of which were
designed by Henry Wilson in 1906 and
1916 after Sedding's death. Inside, the
nave is of four bays with groin vaults over
round clerestory windows, on an entablature supported by giant Corinthian
columns; there are flat panelled soffits
to the aisles, which have round arched
windows. It is simple, bare and all the
more powerful for it.

Royal Court Theatre (223)
1888
Sloane Square, SW1;
tube: Sloane Square
Bertie Crewe and Walter Emden

The theatre has recently undergone a
much needed rebuilding and all that
remains of the Victorian building is the
auditorium and the façade to Sloane
Square. The four-storey façade, vaguely
Renaissance Italian, in brick, stone and
terracotta is rather a jumble and topped
off with an ill-proportioned pediment on
ill-proportioned columns. The auditorium
is more interesting with its two cantilevered balconies with impressively riveted
exposed steelwork. The rebuilding made
much use of modish materials such as
corten steel and polished concrete and
has successfully provided additional facilities, some of which are located in what

were the ladies public toilets under Sloane
Square. Architects for the 1996-2000
rebuilding were Haworth Tompkins.

Holy Trinity Sloane Street (224)
1888–1890
Sloane Street, SW1; tube: Sloane Square
John Sedding

One of the high watermarks of the English Arts and Crafts Movement, few if any
such buildings come as close to realising
the ideal of a total work of art as Holy
Trinity, whose every part is the work of
a notable craftsman or artist. The style is
late perpendicular Gothic but only nominally so; it is very free and relaxed regarding historical precedent. The west front is
in red brick with much stone strapwork
and crenellations and the large west
window is flanked by turrets. The other

elevations, which are barely visible, are in much cheaper brick. The nave is both very wide and high and vaulted in plaster, though it was originally wooden. The aisles are segmentally vaulted normal to the nave and the north aisle is wider than the south, something successfully obscured externally. Most of the internal fittings and decorations bear close attention but the east window by William Morris and Edward Burne-Jones is probably the highlight.

New Scotland Yard, North Building (225)

1888–1890
Victoria Embankment, SW1;
tube: Westminster
Richard Norman Shaw

Norman Shaw's only public commission were these new offices for the Metropolitan Police. It is impossible to put a name to the style of the building, which comprises elements of the Baroque, the Scottish Baronial and the Hanseatic. It is highly original and was most influential. The building is planned around a courtyard with four storeys; the lower two are in granite quarried by convicts on Dartmoor, the upper ones in brick and Portland stone stripes. Each corner has a round tower corbelled from second floor level and capped with ogee domes. The roof is very steeply pitched with three levels of dormers and the north and south elevations end in gables capped with little baroque aedicules. The south building was added in the early 20th century. The building was converted to use as parliamentary offices in the 1970s and the Met were escorted to their hideous 1960s office building in Victoria Street.

Palace Theatre (226)

1888–1891
Charing Cross Road, W1;
tube: Leicester Square
Thomas Collcutt

Built by Richard D'Oyly Carte, the theatre impresario, as the Royal English Opera House, the programme and the building were equally grand. Unfortunately the programme lasted little more than a year before the building was sold to a music hall proprietor.

The entrance façade is onto Cambridge Circus and is concave to reflect its curvature with corbelled and domed tourelles at the corners. Four storeys with attics in a sort of South Kensington French chateau style, the structure is in red brick and pinkish highly detailed terracotta. The auditorium, which seats 1,400, has a flat soffit over three cantilevering balconies – highly ambitious for the time. The saloons and circulation spaces are richly decorated; the marble Grand Stair is particularly lavish.

Castle Street Welsh Baptist Chapel (227)

1889
Eastcastle Street, W1;
tube: Oxford Circus
Owen Lewis

The chapel is an unusual, gauche-looking building but charming. The whole of the street frontage is a loggia supported on four giant Corinthian columns; there are symmetrical stairs in this recess up to gallery entrances. Built in brick with white stone dressings, there are two storeys over the porch ending in large pedimented dormers. Inside, there is a gallery on three sides with decorative iron fronts and a curved panelled soffit.

Garrick Theatre (228)

1889
Charing Cross Road, WC2;
tube: Charing Cross
Walter Emden and Charles Phipps

David Garrick was an actor manager who did much to shape English theatre in the 18th century. The Theatre named for him has a stone façade and six bays with round-headed doors to the rusticated ground floor, a two-storey Corinthian loggia above, and a row of swagged round windows above that. It is perfectly pleasant, although the central column is awkward. The auditorium is buried so that the dress circle is at street level; it has three galleries with columns, which are a little old fashioned for the date. Nonetheless, with its dome, moulded plasterwork and original white and gold leaf colour scheme, it is a very handsome space.

Institute of Chartered Accountants (229)

1890–1893
Great Swan Alley, EC2; tube: Moorgate
John Belcher and Arthur Beresford Pite

Seemingly modest, tucked away on a cramped site, this was a building of considerable influence that continued into the interwar period. Given its charm and vivacity it is not hard to see why it was influential, but Edwardian Imperial Baroque, of which this building is one of the great progenitors, tended to copy only its motifs and rarely the spirit. There are two stone blocks, three

site. The bulk of it is a stone three-storey Italianate early Renaissance Palace with round-headed windows at first floor level over rectangular ones at ground level.

storeys to the west and two to the south with a little octagonal tower and cupola at the junction of the two. The ground floor is divided by knobbly clusters of heavily blocked Tuscan columns, and above the comparatively plain first floor windows is a sculpted frieze continuous on the two-storey section and divided by Doric columns on the higher block. The corner is marked with a sort of attached half lantern, again with cupola and sculpted figures. The double height members room and the domed main reception room are grand spaces with some of the vivacity of the exterior, though with a hint at the pomposity to come.

An extension was added to the rear by Willliam Whitfield (1964–1970) in an aggressively brutalist style of some panache, contrasting ribbed and bush-hammered concrete towers with polished granite and slickly detailed plate glass. The five storeys of offices are ingeniously held over the projecting concrete Great Hall.

National Portrait Gallery   (230)
1890–1895
St. Martin's Place, WC2;
tube: Charing Cross
Ewan Christian

The Portrait Gallery has always been the poor relation, tucked around the back of the National on an awkward cramped

The second floor is blind to the street and top-lit. The gallery was always plagued with awkward circulation and an attempt to resolve this saw the introduction of a two-storey escalator hall in a back yard by Dixon Jones, who, as well as oversee-ing general alterations and refurbish-ments, added a rooftop restaurant with fantastic roofscape views (1998–2000). The rather dreary Duveen Wing to the west of the main building was added in the 1930s by the Office of Works.

Studio House, South Parade   (231)
1891
South Parade, W4;
tube: Turnham Green
Charles Voysey

A house built for an artist, it is some-times called the Tower House. It is a sim-

ple three-storey rectangular volume with a two-storey bay window on the front and a lean-to shed on the back. The walls are rendered and the windows have stone mullions and surrounds, which are now painted. The roof is hipped and shallow pitched in slate with slender iron brackets supporting the projecting eaves. It is very plain and unadorned with almost no detail and remains clean and fresh to this day. The lower floors were the artist's living accommodation and the top floor a single studio space with a large north-facing roof light. The two-storey wing to the west of the tower was added by Voysey in 1894. More than a century old the house still seems youthful and fresh.

St. Paul's Studios (232)
1891
Talgarth Road, W14;
tube: Barons Court
Frederick Wheeler

St Paul's was a speculative development of studios for bachelor artists. Comprising eight three-storey houses arranged in pairs, they make for a most picturesque group on the determinedly un-picturesque Talgarth Road. They are in brick with South Kensington style terracotta dressings and finials beneath steeply pitched hipped slate roofs. The lower ground floor was designed for the housekeeper's occupation with the stu-

dio on the first floor and in the boarded open roof spaces. The chief joy is the studio windows, which rise past the eaves to form barrel-vaulted dormer lanterns like delicate glass bubbles. The tall thin windows off to the side were designed for the easy introduction of canvasses.

Studio House, St Dunstan's Road (233)
1891–1892
St. Dunstan's Road, W6;
tube: Barons Court
Charles Voysey

With its roughcast walls, green Westmoreland slate hipped roof, stone mullioned windows and tapering chimney, this seems like a miniature version of one of Voysey's country houses, entirely lacking the urbanity of his Tower House (no. 231). It consists of very minimal living quarters fronting onto the suburban street with a more generous glass roofed studio space behind. This has proved a reasonable billet for the Hungarian Reformed Church, who assumed residence in 1958 as one unattractive window bears testimony. The railings have all of Voysey's inventive stylishness. It is entirely of its time but, like the Tower House, feels newly minted.

Wesley's Chapel (234)
1891–1899
City Road, EC1; tube: Old Street
Elijah Hoole

Wesley built his chapel initially between 1771 and 1778 to a plain design from George Dance the younger; the bare bones of this chapel remain but it was

screen above and is topped with two unusual turrets. Bands of decorative relief have more than a hint of Art Nouveau about them. The other street elevation is

substantially remodelled by Hoole and the feel is now certainly Victorian rather than Georgian. The chapel is a brick box with minimal stone dressings and brick quoins; the central section has a pediment and a feeble Doric porch. Two levels of round-headed windows reflect the three-sided gallery within. There is a shallow apse at the east end with a half domed ceiling, otherwise the ceilings are flat and panelled. The chapel is flanked by 18th and 19th-century houses, creating a very attractive leafy entrance court. The house on the south side was Wesley's own.

More attractive is the Nonconformist Bunhill Fields Cemetery of 1666, across City Road. It contains the earthly remains of William Blake, Daniel Defoe and Robert Bunyon amongst others. and boasts many monuments and stupendous plane trees.

Bishopsgate Institute (235)
1892–1894
Bishopsgate, EC2;
tube: Liverpool Street
Charles Harrison Townsend

Townsend was accused by Pevsner of 'a reckless repudiation of tradition', and he certainly was a most original architect, though this is perhaps the least original of his well-known buildings, owing something to the Romanesque of Henry Richardson. The Institute was established, with monies from old bequests to St. Botolph's church, for the promotion of education and culture. The street façade, which is all in terracotta, has a vast round-headed entrance with a large

inventive but plainer, and probably the better for it. There are some atmospheric if plain interiors, particularly the flat soffited, clerestory lit Great Hall and the library with its large glazed dome.

Hugh Myddelton School (236)
1893
Sans Walk, EC1; tube: Farringdon
Thomas Bailey

This is a very large and fine example of a Board School by Robson's successor as School Board Architect and shows Bailey's evolution of Robson's initial template. It is three storeys, a 'triple decker', with high ceilings for ventilation and big windows for natural light. The plan is 'H'-shaped, its symmetry reflecting the division of the sexes for teaching. The walls are yellow brick with red brick dressings and beige terracotta on the upper levels. The roofs are steeply pitched and in slate, creating a French chateau feel that is typical of Bailey's schools. Despite the symmetry, the pavilions and towers lend the whole a romantic air. It has been lately converted into flats. The Board Schools, like Georgian houses, have proved very flexible. Many remain in use as schools, many others have been converted to a variety of different uses.

Tate Gallery (237)
1893–1897
Millbank, SW1; tube: Pimlico
Sidney Smith

Some of the architectural ill luck that haunts the National Gallery has touched its British Art sister. Smith was the choice of the gallery's sponsor, Henry Tate, the sugar millionaire. His building is classical with a large pedimented and domed centre block with low wings to end pavilions. The composition is weak overall and in its parts,

however the top-lit interiors function perfectly well as galleries. Apart from the central block, most of the building is single-storey over a basement, a good arrangement for exhibiting art but not for establishing architectural presence. Extensions to south were completed in 1910 and 1926 by Romaine-Walker and Jenkins, the highlight of which is the grand barrel-vaulted Gallery 9. The Duveen sculpture galleries were added in the 1930s in a powerful but simple Roman style with barrel-vaulted ceilings and a domed central octagon. A featureless extension was added to the north-west corner in the 1970s. Recent interventions have included additional galleries in courtyards by John Miller and Partners, and a new basement access arrangement on the south side by Allies and Morrison.

In the 1980s, funds and space were finally found to properly house the magnificent Turner bequest in a separate wing. 'The Clore Gallery', as it called, is one of the final works of James Stirling who, after the Staatsgalerie in Stuttgart, was considered to have been unjustly neglected in his homeland. His small L-shaped wing to the east of the old gallery is a riot of materials, post-modern gestures and bold colour choices – it all seemed a lot cleverer then than it appears now. The top-lit entrance and stair hall is impressive and the traditional enfilade of top-lit galleries at first floor level work well.

Boundary Street Estate (238)
1893–1898
Arnold Circus, E2;
tube: Liverpool Street
London County Council Architects
Department

The most notorious of all London's rookeries, the Nichol, had been immortalised by Arthur Morrison in the popular novel 'Child of the Jago'. When the Housing of the Working Classes Act of 1890 envisaged local authority intervention in housing supply, it was probably natural that the London County Council should look at the Nichol. The new estate has a series of roads radiating from Arnold Circus with its bandstand. The blocks are generally five storeys with glazed brick at ground floor and red and buff striped brick above with round arched doorways and segmental arched windows. Roofs are in slate and steeply pitched. It is pleasant enough in an Arts and Crafts style with a hint of northern Germany. It is still in its intended use today, though improvements have been required. Around the Circus are two Board Schools, Rochelle Primary to the south by Edward Robson (1879) with an unusual covered rooftop play area to the infants' block, and Virginia Primary, a good Thomas Bailey 'triple decker', to the north (1887).

Harrods Department Store (239)
1894–1903
Brompton Road, SW3;
tube: Knightsbridge
Munt and Stephens

Having started as a single room shop in 1849, Harrods grew quickly into the Baroque monster it is today. The building fronting Brompton Road is massive, approaching 150 metres long and six storeys high, faced in pinkish terracotta. There is a continuous series of shop fronts, above which are flat arched windows with Art Nouveau tracery. The centre and ends

project forward, the former with a pediment and an entirely empty show dome. The building to the rear by Louis Blanc (1929–1930) is more restrained, with giant Corinthian attached columns and pilasters bringing some order, and a slightly less lurid shade of terracotta. The most interesting interior is the fish and game hall with its lovely painted tiles by William Neatby.

Passmore Edwards Settlement
(Mary Ward House) (240)
1895–1897
Tavistock Place, WC1;
tube: Russell Square
Smith and Brewer

VICTORIAN

The settlement was founded by the novelist Mary Ward, largely with the money of journalist and philanthropist Passmore Edwards, for the provision of adult education. Although it is clearly influenced by the work of Shaw and Voysey, the building has a vitality and inventiveness all its own and is one of the best buildings of the period. The settlement housed a series of public spaces – hall, library, gym and so on – along with accommodation for the settlers who came to the area with the idea of furthering their own education and that of the poor benighted locals. The building is arranged around a courtyard and is in brick with some high level rendered panels; it is comprised mostly of three storeys with a basement and almost continuous dormers in the steeply pitched roof. The street elevation is exactly symmetrical except for the arrangement of the entrances, which is wilfully anti-symmetrical with the main entrance to the Public Hall in a stone aedicule resolutely to one side. Throughout, both externally and internally, there is a wealth of thoughtful, inventive detail. The building to the east, a school for disabled children, is also by Smith and Brewer for the settlement; although plainer and more overtly classicised, it is still very fine.

Claridge's Hotel (241)
1895–1898
Brook Street, W1; tube: Bond Street
Munt and Stephens

One of the world's most famous luxury hotels, Claridge's is a vast five-storey lump of red brickwork with repeated angular bay windows and large arches at the centres of the façades; the steeply pitched slate roofs have two levels of dormers. The main reception rooms were fitted out by Ernest George and Yeates, of which the entrance hall with staircase and ballroom remain. Between 1929 and 1931 Oswald Milne built an extension to the east and remodelled much of the interior. The brown brick extension is most reticent, even dowdy, from without but inside are the most lavish Art Deco interiors – mostly black and white with lots of zigzag motifs and mirrors.

Prudential Assurance (242)
1895–1901
High Holborn, EC1;
tube: Chancery Lane
Alfred Waterhouse

The Pru, like some other insurance companies, favoured Gothic style buildings, doubtless because of the connotations of great age and solidity. Their headquar-

ters are Gothic with a vengeance – a large three-storey building with many gabled dormers arranged around a series of courtyards. The windows are mostly in the Early English lancet style and the principle material is an aggressive bright red terracotta; there is a large baronial-looking tower in the centre of the street elevation. The symmetry, repetition and stiffness of the façades are scarcely in the true spirit of Gothic architecture. Some of the rear sections were demolished to make way for some awful offices by EPR Architects.

147

Westminster Cathedral (243)
1895–1903
Cathedral Plaza off Victoria Street,
SW1; tube: Victoria
John Bentley

The London Arch Diocese was created in 1850 after the Catholic Emancipation Act of 1829. Difficulties finding a site and funding meant that work on an appropriate church was delayed until 1894 under Cardinal Vaughan, who, realising a neo-Gothic church could never match the nearby Abbey, stipulated an early Christian style, which Bentley transmuted into full-blooded neo-Byzantine. The church has a great nave roofed with three shallow concrete coppered domes with a fourth, slightly smaller over the sanctuary and a semi-dome over the choir. The nave is flanked with narrow aisles with galleries above; beyond these are a series of chapels between the buttresses. The shallow transepts do not project beyond the outer walls of the chapels, although they are higher. Externally, the load bearing masonry is finished with red brick and Portland stone stripes and is heavily articulated, particularly the west front, with many turrets, a great arched entrance and to the north an eighty-six metre Italianate campanile. Inside, it was always intended that the massive load bearing brick struc-

ture would be clad in marble and mosaics; happily, however, this has never proved affordable so, although there are fine marble linings at lower levels, much of the bigger vaults are still exposed, creating a very powerful and atmospheric interior. The side chapels are more finished with much mosaic above the marble. The Stations of the Cross are the most important artwork in the Cathedral, carved in jagged relief by Eric Gill between 1913 and 1918. A recently created plaza outside the west front provides a pleasant refuge from the horrors of Victoria Street.

Horniman Museum (244)
1897–1901
London Road, SE23; train: Forest Hill
Charles Harrison Townsend

Tea merchant Frederick Horniman donated his anthropology, natural history and musical instrument collections to London for educational purposes and he also commissioned a building to house them. The building is highly original; consisting of two halls the street façade is virtually blank with a curved gable reflecting the shape of the hall behind. The

stone gable is enlivened by a vast mosaic by Anning Bell, depicting 'Humanity in the House of Circumstance', as if we were ever anywhere else. The entrance is at the foot of a tower east of the halls with a most remarkable turreted top. A further hall and gable was built by Harrison to the west in 1911 – this is also original but less successful. An extension behind a clunky third gable was added by Allies & Morrison in 2002, greatly increasing the museum's facilities. The very fine Victorian greenhouse to the rear was brought from Horniman's home in Croyden.

Millbank Estate (245)
1897–1902
John Islip Street, SW1; tube: Pimlico
London County Council Architects
Department

Built to accommodate over 4,000 members of the working classes, Millbank is a development of the Boundary Street Estate (no. 238) and an improvement in terms of both open space and facilities, having no shared lavatories or sculleries.

The mansion blocks are symmetrically disposed about a garden to the rear of the Tate Gallery. They are five storeys with steeply pitched tiled roofs, which housed laundry drying spaces. Mostly in red brick with some render at high levels, the sparse detailing is Arts and Crafts in sensibility.

Russell Hotel (246)
1898
Russell Square, WC1;
tube: Russell Square
Charles Fitzroy Doll

A 15th-century French chateau manically enlarged to nine storeys and inflicted on an inoffensive leafy Georgian square, the hotel's vigour and confidence has to be admired, if not its manners. It is a riot of corner turrets, massive gables, bay windows, chimneys and conical roofs

in striped red brick and buff terracotta with steeply pitched slate roofs. The public rooms are lavish, though not quite as frenetic as the exterior.

Whitechapel Art Gallery (247)
1898–1901
Whitechapel High Street, E1;
tube: Aldgate East
Charles Harrison Townsend

The third of Townsend's arts buildings, intended to bring art to the East End, it is no less original than the others. The street façade is in buff terracotta with a large off-centre round arched entrance below a row of square windows. The two

149

turreted end towers frame a blank wall, which was meant to receive a mosaic by Walter Crane that, most sadly, never came about. The gallery was refurbished and extended to the north-west by Colquhoun Miller and Partners in 1988. The neighbouring Passmore Edwards Library was recently integrated with the gallery by Robbrecht en Daem Architecten. The bare but elegant interiors are one of the best places to view art in the city.

Houses, Cheyne Walk   (248)
1898–1899
Cheyne Walk, SW3;
tube: West Brompton/Sloane Square
Charles Ashbee

Cheyne Walk, facing south over the river and (relatively) quiet, has long been a desirable place to live and has housed an astonishing list of major artistic figures, including George Eliot, the Brontes, Vaughan Williams and Turner. Mostly developed in the 18th century, there was a renewed spate of development at the end of the 19th as the erstwhile village of Chelsea became subsumed into the city. Ashbee, who was a notable designer and utopian as well as architect, built a number of houses here, some of which were lost in the war and some shamefully demolished more recently. Nos. 37 and 38 are all that remain, the former of which is plainer, with three storeys, a basement and two levels of dormers in the steeply

pitched slate roof. Very simple in brick and render with white painted windows, it relies on proportion and fine detail for its effect. No. 38 is a little bolder with a large arched window to the basement and an asymmetrical gable with a round window. Both were beautifully fitted out in accordance with Ashbee's veneration for craft, a sense of which can be gained from the fine external railings.

Lloyd's Register of Shipping   (249)
1899–1901
Fenchurch Street, EC3;
tube: Aldgate/Monument
Thomas Collcutt

The register is a rich exercise in Arts and Crafts Baroque in the 'Institute of Chartered Accountants' manner (no. 229) with much statuary, blocking and cupolas. Three storeys in stone, the ground floor has heavily blocked Doric columns with Ionic columns above that and deep recessed window niches at second floor level, also heavily blocked. A dormered mansard roof tops the building. The interiors are very grand and highly adorned. Richard Rogers Partnership built the fourteen-storey extension to the west with their trademark busy steel and glass circulation towers (1997–2000). The planners prevailed upon them to retain the buildings to the street and to set the two new towers back behind a reinstated

St Katherine's Churchyard with their entrances accessed via an archway in the retained street frontage. The combination of old and new architecture plus some fine mature trees is very successful. The office floors themselves are fairly dull both inside and out.

Victoria and Albert Museum (250)
1899–1909
Cromwell Gardens, SW7;
tube: South Kensington
Aston Webb

Webb added the long frontage building to the existing South Kensington Museum buildings, which were and are something of a jumble. A long double height corridor serves the street side galleries and a sequence of very large double height rooms to the north. The elevations in brick and terracotta are a real muddle of stylistic devices, mostly Renaissance but incorporating Romanesque, Gothic and other elements. In general, the principle south façade is too long, low and episodic. Inside, the domed Entrance Hall is impressive and the library rooms upstairs are most atmospheric. To the east, Webb's wing encompasses the extraordinary glass barrel-vaulted double height Cast Courts by Henry Scott (1870–1873). North of these are the North and South Courts erected quickly by Francis Fowke in the 1860s, using innovative glass and iron construction, but much altered in subsequent years. Over the central courtyard from Webb's wing are the refreshment rooms and lecture theatre range by Fowke and Scott, composed of red brick and terracotta in a free Italian Renaissance style. Inside this are some remarkable interiors, including the Ceramic Staircase by James Gamble, clad entirely in ornate majolica, and a series of refreshment rooms by Morris and Co, Gamble and Edward Poynter, all of which are dark and rich. Finally, the northwest corner of the site is occupied by the Henry Cole Wing, formerly the Science Schools by Scott (1867–1872). This is the most convincing of all the buildings on the site, very much in the manner of German Gottfried Semper. It is four storeys in plain red brick with ornate buff terracotta dressings; there is a ground floor arcade to Exhibition Road and an open loggia around the top floor allowing students fresh air between classes.

The museum has embarked upon a long programme of refurbishment of its galleries, employing a range of interesting smaller architectural practices. The most striking of those completed so far is Eva Jiricna's Jewellery Gallery, which is itself jewel-like.

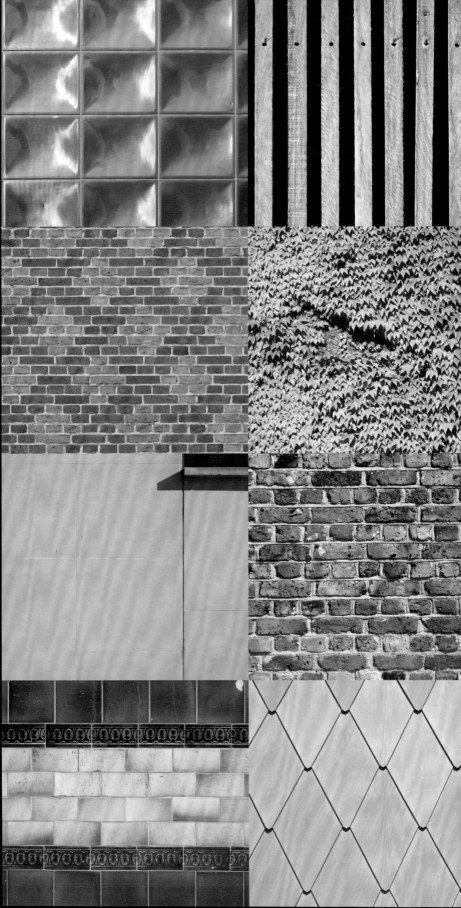

"London, that great cesspool." (251)

Arthur Conan Doyle, Physician and Writer (*1859, †1930)

The reign of Edward VII was short but there is good reason to talk of 'Edwardian' architecture. It is distinctly different from what preceded it, although there is some bleeding of the Edwardian sensibility into the later Victorian period and the interwar years. The rather unfair stereotype of Edwardian England is of a country complacently enjoying the fruits of the previous century's furious efforts, lazily allowing other nations to surpass it and, disastrously, to challenge it militarily. The first Industrial Revolution had indeed greatly increased the size and wealth of the middle classes, but life was still very hard for many, a fact that the Liberal Reforms of the era began to address.

As far as the growth of the city goes, any idea of repose is mistaken as the absolute rate of 60–70,000 per year was similar to that of the preceding century. The growth was now very much directed by the rail and tube networks. The tube in particular expanded greatly in this period, with both new lines and extensions to the older ones. The system was still run by a group of competing compa-nies, each of which built characteristic stations; these often incorporated retail facilities (no. 270) and became a focus of local life. The houses of the new suburbs were once more, as in Georgian times, built in brick with much small scale decorative detail and, nearly always, bay windows; they remain popular homes.

The architecture of the time was still heavily influenced by Arts and Crafts principles with its emphasis on high quality craftsmanship. The influence of continental Art Nouveau is faint, most noticeable in Fuller-Clark's light-hearted projects (nos. 263, 264). Mackintosh, the finest exponent of a British variant of the style, designed only a tiny studio house in London (no. 194). A more widespread influence was a revival of interest in the English Baroque, the so called 'Wrenaissance'. This could produce exquisite, inventive buildings like West Library (no. 265) and Deptford Town Hall (no. 262). In the wrong hands or on the wrong project however, things could turn very ugly indeed; the ponderous Admiralty Arch (no. 277) and Port of London Authority Building (no. 280)

The Heart of the Empire by Neils M. Lund, 1904.

lumber into mind. With a lighter touch in everyway a few architects were drawn to the Mannerism of Michelangelo; only the cleverest and most confident could expect to succeed with this but John Joass (no. 271) and Charles Holden (no. 309) were clever and confident enough for anything.

Theatres and shops are the era's definitive building types. There was an unprecedented boom in theatre and music hall building between 1885 and 1915, with over 200 new venues built across the country by a small band of specialists. The doyen of this group and teacher of most of the rest was Frank Matcham, who designed over eighty. Many have been demolished, but London has hung onto some of Matcham's finest, including the Coliseum (no. 260), London Palladium (no. 278) and Hackney Empire (no. 254). Major department stores from this time include Whiteleys and Selfridges (no. 276) but smaller retail developments such as the beautiful Sicilian Avenue (no. 268) or Fitzroy Doll's exuberant Dillons (no. 272) are more enjoyable. The only major insti-

tution of the period is the uninspiring Science Museum (no. 281).

London has been subject to little planning in a grand manner. For Kingsway however it was decided that the developments lining the new street were to be of sufficient dignity to create a street to compare with those of Paris and Berlin. Kingsway and the Aldwych do have the feel of a tree-lined French boulevard and, while most of the individual buildings are not brilliant, it is a pleasant place to walk. Regent Street, London's other large set piece, was rebuilt at this time; it is grander and more unified than Kingsway but not as pleasant. These streets and others were lit by electricity.

Lutyens' melancholy Cenotaph for the fallen of the First World War (no. 283) might be considered the last monument of the Edwardian era; unsurprisingly it lacks the gaiety that characterised the earlier years.

Wigmore Hall (252)
1900
Wigmore Street, W1; tube: Bond Street
Thomas Collcutt

Only the iron and glass canopy betray the location of this small concert hall behind the well designed if unexceptional terracotta commercial façade. It was built for the German piano manufacturer Bechstein, whose sales room occupied the shop to the street. Similar halls were built by Bechstein in St Petersburg and Paris. Beyond the canopy is a rich panelled corridor leading to the double height foyer and the hall at the rear of the building. The auditorium seats 535 with some accommodation on the small balcony. It has a barrel-vaulted soffit above a simple rectangular hall in an Arts and Crafts tinged Renaissance style with much marble. Behind the stage is an apsidal niche with a large mosaic depicting 'the striving of humanity after the elusiveness of music', by Gerald Moira. The hall is renowned for its acoustic properties.

Central Criminal Court (Old Bailey)
(253)
1900–1907
Old Bailey, EC1; tube: St Paul's
Edward Mountford

Scene of the most grievous criminal cases for London and beyond, the Old Bailey is rich in history and myth and built sinisterly enough on the site of Newgate Prison

(no. 109). Three storeys of rusticated stone make for a foursquare lump of a building. For no obvious reason the central entrance is flanked by pediments on giant Ionic pilasters. The dome above rests on a drum of Ionic columns that is most reminiscent of Wren's work at nearby St Paul's and Greenwich. On top of the dome is the famous statue of blindfolded Lady Justice by Frederick Pomeroy. The interiors too

owe much to Wren, especially the domed Great Hall. The extension to the south is by McMorran and Whitby (1966–1972) in a stripped classical style similar their Wood Street Police Station (no. 370) but not as successful.

Hackney Empire (254)
1901
Mare Street, E8; train: Hackney Central
Frank Matcham

Matcham was the architect in chief to the Edwardian theatre boom, building over 100; his oeuvre suffered proportionately in the post-war theatre destruction boom and perhaps as few as twenty-five remain. The Empire is a fine example with a brick and buff terracotta free Baroque façade topped with a curved pediment and a pair of highly fanciful domes. The auditorium has three levels of curving cantilevered balconies all encrusted in Rococo plasterwork under a coved ceiling with more of the same. The theatre was upgraded and extended by Tim Ronalds Architects (2001–2004), whose new corner building in glass, steel and stone boasts over six metre high 'HACKNEY EMPIRE' super graphics, also in stone.

Euston Road Fire Station (255)
1901–1902
Euston Road, NW1; tube: Euston
London County Council Architects Department

Situated on a corner of the very busy Euston Road, this is the best of a series of such buildings constructed for a growing service. Predominately of five storeys it rises to six at the corner and is mostly of red brick with a stone ground floor and dressings. The steeply pitched slate roof has dormer windows and tall thin chimneys. Under the roof are a number of elegant shallow oriel windows in stone. There are innumerable window types arranged apparently very freely, yet the overall composition has clearly been very carefully considered to produce a delightful picturesque addition to a street that certainly needs it.

St John's Gate (256)
1901–1904
St John's Lane, EC1; tube: Farringdon
John Scott

This is not, as might be imagined, a leftover of the northern wall of the City but rather a leftover of the southern wall of the Priory of St John and originally erected in 1504. A long chequered history and repeated restoration have left little original fabric behind, though the lower part of the wall east and north of the arch does look convincingly old. It was taken over by the re-founded Order of St John in 1874 and is now their headquarters and museum. The archway is vaulted with a room above and is flanked by four-storey blocks with one room on each floor. Scott added offices to the south-east and the impressive first floor Perpendicular Chapter Room with its timber roof and lantern.

Waterloo Station (257)
1901–1922
Waterloo Road, SE1; tube: Waterloo
William Jacomb-Hood, Alfred Szlumper
and John Scott

The designers were all employees of the London and South Western Railway, who built Waterloo as their principle London terminus. They did not attempt the structural gymnastics of the Victorian stations – Jacob-Hood and Szlumper's fully glazed roof is a nine-bay transverse ridge and furrow type supported on flat lattice girders. The roof over the concourse is similar but of a much finer grain and parallel to the platforms. Despite the relative lack of ambition, Waterloo is one of the more pleasant stations to use by virtue of the wide curving, well-lit concourse, which the present operators are spoiling this by filling it full of retail units. The building to the north of the concourse was by Scott. In Portland stone it is a fairly soulless three-storey exercise in Imperial Baroque with attached giant Ionic columns over a rusticated ground floor; the curve to the concourse is its most charming feature. The main entrance, the so-called Victory Arch, commemorates railway staff lost in the First World War.

Snaking sinuously around the west of the Edwardian shed is the new shed designed by Nicholas Grimshaw and Partners, with engineers YRM Anthony Hunt

Associates (1990–1993). This contains five platforms for the Eurostar train. The asymmetrical curved blue tubular steel trusses, glazed to the west, make for a delightfully airy and elegant structure. With the Eurostar services relocated to St Pancras, however, no one seems to know what is to be done with it next.

Buchanan's Distillery Office (258)
1902
Fetter Lane, EC4; tube: Chancery Lane
Treadwell and Martin

Buchanan's distillery is long gone but its offices remain. Treadwell and Martin specialised in small infill schemes in the centre of the City, very often housing upmarket shops. If such work is little more than creating a façade, they at least put everything into it. The Fetter Lane building, four storeys high and five narrow bays wide in stone, is a typically energetic and inventive brew of Baroque, Medieval and Art Nouveau, busy and boisterous with a characteristically picturesque gable. Others of this ilk can be seen at 7 Dering Street, 106 Jermyn Street and 74 New Bond Street, and there are a good many more. Another Treadwell and Martin specialism was public houses, of which The Rising Sun in Tottenham Court Road is a fine example.

Sanderson Wallpaper Factory   (259)
1902
Barley Mow Passage off Heathfield Terrace, W4;
tube: Chiswick Park/Turnham Green
Charles Voysey

Sanderson printed Morris and Co.'s wallpaper designs and were therefore very much part of the Arts and Crafts project. This extension to their main plant is Voysey's only factory and a most original structure. Five bays by two, there are four floors, the lower three of which are lit by large segmental windows between narrow piers, while the upper floor has tiny round windows but was originally

lit by north light roof glazing. The piers, which contain air ducts, have flat tops above the curved parapet walls. The principle material is white glazed brick with blue brick plinths and dressings (now painted black). Like Voysey's other London buildings, it still seems remarkably fresh and modern.

London Coliseum   (260)
1902–1904
St Martin's Lane, WC2;
tube: Charing Cross/Leicester Square
Frank Matcham

Now the home of the English National Opera, the Coliseum was built as a commercial variety theatre and is one of Matcham's grandest remaining theatres. It betrays all his strengths and weaknesses. The terracotta Baroque façade has panache and vigour but is untutored and ill-proportioned. The principle feature is an off-centre tower, which terminates in a revolving electric sign, which, for all its squatness, has become one of the landmarks of the city. The marble-lined foyers and stairs are grand and glamorous. The auditorium is quite stunning; it has three curved cantilevered balconies under a great dome; the décor is free French neoclassical in mostly gold and white. It was, as Matcham's theatres often were, technically advanced with electric lighting, lifts and a rarely used revolving stage.

159

Golders Green Crematorium   (261)
1902–1905
Hoop Lane, NW11; tube: Golders Green
Ernest George and Yeates

The crematorium consists of a complex of buildings with construction continuing into the late 1930s. All of it is in the same red brick Romanesque lending it a decided resemblance to a Italian hill top monastery when viewed from across the attractive grounds to the south. George and Yeates completed the West Chapel and campanile in 1905, the East Columbarium in 1911, the atmospheric cloister in 1916, and, Yeates alone, the Ernest George Columbarium in 1928. Mitchell and Bridgewater were responsible for the East Chapel a decade later. In the grounds are the Philipson Mausoleum, a sombre classical monument by Edwin Luytens, and a haunting bronze, 'Into the Silent Land', by Henry Pegram. Many eminent figures have made use of the services offered here.

Deptford Town Hall   (262)
1902–1907
New Cross Road, SE14;
tube: New Cross Gate
Lanchester, Stewart and Rickards

Reorganisation of London's government in 1900 created twenty-eight Metropolitan Boroughs, all of which needed a town hall. Most of these were built in the Edwardian period, of which Deptford's was by far the best. Like many of the others, it is in a version of Baroque but an unusually lush and lively one. Its seven two storey bays are packed with incident. The centrepiece is a florid oriel window above the entrance and beneath

an emphatic raised pediment topped with a small clock tower. The ground floor windows are recessed behind Tuscan columns and there are statues of admirals in niches between the first floor windows. The double height entrance hall has an elaborate staircase with pink marble columns under a glazed dome in an ornate plaster ceiling; the Council Chamber is a little more restrained though its ceiling is quite elaborate. The

London Borough of Deptford has long been dissolved and the building is now used by Goldsmiths College.

York House   (263)
1903
Riding House Street, W1;
tube: Oxford Circus
Herbert Fuller-Clark

Little is known of Clark; he contributed two fabulous designs to London and was next heard of in Jamaica. York House was the office of plumbing company, T. J. Boulting and Sons. There are five storeys over a basement mostly in red brick, although there are bands of grey and stone mullions and dressings to the windows. Most of the windows are gathered into the six oriels and the corner turrets, which all project above the ground floor level and most of which end in different positively expressionistic ways, as do the many chimneys and the rare bits of blank wall. With all of that and green and gold mosaic adverts and bits of sculpted relief it ought to be a terrible jumble but it fact it all comes together beautifully. There are other interesting buildings of this period on nearby Candover, Foley and Mortimer Streets.

Blackfriars Pub   (264)
1905
New Bridge Street, EC4;
tube: Blackfriars
Herbert Fuller-Clark

Clark's second great and much beloved contribution to the city, the Blackfriars is the most highly wrought pub of the period. The building itself is atmospheric, being the orphaned sharp end of a lost city block. It had been a standard Victorian pub with large stone mullioned lead lighted windows; to this was

added an outsize statue of a friar, mosaic signage, ironwork, enamels and carved relief work. Inside is a riot of copper panels and carvings of monks enjoying the good things in life. To the rear is a tiny extension completed in 1921, a marble and mirror lined barrel-vaulted saloon of the greatest imaginable richness.

West Library   (265)
1905–1907
Bridgeman Road, N1;
tube: Caledonian Road
Arthur Beresford Pite

For the benefit and improvement of the lower classes, many branch libraries were constructed throughout London in the Edwardian period and West Library is probably the highlight. Two storeys over a basement in yellow and purple striped brick, it is not nearly as repulsive as it sounds. The windows are rectangular in round-headed openings divided by un-capitaled columns on the north side. The main block is capped by a delightful wooden lantern influenced by Art Nouveau. The entrance is on the north side in a recessed secondary block, to the west of which is a single-storey children's library. The style, if it can be said to have one, is perhaps early Greek Christian freestyle – it is delicate and refined like an ornamental box. The interiors, seemingly unchanged and barely maintained, are highly atmospheric particularly the top-lit children's room.

Edwin Lutyens
*1869 in London, †1944 in London (266)

It is sadly true that as far as Lutyens and London go, most of the action takes place off stage; he was however the most important architect of his generation and there is much of his work to be seen in the capital. He studied for two years at the South Kensington Schools before working for Ernest George, a successful and talented country house architect. In 1889 at the very young age of twenty he set up on his own with a £100 inheritance and a commission for a small country house.

For his country houses Lutyens, like many of his peers, took the exist-

ing vernacular architecture of Southern England as his starting point but there is a weighty monumentality and an interest in interlocking geometries apparent in even these early countrified projects. Lutyens teamed up with garden designer Gertrude Jekyll and together they produced a string of gorgeous houses. Munstead Wood in Surrey and the Deanery in Berkshire with their warm brickwork, low hanging roofs and lush planting are the very image of the idealised English country house. The Deanery was for Edward Hudson, the founder of Country Life magazine, and this connection was to become invaluable. The magazine constantly publicised and praised the young architect's work and Hudson commissioned Lutyens to design the Country Life offices in Tavistock Street. These are in what Lutyens called his 'Wrennaissance' style; it seems he never considered anything other than a classical style for the City and it soon came to dominate his entire output.

Contacts made through his thriving country house practice helped Lutyens to an extraordinary commission: the building of India's imperial capital at New Delhi. The project involved planning the whole of the new quarter and the detailed design of its centrepiece, the Viceroy's Palace. The project was to engage Lutyens from 1912 to 1929 and established him as a man who could do big jobs. The Palace is a remarkable building; serene and beautifully proportioned it somehow melds classical and Indian tradition without parodying either. It is this kind of visual and stylistic dexterity for which Lutyens is renowned.

Another country house client introduced Luytens to the Hampstead Garden Suburb project, which was not unlike the preceding Bedford Park, but was led by a philanthropic co-operative rather than a developer. Lutyens designed a church, chapel and educational institute along with some houses. A public housing project for Westminster, the Grosvenor Estate (297), is certainly interesting though no more successful than other such projects of the time.

Lutyens' abstract architectonic talents and his position as one of the establishment's favoured sons had him ideally placed for a strange and melancholy influx of work: an unprecedented demand for memorial structures followed the end of World War I. It is easy to get the tone of a war memorial horribly wrong and it is generally accepted that Lutyens mostly got it right. The great arch at Thiepval is powerful and evocative but without bombast and it is hard to envisage how the very simple Cenotaph in London (no. 283) could have been done better. There are further monuments to the Unknown Sailor in Trinity Square and the Philipson family in Golders Green Cemetery (no. 261). It is curious that a man noted for his humour and levity should make such a success of such a sombre line of work.

By the 1920s Lutyens was established enough to be commissioned for a series of commercial buildings in the City and the West End. Britannic House (no. 286), the Midland Bank Headquarters (no. 290) and the very cheeky Crane Bennett Building (no. 300) find Lutyens playing what he referred to as the 'high game', a skilful manipulation of the language of classicism to maintain visual interest in ever larger façades. Lutyens excelled at this; these buildings are urbane, playful, inventive, highly mannered and well proportioned. At the same time there is a facile and heartless quality to some of this work that is not discernable in his houses and memorials.

Lutyens' last great undertaking was a Roman Catholic cathedral in Liverpool. If built, it would have been second in size only to St Peter's. By 1958, fourteen years after Lutyens' death, construction had reached ground floor level but costs were out of control and the project was abandoned. No one who has visited the completed crypt can fail to mourn what has been lost.

163

Viceroy's Palace, New Delhi: main entrance.

Debenham House (267)
1905-1907
Addison Road, W14; tube: Holland Park
Halsey Ricardo

Debenham was a very rich retailer and banker and Ricardo a lone perfectionist with decidedly singular views and theories. Ricardo believed that the general dreariness of the city demanded strongly coloured buildings that were preferably washable to counter the effects of atmospheric pollution. Ceramics were the ideal materials to meet these requirements and virtually the whole of the Debenham House is clad in white glazed terracotta and glazed brick. The Italian Renaissance columns and arches over the lower two storeys are in the former with the wall between in green glazed brick; the attic storey above is in the most vivid turquoise glazed brick and the roof is clad in green glazed pantiles. It presents a gorgeous incongruous appearance on an otherwise mundane Kensington street. The huge house is planned around a central double height hall under a mosaic covered dome. Throughout there are elaborate, decorative plastered ceilings by Arts and Crafts hero Ernest Gimson and wide use of saturated William de Morgan tiling. In size and décor it is no less than a very eccentric palace for a Victorian Medici.

Sicilian Avenue (268)
1905–1910
Sicilian Avenue off Southampton Row, WC1; tube: Holborn
R. J. Worley

Cutting the corner between Southampton Row and Vernon Place, the two ends of this pedestrian passage are marked by a terracotta screen complete with Ionic

columns and urns. The passage is lined with five-storey red brick and terracotta buildings with giant Composite columns over the lower two floors and many projecting oriel windows above, topped off with a terracotta balustrade. The ground floor houses luxury shops behind beautiful bulbous wood and glass fronts. It is all entirely charming.

Methodist Central Hall (269)
1905–1911
Storey's Gate, SW1;
tube: St James 's Park/Westminster
Lanchester and Rickards

The Methodists were inclined to go for unusual styles to differentiate themselves from the more established churches. In this case they chose Baroque and won for themselves what looks like a mitteleuropa Opera House. The building is conclusive proof that size does matter – all the elements that make Lanchester and Rickards' Deptford Town Hall (no. 262) such a charming building are present and correct, but at this scale they charm rather less. The building is dominated by a huge octagonal leaded dome over a bulky stone mass with attached Ionic columns, rusticated ground floor and corners and much carving. Inside, the characteristic modesty of Methodism is entirely forgotten; the staircase and galleried hall under the giant dome are both very much in the grand manner and much the worse for it. The building has

a reinforced concrete frame, which was unusual in Britain at this date.

South Kensington Underground Station and Arcade (270)
1906–1907
Pelham Street, SW7;
tube: South Kensington
Leslie Green and George Sherrin

The tube network was not built to any central plan but rather as a series of isolated, uncoordinated, often competing ventures. At South Kensington two such ventures met and each built a section of the station. The Great Northern, Piccadilly and Brompton Railway's building on Pelham Street is in their house style with dry blood coloured faience cladding and large round arched openings. They were often built single-storey, as here, but with a frame that would allow for building further storeys later; the architect Green designed no less than fifty such in five years before dying aged thirty-three. The Metropolitan District Line station was designed by Sherrin and it includes the charming little shopping arcade at the entrance with glazed roof and decorative iron signage. The operation of the two parts of the station has long since been merged.

Royal Insurance Building (271)
1906–1908
Piccadilly, SW1; tube: Green Park
John Joass

As increasing numbers of large buildings were constructed with steel or concrete frames, architects began to grapple with how this could or should be expressed. Few buildings of the time exploited this new licence so thoroughly and so well as the Royal Insurance Offices. The lower two floors have pairs of Tuscan columns in front of glass shop fronts; the three floors above have a series of canted bay windows in the thickness of the piers between. These are undermined by blind niches, whose putti have seemingly climbed up to stand under the cornice. Above the cornice is an attic storey with more paired Tuscan columns and above that a steep roof with two levels of dormers. Michelangelo is the source of some of the detail, which is mannered and even perverse, but also sharp, sophisticated and stylish.

Dillons (Waterstones) Bookshop
(272)
1907
Torrington Square, WC1;
tube: Goodge Street
Charles Fitzroy Doll

Originally designed as a row of shops, the whole block including the upper floors was gradually taken over by bookseller Una Dillon as it became the principle academic bookshop of the city. Dillons has recently been swallowed up by Waterstones. The four-storey building is made of red brick and terracotta with each of the individual units defined by a steep gable over an oriel window bearing

the arms of Doll's client and their motto 'Che Sará Sará'; the corners sport witches' hatted tourelles. The style is an agitated Gothic with distinct Tudor and Art Nouveau accents. It is crazed but fun.

British Medical Association (273)
1907–1908
Strand, WC2; tube: Charing Cross
Charles Holden

What is now known as Zimbabwe House is a quite remarkable building for its date. It has some classical overtones, even some classical detail and some echo of Lutyens, but this is somehow all subsumed into something subtly new, free, muscular and romantic. The lower two, granite clad, storeys are very high with semi-circular arched openings stretching across both floors. There are three further Portland stone clad storeys with rectangular windows, which recede very slightly. On top is a mansard roof behind a parapet, above which a central three bays and various chimneys on the line of the façade poke up, contributing to the building's picturesque look. The statuary around the second floor windows is by Jacob Epstein and was notorious in its day for its depiction of nudity; sadly, London pollution has long since robbed it of any power to shock. In 2005 however, contemporary artist Neal White launched an exhibition inspired by Epstein's figures in an attempt to reignite the original debates.

Waterlow Court (274)
1907–1909
Heath Close, NW11; tube: Golders Green
Mackay Hugh Baillie Scott

Scott was one of the most prolific Arts and Crafts architects, but one with an unfortunate tendency towards the twee and whimsical. There is a little of that at Waterlow Court in the fake half timbering, for example, but overall it is quite forceful and one of his better efforts. It was built by the Improved Industrial Dwellings Company to provide small flats for single ladies about whose safety in the wicked city there was much public concern. Two storeys with a dormered attic it is arranged around a courtyard, which is the most enjoyable feature of the design. Entered via a timber lychgate and an arched entryway, the court is cloistered with large round arches in white painted brickwork, while the rest of the design has an admirable simplicity and directness.

Hampstead Garden Suburb (275)

1907–1938
Parker and Unwin, Edwin Lutyens

ENSEMBLE Social reformer and writer, Henrietta Barnett, had campaigned for the retention of open land around her home in Hampstead: the Heath Extension. Following this she proposed a new settlement around the Extension to accommodate people of all classes as an alternative to the often dreadful conditions in the city. Parker and Unwin, who were at the centre of the Garden City movement, were appointed to design the master plan and later some housing. It was to be a 'Garden Suburb' rather than a Garden City and would therefore provide no employment, but everything required in a residential area: houses, schools, churches, shops and community facilities. Through co-partnerships of interested individuals, much of this was built, although far fewer shops than originally intended, and the housing for the lowest classes was never materialised. It is now an upmarket suburb with wide and leafy streets, low densities and perimeters marked by hedges rather than walls. Most of the housing is by professional architects. Luytens was employed for the plan and erection of most of the buildings in the centre of the suburb, including St Jude's Church, the Free Church, the Henrietta Barnett School and the Henrietta Barnett Memorial. Aside from the churches, it is all in grey brick with red brick dressings and red tiled roofs; the style is 'Wrenaissance' with hints of Queen Anne and Norman Shaw and it is all most accomplished. St Jude's is an anomaly that combines Old English, Gothic and Renaissance exterior features with a barrel-vaulted and domed Byzantine interior. Some consider this a virtuoso display of Lutyen's renowned ingenuity and eclecticism, but it may just be a muddle. The church's spire, which was added in 1935, is certainly magnificent considered in isolation. The Free Church is not dissimilar but has a dome rather than a spire and is much plainer.

St Jude-on-the-Hill, Hampstead Garden Suburb.

left: The Institute, Hampstead Garden Suburb.

Selfridges Department Store (276)
1908–1928
Oxford Street, W1; tube: Bond Street
Daniel Burnham, Albert Millar,
Francis Swales, Sir John Burnet and
Thomas Tait

Harry Selfridge was a retail pioneer whose methods had made him a fortune in Chicago; bored of retirement, he decided to try out the same methods in London. Along with his notions about retail he brought with him American architectural gigantism. The store, which was built in stages, is truly vast at twenty-one bays by eight and five storeys. The ground floor has shop windows between squat square Tuscan pillars, above which are vast three-storey Ionic columns with highly ornate shafts. The top floor has punched windows in what is effectively the entablature of this monstrous order. The centrepiece over the main entrance comprises a great winged figure and clocks. The inside was planned for maximum flexibility and has been constantly altered, but one of the escalator wells shares some of the heroic scale of the exterior.

Whiteleys, another large department store, was being built at the same time in nearly as grand a manner by Belch-er & Joass in Queensway, Kensington (1908–1912).

Admiralty Arch (277)
1908–1911
The Mall, SW1; tube: Charing Cross
Aston Webb

Although the result of a competition for improvements to The Mall and for a national memorial for Queen Victoria, the Arch is as much office building as triumphal arch. The three arched portals are flanked by tapering curving four-storey Portland stone office blocks and three storeys are cleverly squeezed in over the arch. The façades are concave and tapering on both sides, which helps to disguise the shift in axis from The Mall to the Strand. Inside the north arch, there is a nose carved in the wall, the purpose of which is unknown. In 2002, the Admirals made way for the Cabinet Office.

London Palladium (278)
1909–1910
Argyll Street, W1; tube: Oxford Circus
Frank Matcham

The elevation to the street is all that re-mains of a previous incarnation of the theatre by Owen Lewis of the 1860s. It is a simple seven-bay temple front in stucco with giant Corinthian columns on high pedestals. Matcham removed the three central columns to allow a wider entrance and fitted an elaborate steel and glass canopy. The interiors are all Matcham's work. The auditorium has a capacity of 2,270, making this theatre one of the largest in the city, although it could seat a massive 3,340 when it first opened. This is accommodated with only two cantilevered balconies, because the auditorium is so wide. The style is the usual French Baroque/Rococo in mostly white, pink and gold and the ceiling of the auditorium is a segmental vault with a large lantern. Matcham loved techno-logical gadgets, and here he installed a box-to-box telephone system for a use that is now a mystery.

Michelin Building (279)
1909–1911
Fulham Road, SW3;
tube: South Kensington
François Espinasse

A good humoured and exotic addition to Kensington, the ground floor of the building was a service bay for the fitting of tyres with the Michelin office in Britain on the floors above. There is red and yel-low brick, blue, green and white faience, decorative ceramic spandrel panels and signage, and painted tiled panels depict-ing racing triumphs in Michelin tyres. At the gable there is a large arched window flanked by round towers, which are topped with glass domes representing piles of tyres; these are lit from within at night.

Its well-disguised use of a concrete frame was still unusual in Britain at the time. Three of the large first floor windows have stained glass depicting Bibendum, the tyre company's 'Michelin Man' mascot. It now serves as a luxury shop and restaurant. It is hard to imagine a city of buildings like this, but it would surely be fun.

Port of London Authority Building
(280)
1912–1920
Trinity Square, EC3; tube: Tower Hill
Edwin Cooper

The Port of London Authority has responsibility for about 150 kilometres of the Thames, which in 1912 was still one of the busiest ports in the world. Naturally, such an authority would wish to have a building that reflected the gravity of this responsibility. Cooper's building is square with one corner shaved off for the main entrance. It is organised around a central square space, which until the last war had been roofed with a thirty metre concrete dome; this space was partially built over in the 1970s. Three storeys over a basement with an attic and dormers, the building is massive and the sense of weight is emphasised by the rustication of the stone throughout. The entrances on the diagonal and lesser ones at the other corners have recessed porticos with giant three-storey Corinthian columns in antis. If this was not enough, there is a huge tower over the main entrance holding nothing but niches for monumental sculptures, most notably 'Old Father Thames'. The entrance hall and other interiors are similarly monumental and heavy.

Science Museum   (281)
1913–1928
Exhibition Road, SW7;
tube: South Kensington
Richard Allison

Despite its marvellous collection, the Science Museum feels a little like the poor relation amongst the Albertopolis museum triumvirate. Hemmed in by the Natural History Museum and Imperial College, it has limited frontage to the street. Allison's building is a commonplace Beaux-Arts exercise with a rusticated ground floor and attached two-storey Ionic columns with an attic above. It is planned around a series of halls heading westwards into the site, some of which have galleried double and triple height spaces. Recent additions have been more exciting.

Wilkinson Eyre's Materials Gallery Bridge (1997) is quite extraordinary – the deck comprises laminated sheets of glass running across the span and the whole structure is suspended from the building by a spider's web of tiny wires. It is impressive and frightening in equal measure.

The westernmost hall is the Wellcome Wing by MJP Architects (1998–2000). It is a vast room with three levels of progressively smaller galleries with a curved volume, an Imax cinema, hanging in the void. The space is eerily lit by a massive blue window that occupies most of the west elevation. It is an exciting, even dramatic, and busy space.

Holland House (282)	**Cenotaph** (283)
1914–1916	*1919–1920*
Bury Street, EC3; tube: Liverpool Street	*Whitehall, SW1; tube: Westminster*
Hendrik Berlage	*Edwin Lutyens*

A boon for any city, London is lucky to have a building by the leading Dutch architect of his generation; it is a pleasant building and a reminder that globalisation is nothing new to the city of London. The building was erected for Dutch shipping tycoons, the Kröller-

Müllers. The main wing to Bury Street has five storeys with a smaller four-storey section to the east. Over a black granite plinth the façade is divided by grey green faience ribs spaced more closely than the steel frame behind, and between these are windows and spandrel panels with bosses in the same faience as the ribs. The granite plinth rises up at the entrances and corners, on one of which is carved a moderne ship's prow. The entrance hall and staircase retain their original and strikingly colourful décor, which was created by Bart van der Leck and Henri van de Velde in 1916 after a Kröller-Müller Berlage split. The façades are a frank expression of the repetitive nature of the building's frame construction, fifteen to twenty years ahead of contemporary British practice.

The Cenotaph is the principle National War Memorial constructed in the wake of the catastrophic 1914–1918 conflict. It is easy to imagine the pressure that even the cocksure Lutyens must have felt in designing such an emotionally charged object, with the Empire looking on and ready to criticise. The general consensus is that, through restraint, he succeeded. Comprising a tall, subtly tapering rectangular block of Portland stone with an abstract coffin at the top and wreaths carved into the two short sides. It is exceedingly muted but with a sombre brooding presence. It is the scene of an annual ceremony at 11am on the Sunday closest to 11th November.

VIRGINIA PRIMARY SCHOOL

THE
JOLLY
BUTCHERS
TRUMAN
HANBURY
BUXTON
& Co LTD

ADT

"Our task? To make Britain a fit country for heroes." (284)

David Lloyd George, Prime Minister (*1863, †1945)

The end of the war saw Britain traumatised, demoralised and indebted. A single positive consequence of the conflict was the recognition that the whole country had struggled together; it was no longer possible to deny large sections of society voting rights and universal adult suffrage was finally granted in 1928. The economic slump of the 1920s and 1930s brought terrible poverty and conflict in its wake. The old industrial areas of the North, Wales and Scotland suffered great deprivation while the Midlands and the South East, centred on London, fared better. The new motor, aviation and electronics industries were concentrated in these areas.

London continued to grow, though it was superceded by New York as the world's most populous city in 1925. Much of the growth continued to be associated with the underground; the Metropolitan Railway actively advertised the joys of living in 'Metro-land' in a bid to fill its trains and sell housing plots. 1930s houses tended to be of two storeys and semi-detached rather than terraced. Stylistically, a watered down Arts and

Crafts, Tudor with fake half-timbering or a very light Deco were common. A sudden aversion to large trees, replaced with fruit trees or no trees at all, lend these districts a strangely denuded air.

The architectural scene was chaotic with competing, opposing approaches. Arts and Crafts faded away except for some small scale housing. Some architects, pre-eminently Lutyens, picked up the threads of Edwardian Wrenaissance Baroque and carried on in the Grand Imperial Manner (nos. 290 and 300). For others, this was perhaps too celebratory and backward-looking and there were fewer and fewer clients with the pocket or stomach for such swagger. From America came a different sort of swagger: bluff no nonsense commercial buildings in vaguely classical or Deco overcoats (nos. 285, 287, 292).

Art Deco, imported from the across the channel, was usually employed for new building types often associated with new modes of transport. The Daimler Garage (no.310) and Victoria Coach Station (no. 312) are good examples. Art Deco was also commonly employed for the new

Arnos Grove Underground Station.

factories springing up on the city's periphery. The Great West Road in Brentford, the 'golden mile', has a famous string of Deco factories. For all their virtues such buildings betray the thin flashiness and over reliance on surface graphic devices that are characteristic Deco weaknesses. Some Art Deco influenced buildings in London however combine graphic élan with material and spatial richness: the Royal Horticultural Society Exhibition Hall (no. 291), Simpsons (no. 326) and St Olaf House (no. 306) are wonderful buildings.

The 1930s saw the arrival of the Modern movement. The early buildings are all by refugees from the continent who taught the first generation of natives how to do 'Modern'. Striking examples in the optimistic white mode are London Zoo Penguin Pool (no. 318) and Highpoint (no. 320), both by Bertold Lubetkin, who had arrived from Russia via Paris and brought elements of both these important Modernist architectural cultures with him. Lubetkin's best pre-war building is modest but intensely evocative of the time; Finsbury Health Centre (no. 328) embodies the social and aesthetic hopes of the coming generation of 'heroic Modernists' like no other building in Britain.

The 1920s and 1930s saw considerable expansions of the underground network, which was nationalised and united within London Transport in 1933. Expansion and consolidation was led by Frank Pick and his chosen architect Charles Holden. Holden's stations are so ubiquitous and consistent that London is scarcely imaginable without them. They embody all the disparate currents of contemporary architecture: a solid classical framework, some Deco motifs, Modernist construction with hints of the Arts and Crafts. Barely altered the stations are in daily use; Arnos Grove, Rayners Lane, East Finchley and Chiswick Park (no. 313) are good examples. In town in a necessarily different vein, Holden was the architect for Piccadilly and St James's Park stations.

On 1st September 1939, twenty years after the last peace, London was at war again and about to face its worst trial since the Great Fire.

Bush House (285)
1920–1923
Aldwych, WC2; tube: Temple
Harvey Corbett

For a long time the headquarters of the BBC World Service, Bush House was origi-nally built with American money and by an American designer as a trade centre. It terminates The Kingsway, the most grandi-ose of the Edwardian street improvements, in the most emphatic manner. Comprising a huge pedimented gable in Portland stone, under which is a semi-circular niche made with a great arch in front of a half dome coffered soffit, there is a screen under the arch with three-storey Corinthian columns bearing the inscription, 'Dedicated to the friendship of English-speaking peoples'. It is hard to see how the World Service could have found a building less in keeping with their ethos and self-image but they seem to have been happy there.

Britannic House (286)
1921–1925
Finsbury Circus, EC2; tube: Moorgate
Edwin Lutyens

A large office building for the Anglo-Persian Oil Company, Britannic House is seven storeys in Portland stone. The ground floor is rusticated with round arched windows and the two floors above form a sort of extended plinth with small rectangular windows. On top are three-storey attached giant Corinthian

columns supporting a small attic storey under a steeply pitched slate roof. In the usual Lutyens manner it manages not to repeat itself bending the classical rules well beyond the breaking point. The interiors were skilfully reordered by Inskip and Jenkins (1987–1989), who re-

tained Lutyens' grand circulation spaces and built a smooth semi-circular glass roofed atrium in what used to be two light-wells.

Adelaide House Offices (287)
1921–1925
King William Street, EC4;
tube: Monument
Sir John Burnet and Thomas Tait

These offices were one of the first City buildings to abandon the increasingly difficult pretence of being a classical palazzo – at eleven storeys it is simply no longer possible. Nonetheless, there are vestigial classical references, including hints of columns at the corners and strongly projecting cornices. Otherwise, it comprises rows of windows divided by vertical Portland stone strips and spandrel panels, a prototype modern office building imported from Chicago via Liverpool and Glasgow. With its granite plinth and entrance and strip at 'capital' level, it is elegant in a grim grey sort of way and a harbinger of much more of the same, and worse, to come.

Liberty's Department Store   (288)
1924
Great Marlborough Street, W1;
tube: Oxford Circus
Edwin T. and Edwin S. Hall

Since its foundation in 1875, Liberty & Co. had become so closely identified with the sale of items in the English Arts and Crafts and the Art Nouveau styles that the latter is known in Italy as 'Stile Liberty'. This might explain the choice of style for their 1920s store extension,

as anything 'Old English' in the centre was highly anachronistic by this time. From the outside, the vast neo-Tudor mass does look out of place and time. The glory of the building, however, is its wonderful interior arranged around three four-storey top lit atria and formed in chunky but stylishly detailed timber sections. These were retrieved from two decommissioned Royal Navy ships, HMS Impregnable and HMS Hindustan. The building still serves beautifully as an upmarket, glamorous department store and tourist attraction.

Rudolf Steiner House   (289)
1924–1926
Park Road, NW1; tube: Baker Street
Montague Wheeler

One of the wilder shores of spiritual life in late 19th and early 20th century life was an interest in, first Theosophy, and later Anthroposophy. The headquarters of the Great British Anthroposophical Society houses a lecture theatre, meeting rooms, bookshop and offices along with other amenities. The four-storey Portland stone façade looks at first glance like a standard neo-Tudor bit of urban London, but a closer look reveals some unusual fairytale curves around the windows and shop front canopy. The staircase inside is a curvy expressionist echo of the Goetheanum. A recent café area by Nicholas Pople is centred around a joinery formed tree.

179

Midland Bank Headquarters   (290)
1924–1939
Poultry, EC2; tube: Bank
Edwin Lutyens, Gotch and Saunders

This is Luytens playing his 'high game' furiously, producing a huge commercial building that gives the appearance of a mannerist Palazzo, striving not to repeat himself without the changefulness ever looking contrived. The ground floor has round arched windows with residual Doric pilasters in the reveals; above that is a mezzanine floor and above that three-storey arched openings under a small cornice. At the top are recessed attics with a central arch feature topped by a dome. The building recedes for a bay at the ends above the mezzanine level, on which are seated sculptures of a boy with a goose. All the stone on the street frontage is rusticated while the recessed plains are smooth. It is all cleverly done. The banking hall is lavish, with rows of square Corinthian columns of green marble. Some other interiors survive. The Bank lately moved out and the fate of this building is unknown.

Royal Horticultural Society,
Lawrence Hall   (291)
1926–1928
Greycoat Street, SW1; tube: Victoria
Easton and Robertson

Lawrence Hall is an Exhibition Hall for a charity dedicated to the promotion of horticulture, who hold regular flower shows here. The exterior is brick neo-Georgian with Deco overtones and looks a little like a cinema without the film posters, but betraying nothing of the hall that lies within. The convex entrance screen leads to a subtly streamlined foyer with steps leading down into the hall. This comprises eight bays divided by vast concrete arches; on the inside the profile is elliptical and on the outside stepped to provide for four levels of clerestories of diminishing height. The flat concrete roofs of the clerestories provide lateral stability to the arches. Aisles to the sides

and the topmost flat roof are further lit with glass lanterns, while the east gable façade has three vertical strip windows. It is exhilarating and highly evocative.

Ideal House   (292)
1927–1929
Great Marlborough Street, W1;
tube: Oxford Circus
Raymond Hood and Gordon Jeeves

Ideal House was built for the American National Radiator Company. Hood was an important American architect of the time and the principle architect of a much bigger building for the same client and the Rockefeller Centre, both in New York. The London building is a sharp rectangular block of black polished granite with regularly spaced windows, seven storeys high with seven bays to the south. There were originally only four bays to the west but a further seven were added in the 1930s. The shiny blackness is relieved by intensely colourful decoration to the ground floor and the cornices in enamelled metal. The motifs are Art Deco floral with Egyptian and Oriental overtones.

55 Broadway,
London Underground Offices   (293)
1927–1929
Broadway, SW1; tube: St. James's Park
Charles Holden

London Underground was consolidating the network of separate tube lines into a single system and wanted a building to express their newly won importance; No. 55 was the tallest building in the city when it

was completed. The plan is cruciform with one wing to the east longer than the others, while the ten-storey wings step back at the upper levels. The central service core extends the highest at fifty-three metres, presenting a stereotypical 'New York' style ziggurat appearance. There are two-storey infill ranges between the arms of the cross. The architecture is

fairly muted with circular granite piers at ground level with abstract block capitals; otherwise there are simple rectangular windows in the Portland stone walls. Relieving this is sculpture by leading and, in some cases, controversial sculptors of the day, including Jacob Epstein, Eric Gill and Henry Moore. The building accommodates a marble lined underground station and, since 1988, a shopping arcade as well as London Underground's offices.

Oxo Tower   (294)
1928–1929
Barge House Street, SE1;
tube: Blackfriars
Albert Moore

Until recently, this was a largely utilitarian eight-storey red brick box with minimal stone dressing to the river front and punched windows. It was built as cold stores for the Liebig Extract of Meat Company. The one flourish was a three-storey rendered Deco tower with windows spelling 'OXO' on all four sides, 'oxo' being the company's well-known stock cube. The oddly emblazoned tower has become a renowned, if surreal, city landmark. After a long contest, the building came into the hands of the Coin Street Community and was refurbished as a mixed-use building by Lifschutz Davidson Sandilands (1994–1996). They built a glamorous steel and glass restaurant on the roof, which has terrific views, and opened up a two-storey colonnade by the waterside, both of which have been well received.

Daily Telegraph Building (295)
1928–1931
Fleet Street, EC4; tube: Blackfriars
Elcock and Sutcliffe, Thomas Tait

A great hulking mass in Graeco-Egyptian Deco Portland stone, the building certainly contrasts sharply with its near neighbour, the Daily Express (no. 304). The granite half basement has strange elongated octagonal windows below rectangular windows up to a cornice, with the entrance in the middle. Above are six giant, four-storey fluted columns in antis with abstract lotus leaf capitals; between the columns are bronze windows with stone spandrel panels. Tall vertical windows to the end bays mark staircases and further storeys above are deeply set back from the façade. There is a large amount of vaguely Egyptian relief to stone edges throughout. The original entrance hall has been preserved and is suitably lavish.

Conway Hall (296)
1929
Red Lion Square, WC1; tube: Holborn
Frederick Mansford

Conway Hall is the home of the South Place Ethical Society, founded in 1793 as a Philadelphian Protestant group, who had severed their already tenuous relationship with God by 1880 and have remained strictly secular. The building has two halls, a library, a bookshop and

offices. The main entrance to Red Lion Square is framed by a two-storey arched opening in grey brick with red brick and stone dressings, and there is a curved balcony over the door. The foyer has some idiosyncratic classical detailing that bears similarities to the contemporary work of the celebrated Slovene architect, Plečnik.

The main hall is galleried on three sides with a shallow barrel-vaulted ceiling with roof lights that are now obscured. Tight budgets have seen few other changes since 1929.

Grosvenor Estate (297)
1929–1930
Page Street, SW1; tube: Pimlico
Edwin Lutyens

As social housing, jointly developed by the Grosvenor Estate and Westminster Council, it is a fairly surprising job for the darling of a rich establishment, but Lutyens seems to have given it serious attention. There are five 'U'-shaped, six-storey blocks disposed either side of the street. Inside are typical deck access balconies creating stripes with rendered fronts. Elsewhere, the walls are yellow brick with regularly placed white painted windows. The squares formed by the corners of four windows are all rendered lending the building a chequered super graphic appearance; it is simplistic but memorable. Between the blocks on the street are little Lutyenesque classical pavilions with pyramid roofs serving as shops, hairdressers and so on. Surprisingly, these all seem to be still in use.

Savoy Theatre (298)
1929–1930
Strand, WC2; tube: Charing Cross
Bertie Crewe, Frank Tugwell and
Basil Ionides

The Savoy was built by theatrical impresario, Richard D'Oyly Carte, in 1881 and was much identified with his produc-

tions of Gilbert and Sullivan operettas. A man who did not believe in idleness, in 1929 he ripped out the interior and

rebuilt it. By this time, the theatre had been subsumed into D'Oyly Carte's other venture, the Savoy Hotel. The new theatre is Art Deco with much use of aluminium leaf. There are two curved balconies with fluted aluminium fronts and in front are vast coffered aluminium slanting walls to the stage with a similarly coffered ceiling above. The colours of the upholstery and curtains are luscious. The foyers are in a similar vein and similarly lush. The whole was burnt out in 1990 but, built only three years later, it had been fully restored by William Whitfield and Partners.

Olympia Exhibition Halls (299)
1929–1930
Hammersmith Road, W14; tube: West
Kensington/Kensington Olympia
Joseph Emberton

The halls themselves were constructed in 1885 by Henry Coe as the National Agricultural Hall, with pleasant barrel-vaulted sheds, lattice trusses and partially glazed roofs. Emberton's new frontage building is clearly meant to impress with its size and modernity. Six storeys in rendered brickwork on a concrete frame; it has long continuous strip streamline windows and integrated Art Deco super graphics. The central entrance section is recessed with tall vertical piers. Emberton was also responsible for the simple and direct garage building to the rear.

**Crane Bennett Ltd. Office and
Showroom** (300)
1929–1931
Pall Mall, WC1; tube: Piccadilly Circus
Edwin Lutyens

Now the Banco Sabadell, this is one of
Lutyens' most playful elevations and one
of his most charming. The narrow façade
has seven storeys; the bottom three form
a plinth in smooth undecorated stone and
there is a large asymmetrical arched opening flanking a much smaller door case.
Above this are three regular openings and
then two-storey attached columns and pilasters in Lutyens' own Delhi order, with
little bells where the volutes would be on
a Corinthian capital. The two attic storeys
end in a pedimented gable. Despite the
introduction of emphatic asymmetry, the
composition is beautifully balanced and
proportioned.

Battersea Power Station (301)
1929–1939
Battersea Park Road, SW8;
tube: Sloane Square
Giles Gilbert Scott

One of the iconic buildings of London,
Battersea Power Station is currently lan-
guishing in a state of uncertainty and
increasing disrepair. The construction of
such an enormous power station so close

to the centre of the city inevitably led to
concern regarding both its appearance
and pollution. The former was addressed
by the appointment of Scott as some kind
of exterior stylist, and the latter by innovative exhaust gas scrubbing technology,
although what protection this afforded
the air was offset by draining the residue
into the Thames! One of the largest brick
structures ever built, albeit with a steel
frame, it was built in two identical halves,
the second, east section between 1944
and 1945. The massive brick box with its
four corner towers and huge fluted columns is simple, direct and very powerful.
The interiors of the first phase, some of
which can still be seen, were remarkably
plush and costly for such a utilitarian
building; the Art Deco Control Room, for
example, is wonderfully Flash Gordon. A

series of feckless developers and heritage
bodies have left the structure partly un-
roofed and with an unknown future.

Hanover Primary School (302)
1930
Noel Road, N1; tube: Angel
*London County Council Architects
Department*

A most unusual and charming building
on a long thin canal side site, the school
has two greatly contrasting elevations reflecting its different outlooks and orien-
tations. The site steps sharply across its
narrow dimension so that the first floor
is nearly at road level. The structure is of
yellow brick with purple brick dressings
and white painted wooden windows. To
the north (street) side, the long central

part of the elevation is recessed behind square brick columns with 'Tuscan' capitals, which rise all the way up to support the flat roof and brick parapet. This part of the school has three floors of classrooms on the south side with corridors behind the giant colonnade; at each end are the blocks containing the boys' and girls' entrances and stairs, which project to end the colonnade. At the east end is a further three-storey block containing the school hall and other common facilities. To the west across a yard is a charming caretaker's house. The south elevation, to the canal, is a series of many paned glazed wooden screens between brick piers and concrete floors with continuous iron railed balconies. The roof, which serves as a playground, also has iron railings.

Adelphi Theatre   (303)
1930
Strand, WC2; tube: Charing Cross
Ernest Schaufelberg

The current building is the fourth on this site. It is normally described, rightly, as Art Deco but there is a definite mitteleuropa expressionist air about the place. The narrow façade to the Strand above the canopied entrance is clad in (now painted) white tiles, while black stripes at high level serve as a cornice with 'ADELPHI' above in block lettering; there is a single asymmetrically placed irregular octagonal window to the Dress Circle bar with jagged tracery. The interior is similarly angular and crystalline with strictly no curves. The auditorium has two cantilevered concrete balconies under a faceted soffit.

Daily Express Building   (304)
1930–1933
Fleet Street, EC4; tube: Blackfriars
Owen Williams, Ellis and Clarke

Ellis & Clarke were the architects but the engineer Williams is normally credited with the design. The lavish Art Deco front-of-house interiors were by Robert Atkinson. Constructed for the legendary press Baron, Lord Beaverbrook, it housed the journalists and presses of the Daily Express, at the time the biggest selling newspaper in the world. The eight-storey, streamlined and curved façade is unique in Britain apart from its near twin in Manchester. The materials are glass, black Vitrolite and chrome and the effect is sleek, elegant and rich. The design cleverly housed what was effectively an industrial process in the heart of the city, right up to the newspaper revolution

of the late 1980s. It is otherwise notable as the home of the beautifully illustrated Rupert Bear cartoon, beloved of generations of British children.

Broadcasting House (305)
1931
Portland Place, W1; tube: Oxford Circus
George Val Myer, Raymond McGrath

Myers was a, not very distinguished, commercial architect who gained this prestigious commission via the BBC's landlord for the site. What he produced is a vast, coarse lump of a building – eight storeys in Portland stone with rows of Georgian proportioned unadorned punched windows. The entrance is at the south end, which is semi-circular and recedes at the upper levels. Eric Gill was responsible for the fine carvings of Ariel and Prospero. The building is arranged around a block

of studios in the middle of the plan with offices and ancillary spaces arranged around the perimeter. The interiors were more interesting and were supervised by McGrath, with work by Serge Chermayeff and Wells Coates, but have been much altered in subsequent years.

A large extension is currently under construction to the north and east by MJP Architects, begun in 2005. The intention seems to be to compensate for the lack of detail on the original building by introducing an awful lot on the new one.

St Olaf House (306)
1931
Tooley Street, SE1; tube: London Bridge
Harry Goodhart-Rendel

Goodhart Rendel was a self taught architect who became a leading writer, teacher and church designer. On the evidence of Olaf House, it is a shame that he did not do more secular buildings. There are façades to the river and Tooley Street, the latter of which is six storeys in plain Portland stone with four long horizontal oriel windows over the wide entrance. There are stepped punched windows to stairs in the ends and an incised carving of King Olaf in the south-west corner. The river elevation is more flamboyant; a storey higher, it is divided by plain round columns and is in granite to the riverside arcaded walkway with limestone above. Over the walkway are five bands of strip steel windows with canted ends. The central section of the façade has three vertical oriel windows in a field of gilded relief panels. At the top is

a 'HAY'S WHARF' Art Deco super graphic. It is both fancy and rational and easily one of the best buildings on the river.

Royal Masonic Hospital (307)
1931
Ravenscourt Park, W6;
tube: Ravenscourt Park/Stamford Brook
John Burnet, Thomas Tait and
Francis Lorne

One of the architectural problems of theatre design is that most of the spaces need to be unlit and designers usually try to find some way around this. In this instance the architects chose to celebrate the problem and present a reasonably successful, almost blank façade to the street. The ground floor has a rusticated stone lower part with a continuous cast stone relief above depicting

A large rambling complex, as hospitals tend to be, it has been extended many times. Generally the materials are red brick with steel windows, flat roofs and concrete decks. A three-storey, 'T'-shaped entrance and administration wing faces the park with a large, rich, sombre entrance hall and stairs. The 270 beds were accommodated around a five-storey, three-sided courtyard, open to the south, behind the entrance block. The ends of the wings step back progressively and end in large semi-circular, open 'sun terraces' with nautical style railings. The inspiration is undoubtedly the Dutchman, Dudok, though contemporary American hospital planning was studied as well. The hospital was privately and generously funded, thus the materials and décor throughout are opulent by normal hospital standards.

Saville Theatre (308)
1931
Shaftesbury Avenue, WC2; tube: Tottenham Court Road/Leicester Square
Thomas Bennett, Bertie Crewe

'Drama Through The Ages', sculpted by Gilbert Bayes. It is interrupted only by the entrance, which has the only window arched above it. Above the frieze is banded rusticated red brown brickwork with some cast stone paired medallions. One can speculate whether the design would work so well without the mature trees on this stretch of the street. Unfortunately the original interiors were destroyed when the building was converted into a cinema in 1970.

Charles Holden
*1875 in Bolton, Lancashire,
†1960 in Harmer Green, Hertfordshire (309)

Holden was born in Bolton in 1875, the son of an unsuccessful draper. After various clerical jobs he was articled to a Manchester architect, Everard Leeson, and attended classes at the Municipal School of Art. In 1897 he submitted a design for the Royal Institute of British Architects Soane medal; Holden's design for a market hall came only third but it was widely publicised and to this day is routinely included in accounts of the Arts and Crafts Movement. Perhaps on the strength of this success Holden was employed in 1887 by Charles Ashbee, a leading Arts

and Crafts architect, designer and social theorist. Holden stayed only two years before he joined the office of established hospital architect Percy Adams, apparently in search of a more pragmatic and productive environment.

The first architectural indications of Adams' new employee are at the Belgrave Hospital for Children; although this building was planned by Adams the façades received a makeover from Holden. A more equal collaboration can be detected in the pair's next project, the British Seaman's Hospital in Îstanbul. This highly romantic building can be located by its little tower nestling below the Galata Tower in the classic view of Pera from Süleymaniye. Holden's next job won in competition was the Bristol Central Library, an icon of the Arts and Crafts Movement. Externally the library is a wonderfully free exercise in neo-Tudor with classical overtones. Although the interiors are certainly fine they are more traditionally classical. At this time Holden began to receive commissions in central London; first was an extension to the Law Society (no. 160) followed by the British Medical Association building (no. 273) in the Strand. Both these buildings are in a highly mannered classical style; in the case of the latter the connection with classicism is tenuous to the point of breaking. The buildings share a tremendous youthful brio and panache.

After an underproductive war Holden was appointed to work with what became the Imperial War Graves Commission. By 1920 he was promoted as the fourth 'Principal Architect' and was involved in work for the commission up to 1928. His cemeteries are generally in a stripped classical style but some, such as Corbie and Tournai, are even more severe, resembling megalithic structures in their stark elemental heaviness.

Holden had met Frank Pick in 1915 through their common membership of the Design and Industries Association. Pick, who held various influential positions in London Underground, has been described by Pevsner as the greatest patron of design of the 20th century. He certainly believed strongly in the importance of good design and a distinctive visual identity and was intent on imposing them on the chaotic system in his charge. After a few small jobs Holden was appointed to design a whole series of stations when the Northern line was extended south in the mid 1920s. The new stations were, as Pick intended, distinctive with simple white limestone facings and double height ticket halls lit with large high level windows. There are traits of both Deco and Modernism in the styling. Further stations were required for the extension of both ends of the Piccadilly line in the early 1930s. These are generally in brick with large expanses of steel windows, while much of the structure and the platform canopies are concrete. Particularly good examples include Arnos Grove, Southgate and Chiswick Park (no. 313). The Deco overtones are quieter in this batch of stations and the Dutch and Scandinavian Modernist influence more pronounced. A common basic language is used for all the stations, which also offer tremendous variety. They have lasted wonderfully well and are much loved.

Holden also designed a headquarters for the Underground (no. 293), which includes St James's Park Station underneath; it was the tallest building in London at the time and has a hint of Manhattan about it along with Holden's usual influences.

Holden's last big job was for the University of London, planning a campus to house the university's central facilities and some of the smaller colleges. The proposals envisaged a vast swathe of building with many courtyards marching through Bloomsbury. Thankfully, only about a quarter of this was ever built. This 'fragment', Senate House (no. 315), is still a substantial building and its book stack tower has become the symbol of the university as both client and architect intended.

Sketch design for an entrance to Tooting Broadway Underground Station, London.

Daimler Garage (310)
1931
Herbrand Street, WC1;
tube: Russell Square
Wallis, Gilbert and Partners

The garage is an example of the per-ceived affinity of Art Deco and the new modes of transport. It was built to house cars owned by Daimler and those of sub-scribing private owners. The ramp up through the building is housed inside a vast drum in front of the four-storey slab at the rear of the site; there are lower blocks to the front. Two stair towers are emphasised with vertical windows in decorated surrounds. Otherwise, the materials are white render on concrete with steel windows with characteristic horizontal emphasis; the panels between the windows are incised in line with the window transoms to maintain the sense of restless motion.

Granada Cinema (311)
1931
Mitcham Road, SW17;
tube: Tooting Broadway
Masey and Uren, Theodore Komisarjevsky

The 1930s saw an explosion of cinema building in London and, like the Edwardi-an theatres before them, the puzzle now is

what to do with them all – many, like this one, become bingo halls and a less romantic fate is hard to imagine. Many of the boom cinemas were extravagant and romantic and none more so than the Tooting Granada. The exterior is dull enough with giant Corinthian columns in antis over the entrance. The interior

by the set designer Komisarjevsky is a different kettle of fish entirely. The double height baronial foyer, the vaulted and arcaded Moorish style Hall of Mirrors, and the vast 3,000-seat, two-dimensional fretwork Gothic auditorium are all packed with lavish decorative plaster detail. There is much to enjoy, quite apart from the Bingo.

Victoria Coach Station (312)
1931–1932
Buckingham Palace Road, SW1;
tube: Victoria
Wallis, Gilbert and Partners

It is highly doubtful that any road jour-ney over our tiny islands could have the allure of, say, the Silk Road or Route

66. Nonetheless, Victoria Coach Station has a slight but definite scent of the romance of travel; buses can be taken to Ireland, Cornwall, Aberdeen and even the continent. The buses dock in an inner courtyard with a partially glazed roof, surrounded on two sides by offices in six-storey blocks, which are in render with a strong streamlined horizontal emphasis. The entrance on the corner, where these blocks meet, is higher and with a pronounced vertical emphasis. It is all a little grimy, but who would have bus travel any other way?

Chiswick Park Underground Station (313)
1931–1933
Acton Lane, W4; tube: Chiswick Park
Charles Holden

From its creation in 1933 until the war, London Underground under Frank Pick

became a very dynamic organisation, overseeing massive expansions of the network to the limits of London and establishing new lines. Holden was the architect for much of this expansion, leaving behind a wonderful legacy of instantly recognisable, airy, Scandinavian classical Deco stations peppering the outer suburbs, they are pleasant, rational and hardwearing. Chiswick Park is all these things. Here the ticket hall is a double height brick drum with a single central column and large steel windows. The black glazed brick at lower level and the steel shop fronts are just as they were, seemingly impervious to wear. It is largely unchanged, because no change has proved to be necessary.

There is a brick tower to counterpoint the roundness of the drum and to mark the station from a distance. The pleasant but crude platform canopies are of reinforced concrete.

Royal Institute of British Architects (314)
1932–1933
Portland Place, W1; tube: Regent's Park/ Great Portland Street
George Grey Wornum

It was perhaps inevitable that the RIBA would end up with a slightly unusual building. It is not, however, badly designed being the winner of a prestigious, very popular competition. The peculiarity lies in its architectural preoccupations which were only briefly fashionable during a time when little was built. It is in the Scandinavian Modern neoclassical manner with the slightest of hints of something more sinister from contemporary Italy. A simple four-storey limestone block, it has minimal moulding, stark punched windows and some reliefs that are entirely of their time. The entrance is topped with a large two-storey window and flanked by peculiar freestanding stone pylons. The interior is richer and planned around a grand staircase. The recessed and even plainer upper storeys were added in the late 1950s.

Senate House, University of London (315)
1932–1937
Malet Street, WC1; tube: Russell Square
Charles Holden

London's many and various educational institutions are nearly all constituent entities of the University of London; Holden's building houses the Corporate Headquarters and Library of the central body as well as acting as landlord to a variety of the smaller constituents. Holden's original master plan envisaged a much larger development, but the approaching war and changed priorities caused this to be abandoned in 1937. What was built were two large blocks assembled around courtyards; the blocks are six-storey with a granite base and Portland stone above, with very simple rectangular punched windows and very little detail to the stonework. Between the two lower blocks is a nineteen-storey tower with a stepped ziggurat Manhattan-like profile, which houses the Library's stacks and is a symbol and landmark of the university. It seems entirely appropriate that the university's icon should be filled with a million books. The open undercroft to the tower, and interiors such as the Library Reading Room, the Senate Room, and the entrance hall and staircase are large-scaled, sombre and classical, with Art Deco and Arts and Crafts overtones. The building's imagery is strikingly unique for London – this and its use by the Ministry of Information during the war led George Orwell to use it as his model for the Ministry of Truth in the novel, '1984'.

Peter Jones Department Store (316)
1935–1937
Sloane Square, SW3;
tube: Sloane Square
Slater, Crabtree and Moberly

Although by no means the first curtain wall building in Britain, Peter Jones is the first building in London with a full, recognizably modern curtain wall. It is also elegant with a pleasing contrast between the horizontal spandrel panels and the vertical steel mullions. The curved corner to Sloane Street and the recessed fifth floor also contribute to the elegance and interest of the composition; how much so can be judged by the lack of these features in the otherwise identical extension to the west of 1937. Recently subject to a thorough overall by John McAslan and Partners (2000–2004), the store now houses a minimalist curvaceous escalator atrium cut through all six floors of the building and a rooftop restaurant. Around the back in Cadogan Gardens is a small building with similar details, which was built first as a test bed for some of the novel technologies being employed. Next door, and now part of the store, is a pleasant Arts and Crafts, Queen Anne studio house by Arthur Mackmurdo from 1893.

Gorilla House, London Zoo (317)
1933
Regent's Park, Prince Albert Road, NW1;
tube: Regent's Park/Camden Town
Tecton Architects

Tecton it was, lead by Russian émigré Bertold Lubetkin, who brought Corbusian modernism to Britain, and the Gorilla House was their first project. It is a cir-

cular structure, one half containing the animal's winter quarters in horizontally ribbed, white painted concrete with high level windows. The other half was a roofed open cage for the apes' use in the summer and, transformed by sliding screens, an indoor viewing room for visitors in the winter. It is ingenious and quite unprecedented for Britain at that time.

Penguin Pool, London Zoo (318)
1934
Regent's Park, Prince Albert Road, NW1;
tube: Regent's Park/Camden Town
Tecton Architects

Perhaps the single most pervasive icon of Modernism in Britain, the Penguin Pool is a very modestly sized structure. A white concrete wall with various viewing holes surrounds an elliptical pool. Around the edge are stepped ramps and small nest-

ing box enclosures. Across the middle of the pool are two interlocking spiral ramps, incredibly thin concrete ribbons twirling in the air. The engineering was by pioneering Anglo-Dane Ove Arup. Wonderful as it is to look at and beautifully restored by Avanti in 1987, it seems the penguins had never taken to it and it now serves as a 'water feature'.

Hornsey Town Hall (319)
1933–1935
The Broadway, Crouch End, N8;
train: Crouch Hill
Reginald Uren

Plainly indebted to Dudok's Hilversum City Hall of 1931 in its use of brick, asymmetric chunky massing and vertical emphases including a tall tower, the town hall differs from Hilversum in having much darker bricks and lacking the strong horizontal accents in the Dutch design. It is 'L'-shaped with three storeys, although one wing has double height spaces to the upper part. The tower is located close to the corner. Slight stone trimmings around the entrances and the double height windows to the main spaces relieve the brown brick. The interior is rich but restrained; the top-lit entrance hall with its marble staircase with decorative steel balustrading is impressive, as are the Council Chamber and Assembly Hall. Hornsey was dissolved as a borough in 1965 and the building languished for a period; it is now being refurbished as an Arts and Community venue.

Highpoint Flats (320)
1933–1935
North Road, N6; tube: Highgate
Tecton Architects

High up in the leafiest of London suburbs, Highpoint I was originally conceived as worker's flats for Gestetner, although at some point this morphed into the speculative building of large flats for the middle classes. It has become burdened with all manner of rhetorical significance and, to this day, people point to it as proof that Modernism and high-rise living really work. The building is of eight storeys on a double cross plan with a flat in each arm of each cross on every floor. The flats are large and well-lit by large expanses of steel window and the common spaces are similarly huge and gleaming. The ground floor is on pilotis, the walls are white rendered concrete, the windows punched and, apart from a slight swell to the solid balcony balustrading, there is no further architectural expression. It does feel fresh, clean and bright, but not much imagination is required to see how, denuded of trees and much enlarged, the same elements might have a very different feel.

Highpoint II, where Lubetkin lived himself, followed in 1938. It is much smaller with three stacks of four maisonettes in a straight line and penthouses on top. The palette of materials is richer with tile and brick infill panels and expressions in some façades of the structural framing. The entrance canopy has the famous pair of caryatids copied from the Erechtheum – Lubetkin's droll comment on the traditionalist resistance he had encountered from local residents and officials.

Courtauld House, Eltham Palace (321)
1933–1937
Court Yard, SE9;
train: Eltham (from London Bridge)
Seely and Paget

Stephen Courtauld of the very wealthy textile family took a lease on the remains of the old palace (no. 19), which he refurbished, and built himself a new house attached to the south of the Great Hall. The house is most curious; the exterior in red-brown brick with beige stone dressings and steeply pitched tiled and leaded roofs is in a roughly 17th-century French style incorporating some fragments from the 15th or 16th-century house. Internally however, it is all very different; every technical advance of the time is incorporated and the styling is streamlined Art Deco at its glitziest. The circular entrance hall with its concrete dome lit with hundreds of circular lenses is particularly striking. The strange juxtapositions do not feel perfectly resolved, but it is certainly interesting and unique.

Isokon Flats (Lawn Road Flats) (322)
1934
Lawn Road, NW3; tube: Belsize Park
Wells Coates

The Isokon building was both a develop-ment and an experiment. The owners of Isokon, a company making modern plywood furniture, decided to build a small number of minimal flats for young urban professionals as an alter-native to the squalid single rooms they were customarily obliged to inhabit. The building has four storeys and is in a very slightly pinkish render. The street façade is strongly abstract and sculptural with, of course, a flat roof and open access decks and stairs expressed with solid balustrading. The garden side is more straightforward with punched windows in the render and individual balconies to the flats. The interiors of the flats were indeed minimal with single bedsit rooms and tiny bathrooms and kitchens. A communal kitchen was supposed to compensate for the latter, with each flat having a dumb waiter to the ground

floor. However, the kitchen closed in 1936, leaving the inhabitants to survive as best they could. A bar was opened in the kitchen's stead, which became the haunt of young bohemians of the time and the East European émigré artistic community.

Sun House (323)
1934–1935
Frognal Way, NW3; tube: Hampstead
Maxwell Fry

Hampstead's collection of white early modern houses is such an established part of its identity that it is difficult to imagine how striking and controversial they were when they first appeared. The

Sun House was one of the first and best of them. The site slopes steeply, which Fry exploited to step the section such that the main living spaces are elevated on one side over a large south-facing balcony. Otherwise, it is quite a simple rendered concrete box with continuous strip windows of differing heights with a sun terrace on the flat roof. For all its simplicity, it is very carefully and art-fully arranged and proportioned.

Apartment Building, 59–63 Princes Gate (324)
1935
Princes Gate, SW7;
tube: South Kensington
Adie, Button and Partners

Muscular and direct, this vaguely Deco apartment block blends in with the white architecture of this part of West London surprisingly well. It is ten sto-reys, the top two of which are succes-sively stepped back, and the entrance is in the middle between two banks of

and otherwise there are simple punched windows. Norman Foster added a polite, glazed extension to the south. Altogether less well mannered are the alterations to the house immediately north; this has the same dates as the Cohen house and was by Gropius & Fry; you have to look hard now to discern traces of their original design

Simpsons Department Store   (326)
1935–1936
Piccadilly, SW1; tube: Piccadilly Circus
Joseph Emberton

The streets around the east end of Piccadilly have long had a reputation for upmarket men's clothing; Simpsons, who invented a novel self-supporting trouser, were an important fixture of this trade. The Piccadilly façade was the first in Britain to boast an uninterrupted glazed shop front that curved concavely to the street to minimize reflections. The four floors above have simple strip windows between stone spandrel strips; above them is a recessed attic under an elegant concrete canopy filled with glass lenses. The rear section to Jermyn Street is from the 1950s. The roof top extension (1962) by Architects Co-Partnership is best viewed close up, when it disappears from sight. Inside, the old arrangement of a series of small rooms has now been lost but the stairs, toilets and lifts are all original and stylishly evocative of the

wide concrete balconies. The rendered façade is incised with horizontal lines corresponding to the transoms of the steel windows, recalling the rustications of the 19th-century buildings in the area. Corner windows help to dematerialise what is a substantial lump of building and add a little moderne zip to the façades.

Cohen House   (325)
1935–1936
Old Church Street, SW3;
tube: South Kensington
Erich Mendelsohn and Serge Chermayeff

The brief partnership between German exile Mendelsohn and Russian born, British raised Chermayeff was instrumental in introducing continental Modernism to Britain. This well-proportioned house still looks quite strikingly fresh and new today. The rendered façade to the street has a single-storey volume hard on the pavement with a long strip window. The second storey is recessed except at the south end, which juts forward to align with the lower block; upstairs is one large window marking the stair and hall

age. It was acquired by a book chain in 1999, who have replaced the beautiful original signage by Bauhaus professor László Moholy-Nagy with their own banal logo.

Ibex House Offices (327)
1935–1937
Minories, EC3; tube: Tower Bridge
Fuller, Hall and Foulsham

The most extensive example of 1930s streamlining in London, the offices comprise ten storeys of bands of steel windows alternating with buff glazed terracotta spandrel strips. The effect is heightened by rounded corners and recessed upper storeys with nautical style steel railings to the terraces. Central vertical features offset the extreme

horizontality, with continuous windows in shiny black granite surrounds and semi-circular glazed staircases.

Finsbury Health Centre (328)
1935–1938
Pine Street, EC1; tube: Farringdon
Tecton Architects

The Health Centre was the first piece of the Finsbury Plan, an ambitious attempt by the eponymous borough to improve the lives of the poor urban working classes in their area. It is also the first totally Modernist building procured by

the public sector in Britain. It is therefore of great social and architectural importance and in both respects prefigured much that was to come over the following twenty years. The 'H'-shaped building has two storeys with a basement and is flat roofed throughout. The central section houses the entrance, reception, waiting room and toilets at ground floor

level, with a lecture theatre and terrace above. It is expressed as a glass block and buff tiled concrete screen wall and the interior is light and airy. The business end of the Centre is located in the two side wings, which house the treatment and consultation rooms. These have a 'one room and a corridor' plan, again prioritising natural light and airiness. The wings have tiled gables, ends and parapets with hardwood curtain walling and enamelled glass spandrels between. Some of the Centre was refurbished very well in the mid 1990s by Avanti, but lack of funding has halted the renovations and the future of the Centre is in doubt.

Barkers Department Store (329)
1935–1939
Kensington High Street, W8;
tube: High Street Kensington
Bernard George

Above a continuous canopied shop front, four-storey high bronze windows between stone clad steel frame elements rise up to meet two receding attic storeys. There is almost no trace of historical detailing. The most striking elements are the two stair towers, which extend the full height of the building, with a continuous 'V'-shaped bay window of many tiny panes between stone planes. At the top, the windows turn into large undulating lanterns the full depth of the stair. There are some interesting relief carvings at

the lower levels of the stair walls. Still used as retail at the lower levels, though Barkers no longer, the upper levels are now offices. To the west is one-time sister store Derry and Toms, also by George (1929–1931). Less flamboyant and more classical, it is topped with Europe's largest roof garden.

Florin Court (330)
1936
Charterhouse Square, EC1;
tube: Florin Court
Guy Morgan and Partners

Much loved by location managers of 1930s dramas, Florin Court was built as London apartments for City businessmen and professionals. Ten storeys, the façade is strongly modelled with the centre deeply recessed, while the internal and external corners to these steps are curved and glazed. The top two floors recede progressively to a communal roof terrace. Pinkish brickwork and steel windows dominate the walls. The spandrel strips are expressed continuously with thin pre-cast concrete top and bottom strips, whereas the windows are not continuous, but have brick infill panels. Originally, there were squash courts, a bar and a dining room. A basement

swimming pool was added in the 1980s in clumsy period style.

Kensal House (331)
1936–1937
Ladbroke Grove, W10;
tube: Kensal Rise
Maxwell Fry

The development was sponsored by the Gas Light and Coke Company as a demonstration of new ideas about working class housing and new domestic gas technology. Fry answered to a project board of reputable architects and the social reformer, Elizabeth Denby. The housing is arranged in two parallel blocks running north to south, the longer of which to the back of the site curves gently beyond the end of the front block. The rendered six-storey blocks are arranged around staircases with no decks or corridors. The east elevations have regular punched windows to the bedrooms and the west side has balconies to the living spaces. Behind the housing is a radially planned, single-storey, steel framed nursery school, which, in the light of its main ideas at least, is easy to imagine being built very similarly today.

Brockwell Park Lido (332)
1937
Dulwich Road, SE24; tube: Brixton,
train: Herne Hill (from Victoria and
London Bridge)
London County Council Parks
Department Architects

1930s notions regarding health and fitness, sunlight, and air led to a slew of lidos constructed throughout Britain in the period. The well-known deficiencies of the British climate and local authority maintenance regimes have meant that many have been lost, a fate that threatened Brockwell Lido. It was saved by public pressure and is now back in use after a recent refurbishment by Pollard Thomas and Edwards. The pool is surrounded by low ranges of brownish brick buildings housing changing rooms and other facilities. On the north side stands only a small pavilion and the perimeter is completed with walls and terracing. The architecture is charming in a discreet, rambling way. The recent extension to the south range, adding further leisure facilities, was done well and sympathetically.

Mytre House Mixed Development (333)
1937–1938
John Street, WC1;
tube: Holborn/Chancery Lane
D. E. Harrington

The site is a narrow wedge with the thin end on John Street, where there is an eight-storey office building that drops to three storeys after six bays along Roger Street. To the rear in the mews is The Duke of York pub on the ground floor below offices and a four-storey apartment block. The ground and first floor of the offices are divided by attached pilasters in reconstituted stone, while the storey above is in red brick laid to form vertical ribs between the steel windows. The body of the tower has punched windows in plain brickwork and the ribbing returns at the topmost storey, which is recessed with a concrete canopy and perky little circular turret. The housing to the rear is plainer but curved balconies, a steel oriel window to the stairs and patterning to the brickwork provide plenty of visual interest. The separate parts of the development are all individually successful, even refined, and they are aggregated equally successfully. While the

basic pattern is a classicised Art Deco, there is more than a hint of Amsterdam School brick expressionism, especially towards the rear.

Houses, 1–3 Willow Road (334)
1937–1939
Willow Road, NW3; tube: Hampstead
Ernö Goldfinger

The middle and largest of the little terrace of three houses was Goldfinger's

199

own family home until his death in 1987. Controversial among local residents when it was built, it became the first modern house to be purchased by the National Trust and is now a museum. From the road, the terrace has three storeys, but a fall across the site allows for garden rooms at basement level on the other side. The concrete frame is partially exposed at ground and first floor level and there are large concrete framed openings on the two long first floor façades, one of which has a long balcony facing the garden. Punched windows in reddish brown brick under a flat roof occupy the rest of the exterior. Inside, the houses are arranged around central spiral staircases and the rooms are light and airy. Goldfinger's own house makes much use of sliding and folding partitions, allowing the space to be configured in a variety of ways.

Imperial Airways Empire Terminal (335)
1937–1939
Buckingham Palace Road, SW1;
tube: Victoria
Albert Lakeman

This terminal of Imperial Airways, which ultimately became British Airways, allowed London passengers to check in before transfer to Croydon Aerodrome or the Flying Boats at Southampton Dock. The building in Portland stone is centred

on a ten-storey clock tower, either side of which are two short concave curving five-storey wings with horizontal strip windows. The space between the wings in front of the tower is filled with a single-storey entrance area, topped with a large sculpted group entitled, 'Speed Wings Over the World', by Eric Broadbent. The

building clearly seeks to embody the thrill, wonder and romance of air travel and it may be that it tries a little too hard. If so, it has been brought down to earth in no uncertain terms being the home now to the resolutely unromantic National Audit Office.

Waterloo Bridge (336)
1937–1942
Waterloo Bridge, WC2/SE1;
tube: Embankment/Waterloo
Rendel, Palmer and Tritton,
Giles Gilbert Scott

Completed during the war years, Waterloo Bridge was sometimes referred

to as "the ladies' bridge", alluding to the women employed in the latter part of its construction. There are five spans of approximately seventy-three metres, which are achieved not, as it may appear, with arches but with balanced cantilevered concrete box beams with central spanning elements. The elegantly profiled arches clad with Portland stone are only at the two edges of the bridge and this doubling up of the arches and the interplay between the two adds to the visual interest of the bridge at embankment level. Scott's detailing of the steps and other features has an unusual organic Deco character.

Institut Français (337)
1938
Queensbury Place, SW7;
tube: South Kensington
Patrice Bonnet

The Institut was founded in 1910 for the promotion of French culture in London. It commissioned French architect Bonnet to design its first purpose-built premises. It is certainly exotic, though it would be scarcely less so in Paris then it is in West

London. Mostly red brick in an expressionist Deco manner, it feels more Dutch or German than French or English. The street elevation has a low ground floor divided by stone basket weave columns between square openings; above are double height triangular headed 'Gothic' windows with elaborate ceramic tracery. The top storey is blind under a projecting brick cornice and is decorated in relief with brick diamonds containing sculpted birds and a snake. The entrance is to the south off an alley and over the entrance is a remarkable glazed stepped lantern with more frenetic ceramic tracery. The entrance hall is impressive, as are the double height galleried library and the theatre, which has been converted into a cinema.

E. Pellicci's Café (338)
1946
Bethnal Green Road, E1;
tube: Bethnal Green
Achille Cappucci

The best remaining café interior from the 1940s, it is still in use as a family run café. The shop front is in stainless steel with primrose yellow Vitrolite fascia and stall riser with the Deco chrome legend, 'E. PELLICCI'. The tiny, cramped, and in winter steamy, interior has a low panelled ceiling and the walls are lined above dado level with marquetry panels and Egyptionate pilasters. It is most atmospheric. The café at the south end of Essex Road has an interior of similar quality but is now run by a chain of sausage and mash shops.

"Our people have never had it so good." (339)

Harold Macmillan, Prime Minister (*1894, †1986)

When the end came in 1945, London had been at war for over five years. The city was grimy, exhausted and very badly damaged; over 110,000 buildings had been destroyed, 310,000 seriously damaged and 30,000 of its residents had died. Worst hit was the old City and the East End around the docks but there was damage throughout. The nation was determined to build a better society on the ruins and the new socialist government promised homes fit for heroes, free health care, schooling to degree level and pensions for the old. Even before war damage the social infrastructure for all this had never existed. Building this new world was a tall order for a weary, bankrupt Britain and would require unprecedented levels of state management and planning. One aim of the plans was to permanently limit London's growth and to this end the city was girded with a 'green belt'. Other planning priorities were a huge expansion of the road network and a more rigid and proscriptive approach to land use zoning.

The old City had lost about a quarter of its fabric and private rebuilding was slow.

The City Corporation took it upon themselves to build Golden Lane (no. 353) and then the much larger Barbican (no. 381) on flattened areas north of St Paul's. These were predominately housing, but also included retail and leisure facilities and an arts centre in the Barbican. In and around the Barbican are high level walkways that were part of a network planned to cover the whole City; this madcap plan was quietly dropped in the 1970s. Commercial development when it came was generally in an inoffensive, undistinguished Modernist style; it was only in the 1960s that budgets allowed for more striking modern buildings (see nos. 376, 392, 396). The finest office developments of the period, Congress House (no. 349) and the Economist Building (no. 368) are both in the West End.

The priority in the wider city was to replace housing lost to the Blitz and subsequent slum clearance. The densities prescribed in the new plans for the East End were well below pre-war levels and much of the displaced population preferred to live in the outer suburbs anyway, causing London's first population

left: Post War London.   Festival of Britain.

decline since 1666. Some of this generation of housing continues to inspire affection; Churchill Gardens (no. 341), Trellick Tower (no. 385) and Golden Lane are all popular places to live. Most of it, built too quickly too cheaply, failed spectacularly and some has already been demolished. Robin Hood Gardens (no. 386) gives a good idea why. Private sector housing was scarcely more successful, although shining exceptions are the Span Developments (no. 354) and Denys Lasdun's St James's Apartments (no. 358).

The first great post-war cultural project was the Festival of Britain in 1951. Ostensibly this was to celebrate the centenary of the Great Exhibition, although conservatives saw it as a propaganda exercise for the socialist government. Its great theme was the wonders of technology past and the wonders to come in a bright future. The architecture had its part in this and was as modern, futuristic and optimistic as could be devised. All that remains of this is the Royal Festival Hall (no. 342) and its bright and airy Scandinavian Modernism is still redolent of the optimism of the time. The rest of the Festival

sites were cleared and lay empty until the Greater London Council developed a new centre for the arts in the late 1960s. The first group of buildings housed the Hayward Gallery and Concert Rooms (nos. 374, 375) executed in Brutalist fashion with raw jagged shapes, dirty windowless concrete and hidden entrances. They signal a general change that had taken place in post-war architectural thought, away from the gentle Scandinavian model in favour of harsher more expressive forms. Lasdun's later National Theatre (no. 372) successfully makes the case that not all Brutalism is bad for you; the concrete here is used to good effect to produce one of the period's best buildings.

If one London building from the period can take its place in the pantheon of sixties icons alongside Concorde, the Mini (skirt and car), the E-type and the Marshall Amp it is the GPO Tower (no. 365), a communications relay with revolving restaurant clearly forged in 'the white heat of the technological revolution'.

Spa Green Estate (340)
1946–1950
Rosebery Avenue, EC1; tube: Angel
Tecton Architects

The site had been identified in the Finsbury Plan for slum clearance and redevelopment before the war, and a reduced scheme was therefore ready for commencement soon after the hostilities ended. There are two large eight-storey blocks, each arranged around three stair cores facing each other across a landscaped garden. The inner faces are brown brick with simple punched windows to bedrooms. The outer faces have a livelier composition of brick and rendered fronts to the recessed access balconies. Overall, the appearance is a little spartan and grim. The third four-storey cranked block, facing Rosebery Avenue behind a screen of mature plane trees, is more attractively varied with tiles as well as render and brickwork and is also more in scale with the surrounding streets.

Churchill Gardens Estate (341)
1947–1962
Churchill Gardens Road, SW1;
tube: Pimlico
Powell and Moya

Like Spa Green (no. 340), Churchill Gardens was being envisaged before the war on a site occupied by run-down, small-scale industry. The scheme was expanded as a consequence of the need

for more housing after the conflict. Powell and Moya were barely qualified when they won the competition with a scheme much influenced by pre-war Dutch and German social housing projects. There are a series of long seven-storey blocks along Lupus Street on the northern boundary of the estate, with ground floor shops and three sets of maisonettes above. Behind this and towards the river are a series of nine-storey to eleven-storey blocks running north-south with a few lower blocks orientated east-west, while terraced houses occupy the river embankment. The final phase at the east end of the site abandons the block typology for a snaking, continuous six-storey terrace. Whilst there is variation across the nearly thirteen-hectare site, the essentials generally comprise a white painted exposed concrete frame with yellow brick infill and white painted windows. The flat roofs have characteristic large white drums housing water tanks. The spaces between the blocks are well planted and, crucially, well maintained. Like all of the architect's work it is high-quality, but self-effacing and undemonstrative, although such a large site perhaps presents these virtues to excess. Successful as it has been as a housing scheme, it does not entirely convince as a piece of urban fabric, having more of a suburban feel, which is hardly appropriate only ten minutes walk from Victoria Station.

Royal Festival Hall (342)
1948–1951
Belvedere Road, SE1;
tube: Embankment/Waterloo
London County Council Architects
Department

The concert hall was London's contribution to the Festival of Britain, the government of the day's attempt to cheer up a tired population. The hall is in the middle of the plan and elevated up above ground level; the foyers and ancillary spaces are arranged around the hall and under its raking floor. The foyers are open to the various stairs leading to the upper levels and this complicated and dynamic large space is the principal joy of the building. The hall itself has a single balcony level with a series of small boxes cantilevered out from the flanking walls. There have been some slight changes recently in an attempt to cure poor acoustics. The building's organisation is faithfully expressed externally, the blank volume of the hall with its vaulted roof appearing above the stone and glass façades of the foyers. The latter were expanded in the 1960s, when the light-hearted original façades took on a more rationalist look. What now serves as a restaurant at second floor level took its final form at this time – a wonderful double height space, fully glazed and overlooking the river. The building has recently been altered and refurbished by Allies and Morrison (2005–2007) and once again has a fresh and cheery look.

Stockwell Bus Garage (343)
1950–1954
Lansdowne Way, SW8; tube: Stockwell
Adie, Button and Partners

The huge roof, formed of nine barrel vaults which cantilever from great reinforced concrete arches spanning fifty-nine metres, was designed to shelter 200 buses. Each vault is divided by a continuous roof-light at the apex. It is an exhilarating space, and the notion that all of this was considered worthwhile for a mere bus garage only increases one's exhilaration. Much of the infill between the frame and arches is glass or large concertina doors with some brick panels at low level. There is a low range of brick ancillary accommodation to the rear. The reinforced concrete engineering was by A. E. Beer and Partners.

Skylon (344)
1951
South Bank, SE1;
tube: Embankment/Waterloo
Powell and Moya

DEMOLITION The Skylon was the 'vertical feature' of the Festival of Britain and took the form of an apparently floating cigar shaped needle. The structure of the

needle was steel and was clad in aluminium louvers. In daylight it had an improbable insect-like appearance, but the structure was most spectacular by night. Lit from within, the tensegrity cable structure that supported it disappeared into the darkness to leave a ghostly, glowing shaft hovering above the South Bank. When the Festival ended, a new government, which wanted nothing to do with its predecessor's popular festival, refused to pay for the Skylon's relocation and it was torn down for scrap. Since then, its rebuilding has been ceaselessly discussed, most recently in relation to the Olympic developments. It will surely happen one day. Felix Samuely was the engineer.

Time Life Building (345)
1951–1953
New Bond Street, WC1;
tube: Oxford Circus/Bond Street
Michael Rosenauer

The street façades are unremarkable, with six storeys of punched windows in Portland stone grouped into bays of five with the cills extended to form continuous string courses. There is a seventh recessed storey and a small two-storey section to the south. The building is notable for the artworks lavished upon it, the most notable being the reliefs

in the parapet wall to the second floor terrace by Henry Moore. There is also a bronze reclining figure by Moore on the terrace. The building was paid for in American dollars and was exempted from the materials rationing of the time.

The interiors are rich, particularly the sequence of spaces from the entrance up to the terrace. These were overseen by Hugh Casson and Misha Black, who were heavily involved with the Festival of Britain at the time.

Hallfield School (346)
1951–1955
Hallfield Estate, W2;
tube: Bayswater/Paddington
Lindsey Drake and Denys Lasdun

Lasdun had worked with Lubetkin on the design of the earlier estate, of which the school has become a centre point. The school is highly articulated and romantic. The juniors are housed in a curving two-storey block to the north, with glazing between a closely spaced concrete frame under a flat roof. The infants are located in a series of lower buildings huddled informally around intimate leafy courtyards to the south. It is generally considered one of the finest of the many post-war schools and it has an influence on the planning of schools to this day. In 2005, Caruso St John Architects completed a pair of characteristically thoughtful and self-effacing, rendered, flat roofed classroom blocks.

BBC Television Centre (347)
1951–1960
Wood Lane, W8;
tube: White City/Wood Lane
Norman and Dawbarn

It is perhaps only the Houses of Parliament that have had a more central role in post-war British life than Television Centre. The original building, one of the first of its kind, has an eight-storey, curtain wall clad, circular office building around a circular courtyard. This is exposed and raised on piloti to the west forming an entrance way; elsewhere it is surrounded by lower radial studios connected by an outer runway to the scenery workshops. Of necessity, the studios are blind and are clad in brick with some curious little 1930s or 1950s style decorative embellishments. Reflecting the huge expansion of the role of the media, the building has been greatly extended in nearly all directions, especially during the 1980s, it's best not to look.

Bevin Court (348)
1952–1955
Bevin Way, WC1;
tube: Kings Cross St. Pancras
Skinner, Bailey and Lubetkin

Lubetkin wanted to call this block of public housing Lenin Court, but the Cold War soon ended that idea. The lack of money that extinguished many of the aspirations for post-war public housing are clearly in evidence in this project – no communal facilities, a single core with long access galleries, no balconies and a much reduced palette of materials when compared to Tecton's earlier schemes. Bevin Court is a 'Y'-shaped block of between seven and eight storeys, with the core at the meeting of the three arms. The faces of the blocks opposite the access decks have a chequered pattern of white concrete and brick panels, not unlike Lutyen's Grosvenor Estate (no. 297). The side on which the decks are situated has very little patterning. The redeeming feature is the central staircase, which is remarkably sculptural and expressive. A central column supports an array of triangular landings in a circular void, connected by stair flight bridges; it is quite stunning.

Congress House (349)
1953–1957
Great Russell Street, WC1;
tube: Tottenham Court Road
David Aberdeen

The home to the Trades Union Congress – the union of unions – is surprisingly progressive for such a notoriously conservative organisation. It occupies half a cramped city centre block in a 'C'-shape around a courtyard. The planning is very fluid, with spaces flowing one into the other with minimal corridor space. The ground floor is fully glazed behind pilotis, allowing views through the building, above which are continuous strip windows in a polished granite wall. The topmost fifth floor is more emphatically articulated. Canopies, balconies, stairs and sculpture are all employed to add interest to what is largely office space. The main meeting hall lies underneath the courtyard, which is paved with large hexagonal pavement lights supported by a steel space frame structure. At the back of the courtyard, in front of a green mosaic wall, is Jacob Epstein's sculpted Pietà, commemorating trade unionists who fell in the war.

Bankside Power Station (350)
1954–1960
Holland Street, SE1; tube: Southwark
Giles Gilbert Scott

Built in the face of opposition in response to power shortages in the late 1940s, Bankside is a huge mass of brickwork on a steel frame, four storeys high and 200 metres long. There is a central campanile style chimney on the north side facing the river. The north, east and west façades have large windows with brick mullions, whereas the forbidding south side has only a row of high level slits. Power generation ceased in 1981 and the building remained idle until Herzog and de Meuron converted it into a modern art gallery for the Tate (1995–2000). Their masterstroke was to leave the colossal machine hall, which runs the full length and height of the building, effectively empty, to be used only for the exhibition of specially commissioned artworks. The fine gallery spaces are all to the north with ancillary

spaces to the south. There is a two-storey opaque glass rooftop extension housing restaurants and bars. A light box on top of the chimney stimulated unfulfilled hopes of a high level viewing gallery.

Bracken House (351)
1955–1959
Cannon Street, EC4;
tube: Mansion House
Albert Richardson

Home of the Financial Times newspaper, Bracken House consisted of two wings of offices separated by a printing hall. When the paper moved out of the city along with all the others, there was little use for the hall, which was demolished. Richardson's office wings feel anachronistic, but have aged better than most of their contemporaries. They have a red sandstone two-storey plinth, a four-storey 'shaft' with bronze windows between red brick pilasters, and a copper clad attic. The corners are chamfered or with engaged circular towers.

Michael Hopkins and Partners were responsible for the new infill building

(1988–1991), which bulges out convexly between the Richardson wings, while maintaining the plinth and attic lines of the older building. The plinth has red sandstone bases supporting a highly refined, skeletal, gun metal structure holding a series of four-storey glazed oriel windows. Internally, the new offices are arranged around a central circulation atrium that is dominated by grey metal and glass block – distinctly post-'Blade Runner'.

Keeling House (352)
1955–1959
Claredale Street, E2;
tube: Bethnal Green
Fry, Drew, Drake and Lasdun

Even at sixteen storeys, it is possible for a tower to look squat, as many post-war housing developments bear witness. Lasdun sought a solution to this at Keeling

House by erecting a cluster of towers accessed by bridges from a central circulation core. The four towers each contain fourteen maisonettes, arranged in pairs side by side with one flat on a single level. Each maisonette is expressed as a single concrete egg crate in the stack. The detailing in concrete and glass is simple but elegant and the proportions are finely judged. Nonetheless, it fails to function in urban terms any better than any other tower deposited amongst terraced streets. Nor did it function well as public housing, although the London Borough of Tower Hamlets may have played some part in that. It has, however, fared very well as middle class housing since its refurbishment by Munkenbeck and Marshall (1999–2001).

Golden Lane Estate (353)
1956–1962
Golden Lane, EC1; tube: Barbican
Chamberlin, Powell and Bon

Although the primary business of the Corporation of the City of London is commerce, they did recognise the need to house the lowly paid clerks and cleaners required for the smooth running of their great money machine. For this purpose, they purchased an area of bomb-ravaged land just north of the City and began building an urban community for 1,000 inhabitants. The centrepiece is a sixteen-storey tower containing single bed flats. It is clad in curtain walling with bright yellow infill panels and has an expressive 'nun's hat' roof termination. Disposed around the tower are four and six-storey blocks of maisonettes with purple-brown

211

brick cross walls, concrete slabs and balcony fronts. Between the cross walls, timber and aluminium screens have bright red and blue infill panels and the roofs are flat. The inventive easternmost block to Golden Lane is in black concrete and white tile. Landscaped gardens and charming pavilion-like sports and community facilities fill the gaps between the blocks. A later phase to the west, on Aldersgate Street, has three storeys of flats above a colonnaded parade of shops. This block, Crescent House, indulges the, by then, prevailing trend of Corbusian Brutalism with exposed concrete vaults and framing, striking a contrast with the gentler Scandinavian Modernist feel of the earlier blocks. The estate has been one of the few of its type to be judged an unqualified success, both architecturally and socially.

Span Housing   (354)
1956–1984
Blackheath Park, SE3;
train: Blackheath (from London Bridge)
Eric Lyons, Cunningham Partnership

Span was a most interesting development company, who, justly appalled at the output of the British housing industry, began to develop high quality modern housing. They were prolific, completing over seventy schemes ranging in scope from three houses to a whole town in Kent. The ingredients were always the same: two or three-storey flat blocks and/ or houses arranged linearly around landscaped common areas, brick cross walls with generally lightweight timber or tile hung cladding with some brick panels, and large white painted windows, often in horizontal strips. The landscaped areas were carefully designed and the responsibility for their upkeep is vested communally in the householders. They make for fabulous places to live, inspiring near religious dedication in their residents. Blackheath Park is very rich in Span developments, with eight schemes on the road itself and a further thirteen in the immediate surrounding area.

United States Embassy   (355)
1957–1960
Grosvenor Square, W1;
tube: Bond Street
Eero Saarinen

If you are carrying a mental picture of Saarinen's expressive, concrete vaulted creations, the American Embassy is a bit of a disappointment. A vast six-storey, stolid rectangular block, it houses 750 staff. The high ground floor is recessed behind concrete columns with gilded aluminium framed glazing. Above is a repetitive chequerboard grid of rectangular windows set in alternately raised and recessed concrete panels; the middle of the Grosvenor Square elevation is topped with a large golden eagle. It is perhaps not surprising that people keep coming here to protest. Security concerns have led to moves to relocate the embassy, leaving Saarinen's building behind to become a luxury hotel.

New Zealand House   (356)
1957–1963
Pall Mall, WC1; tube: Piccadilly Circus
Robert Matthew, Johnson-Marshall
and Partners

Home to the New Zealand High Commission (embassy), this is an early and very prominent example of the podium and tower format in London, presumably modelled on Skidmore, Owings and Merrill's New York Lever House of 1953. It is, however, less of a success, as the podium fails to fulfil its purpose of mediating between tower and street – there is no beguiling courtyard as in New York, but just a large chunk of building. Nor is it as slick and

rest of the chapel, an office development was built incorporating a much smaller chapel that housed the old congregation and the local Upton Baptists, who were also lately homeless. The office building is perfectly period and perfectly unpleasant. The chapel, however, which protrudes from the offices like a small box has a most interesting façade. It is fully glazed behind a complex organic perforated concrete screen formed of highly modelled pre-cast units. Inside is a large and interesting stained glass window across the east wall.

elegant as its model. The podium has five floors and the tower a further thirteen. The lower two floors are recessed behind a colonnade of stainless steel clad columns as is (partially) the fourth floor. The slab edges are expressed and clad in stone, but the building is otherwise fully glazed; the consequence of this and of the poor understanding of environmental comfort of the time is that the building has been shrouded in curtains for 50 years.

Christ Church and Upton Chapel (357)
1958–1960
Kennington Road, SE1;
tube: Lambeth North
Peter Darvall

There was a fine Victorian, Decorated Gothic, Congregationalist chapel by Paul and Bickerdike on this site, but, by the end of the last war, only its tower remained. This chapel had been funded partially by Abraham Lincoln's family, hence the star and stripe decoration on the spire, and the tower is sometimes called the Lincoln Tower. In place of the

Apartment Building,
26 St James's Place   (358)
1959–1960
St James's Place/Queen's Walk, SW1;
tube: Green Park
Denys Lasdun

213

Lasdun's block is proof, if it were needed, that rich people will happily live in concrete tower blocks, although they will of course want balconies facing west over Green Park. It is reminiscent of some of his social housing with its fine proportions and straightforward clean cut detailing, though there are added refinements. The concrete slab edges are clad in granite and each part is even more emphatically delineated and expressed. With eight storeys to the eastern (street) side, there are only six facing the park to allow for higher floor to ceiling heights in the principle rooms. The ground floor is in blue brick, above which there are narrow strips of stone between strips of bronze windows and a recessed penthouse floor. It is timeless and very elegant.

Alexander Fleming House (359)
1959–1967
Newington Causeway, SE1;
tube: Elephant and Castle
Ernö Goldfinger

The developer and the local authority both wanted the maximum amount of development on this site, Alexander Fleming House is the sinister outcome. It originally comprised one eighteen-storey and two seven-storey blocks arranged around a gloomy courtyard, although further blocks were added later. The fabric is as reductive as possible, consisting merely of an expressed concrete frame, a window with blue spandrel panel infill and some windows project forward for reasons that are unknown. The original tenant was the Ministry of Health, but in 1997 the building was converted into apartments and now rejoices in the name, Metro Central Heights.

Millbank Tower (360)
1959–1963
Millbank, SW1; tube: Pimlico
Ronald Ward and Partners

The thirty-two-storey, 118 metre high Millbank Tower is not the worst curtain wall clad office tower and it has earned itself some affection. A relatively small

floor plate lends it a genuinely slender, tower-like profile. The architects chose to model the plan with the north and south façades concave and the east and west convex, which generates a more interesting play of light than a regular box might. It is otherwise fairly straightforward; the curtain wall sections are silver with the vertical emphasized, while the spandrel panels are grey and the glass mercifully clear. There is a two-storey block on pilotis to the river front and an eight-storey block in a curved 'Y'-shape to the rear. 'Millbank' became short hand in the 1990s for the Blair and Campbell regime, which ran campaigns from the building.

Centre Point (361)
1959–1966
New Oxford Street, WC2;
tube: Tottenham Court Road
Richard Seifert and Partners

In its day the most notorious building in London, the developer had struck a deal with London County Council, in which he would build them a traffic route around the site in exchange for permission to build thirty-four storeys. When the building was finally completed, the developer allowed it to stand empty for nine years while he sought a single tenant. That this made some financial sense seemed to exemplify all the futility and greed of the property industry, of which the building was seen as the very prominent physical embodiment. A few booms and busts later, and Centre Point does not now seem quite so dreadful and may even be treasured. Clearly influenced by Milan's Pirelli building, it has a similar long thin plan that makes it appear extremely slender from the north and south. The long sides are gently convex which helps vary its reflections. The tower is entirely clad in futuristic skeletal precast panels. The traffic and pedestrian areas at the base of the tower are still utterly chaotic and recurring initiatives to resolve this have yet to bear any fruit. At the base of the tower there was a banking hall, which is now a bar and a wonderful space with interesting period detail and finishes. The pre-cast and glass retail and residential block to the rear of the site is also interesting.

Commonwealth Institute (362)
1960–1962
Holland Park, Kensington High Street, W8;
tube: Kensington High Street
Robert Matthew, Johnson-Marshall
and Partners

There has always been confusion about what the Commonwealth might or ought to be, and this building seems to embody that confusion rather than clarify matters as was hoped. When it was constructed, the great central volume housed a permanent exhibition about the different countries of the Commonwealth, for the

purposes of education and the promotion of trade. The exhibition hall is housed in a vast 'tent' formed from parabolic concrete shells. Inside, the volume is undivided with multi level galleries and is a striking and exciting space. Outside, the complicated roof shape is clad in copper sheet donated by Zambia, while the walls are in blue green opaque patent glazing; unfortunately, it looks lumpy and earthbound, which was presumably not the desired effect. The building and exhibition became equally ramshackle until the government closed the institute in 2002. The plan is now to demolish the shabby ancillary buildings and refurbish the hall to house the Design Museum, while building three residential blocks that will fund the refurbishment. The competition was won by Dutch firm, the Office of Metropolitan Architecture.

Royal College of Physicians   (363)
1961–1964
Regent's Park, Albany Street, NW1;
tube: Great Portland Street
Denys Lasdun

This building is the Royal College's fifth since their founding in 1518. It is composed of two blocks arranged in a 'T'. To Albany Street is a four-storey block in dark engineering brick with continuous window bands and a recessed top storey. This contains offices and service access and is topped by the President's flat. The second wing in the direction of the park contains the main spaces. It too is four storeys with, at the lower levels, continuous bands of glazing, it is clad in brilliant white mosaics. The uppermost storey overhangs and has a series of vertical slit windows irregularly disposed in a defined band. To the south is a large, dark, brick semi-submerged lecture theatre, which defines the western edge of a semi-sunken garden. To the north, a circular meeting room in a similar style was added by Lasdun in the late 1990s. A superb structure, it is all angular and punchy without being brutal, although one wonders if the 'caring' profession realised it would be such a tough-looking customer. Inside, the pyrotechnics continue with a spatially rich and complex set of principle spaces. The staircase hall in particular is a tour de force of level and

direction changes, galleries and stairs. The library and dining room are also galleried but calmer.

Aviary, London Zoo   (364)
1961–1965
Regent's Park, Prince Albert Road, NW1;
tube: Regent's Park/Camden Town
Anthony Armstrong-Jones,
Frank Newby, Cedric Price

A design team of playboy photographer, Armstrong-Jones, and Price, the perennial terrible infant of post-war British architecture, does not sound promising, and it is the presence of renowned engineer, Newby, on the list that surely explains how the structure was eventually built. It is an early example of both

more naturalistic and more humane zoo enclosures and tensile structures. An array of braced slanting steel structure at the two ends support a cable network clad in aluminium mesh. The height is such that it easily accommodates trees, allowing for a walkway amongst the treetops with their unjustly incarcerated feathered inhabitants.

GPO Tower (365)
1961–1965
Cleveland Street, W1;
tube: Great Portland Street
Ministry of Public Building and Works

The Ministry's architects did not have a great reputation and it may be that conforming rigidly to tight functional requirements, as they were obliged to, enabled them to succeed in this instance. The tower was needed to connect central London with the new microwave communications network and had to be tall enough to clear high buildings in the city centre and hills on the periphery. The tower is a machine for communication and its appearance suits its purpose. The central slip-formed, in-situ concrete core is surrounded by very narrow floor plates for the sixteen floors of the main shaft, which house equipment. Above these are a thirty-five metre section of platforms for the telecom receivers and transmitters. Above that the tower widens progressively for five floors of viewing galleries, a bar and a revolving restaurant. There is a steel lattice tower at the very top. Throughout it is businesslike and utilitarian, clad in very straightforward curtain walling. Its appeal is its extreme slenderness and distinctive profile. Despite the small IRA explosion in 1971, the public floors were not closed for security reasons in 1980, but on account of the corporate laziness and lack of imagination for which British Telecom is such a byword.

Cranbrook Estate (366)
1961–1966
Bonner Street, E2; tube: Bethnal Green
Francis Skinner, Berthold Lubetkin and Douglas Bailey

Looking at this development, it is hard to believe that either the commissioning council or the celebrated architect were thinking beyond the efficient and cheap production of the 600 residential units. Acceptable two-storey houses occupy the perimeter, while further in are haphazardly cranked four-storey blocks of deck accessed maisonettes, and in the middle, six sixteen-storey blocks of flats. The layout might have been contrived for picturesque effect or it might have been, as it seems, utterly random. The façades are of grey brick with panels of grey render and raised panels that are now painted green. There are some attempts at designer stylishness at the base and crown of the towers, and the staircases have some of the Tecton brio of old, but cannot mask the general dismalness, the too small windows and the lack of balconies.

Sir Denys Lasdun
*1914 in London, †2001 in London (367)

Lasdun was born in 1914 into a reasonably prosperous, middle-class family who were able to send him to a private school and the Architectural Association School of Architecture in 1932. The comparatively new full-time architecture schools of the period were very mixed with both traditional practitioners and newly minted Modernists on the staff. Lasdun gradually gravitated towards the latter and on graduation went to work for leading Modernist pioneer Wells Coates, working on Coates' 10 Palace Gate apartment building in Kensington. In 1937 Lasdun built a dis-

tinctly Corbusian house in Newton Road on his own and it was drawings of this house that got him a job with Lubetkin and Tecton, the most successful Modernist architects of their day.

After war service Lasdun worked on the Hallfield Estate in Paddington and, along with Lindsay Drake, saw the project through to completion as Tecton dissolved. Lasdun alone secured the commission for the primary and junior school on the Hallfield site (no. 346). There is little doubt that the British post-war school building programme has been overly praised as the great contribution of Modernism to post-war British life. However, at their best these schools did embody an optimistic light and airy hope for the future; Hallfield, with its intimate planning and landscaping, may well be the very best of them all. The school was followed by a pair of apartment blocks at opposite ends of both the city and the social spectrum. Keeling House (no. 352) in Bethnal Green is social housing while 26 St James's Place (no. 358) in Green Park is socialite housing. Both are elegant and generally successful though Keeling House flirted with demolition at one point. St James's Place's higher quality materials push the elegance to a higher pitch; it also introduces a favourite Lasdun theme of strong horizontal emphasis with projecting concrete floors considered by Lasdun to be akin to geological strata.

Having successfully completed one building on a very sensitive parkside site, Lasdun was presented with another in the shape of the Royal College of Physicians building (no. 363) overlooking Regent's Park in the midst of Nash terracing. The resulting building is one of Lasdun's best, proving his ability to reconcile complex functional requirements with a demanding context and still deliver a building of charm and integrity. Further academic buildings followed in the wake of the College: a whole university outside Norwich, planned along an immense meandering spine following the hillside contours and a new college, Fitzwilliam, and a residential block for Christ's College, both in Cambridge. The Norwich building complex is generally admired but the Cambridge buildings have more mixed reputations. Lasdun's London University buildings have also divided opinion; the vast Institute of Education (no. 382), for example, has some interesting individual elements but is very hard on Bloomsbury. The nearby library for the School of African and Oriental Studies is much more polite.

Lasdun laboured over the National Theatre (no. 372) from 1962 to 1977. It is his masterpiece and London is gradually realising its luck in having it. Theatres are technically demanding and Lasdun met this challenge as well as providing one of the most exciting public spaces in London. Large public buildings place a tremendous strain on their architects. The client is sure to be many-headed, demanding and irresolute and everyone will feel entitled to publicly express whatever opinion occurs to them. Lasdun did well to stick to his principles and if he never seemed to quite regain his pre-theatre vitality, at least he survived it.

Following projects take up where the theatre left off. Office buildings for the European Investment Bank in Luxembourg and for IBM next to the theatre on the South Bank both reemploy the language of projecting concrete slab strata, but lack the contrasting vertical elements and the visual interest of the theatre. A project that could have matched it was Lasdun's scheme for a synagogue in Jerusalem, which sadly got no further than a beautiful atmospheric set of drawings. Lasdun's last building in London is a curious speculative office building on the edge of the City, Milton Gate (no. 411). It is his earlier buildings, however – Keeling House, St James's Place and above all, the National Theatre – that have a sense of proportion, detail and materiality so much finer than any other work of the period.

Hallfield School.

Economist Building (368)
1962–1964
St James's Street, SW1; tube: Green Park
Alison and Peter Smithson

This development of the venerable magazine's site is the epitome of refined 1960s chic. The site is 'L'-shaped with the foot of the 'L' projecting onto St James's and long frontages to Ryder and Bury Streets. In each of the three nodal points is a square tower. The front four-storey tower used to house a banking hall, behind which are fifteen storeys of offices, still occupied by the magazine, and there is an eight-storey residential block around the corner. In each case, the corners of the squares are chamfered off. There are closely spaced vertical ribs and narrow spandrel panels in buff Portland stone with grey aluminium windows. It is extremely simple but beautifully elegant. Almost uniquely for a 1960s development, the tight leftover spaces between the blocks really are akin to those of a medieval city.

Cullinan House (369)
1962–1965
Camden Mews, NW1; tube: Camden Town
Edward Cullinan Architects

This small house at No. 62, designed and built by the architect for his own family, has been influential out of all proportion to its size. Built, of necessity, very simply it showed how vernacular materials and methods could be used stylishly and with a Modernist sensibility. The house runs away from the street to maximise light

and privacy. The ground floor, which houses the bedrooms, is in brick and the upper floor with the living areas is in timber with a distinctly Japanese feel. A concrete structural frame supports

the shallow monopitch roof. Apart from its wider significance, it also set a trend for small architects' houses in this and nearby Murray Mews.

Wood Street Police Station (370)
1962–1966
Wood Street, EC2; tube: St Paul's
McMorran and Whitby

The station also serves as headquarters of the City of London police, the nation's smallest police force. It is planned around a square courtyard that is mostly four storeys. Built of Portland stone and detailed in an anachronistic stripped classical style, it is very plain but for some strange

mannered rustication to the lower two floors. What makes the building interesting rather than curious is the thirteen-storey residential tower that looms up out of one corner. As simply detailed as the rest, with rows of segmentally headed windows under a pitched roof with stone gables, the mini skyscraper has a real brooding presence of the sort that buildings have in paintings by de Chirico. It has a remotely sinister air not ill suited to its function.

St Paul's Cathedral Choir School
(371)
1962–1967
New Change, EC4; tube: St Paul's
Architects CoPartnership

There has been a cathedral choir school from the early part of the 12th century. The current school occupies a set of low buildings to the east of the cathedral. Mostly four storeys, the lower three are clad in Portland stone with the fenestration arranged in full height slots. The top storey is clad in lead, like a mansard, although it does not slope but projects out above the walls below. The school hall is in a lower central block. The design for the school incorporates the tower of Wren's St Augustine at Watling Street, which is all that remains of the church built in the 1690s.

National Theatre
(372)
1962–1977
South Bank, Upper Ground, SE1;
tube: Waterloo/Embankment
Denys Lasdun and Partners

The idea of a National Theatre dates from the mid 19th century, so a mere 120 years passed before it was realised. The building houses three auditoria; the Olivier is a theatre in the round seating 1,160, the Lyttelton, with a traditional proscenium, seats 890 and the Cottesloe is an experimental 'black box' that can accommodate 400. There are considerable front and back of house facilities. It is all expressed as a series of in-situ concrete terraces with glazing between, while concrete lift shafts and fly towers provide vertical counterpoint to the strong horizontals. It is austere and has proved controversial, loathed by the Prince Charles faction and proclaimed by the Modernists as a masterpiece. The former ought to be able to

admit that it is finely proportioned, that its foyers are wonderfully exciting spaces and that its auditoria work well. The latter might concede that planar concrete does not weather well in a wet climate, that its relationship to the embankment is more confused than it might be and that there is no relationship at all with the street to the rear. It is, then, a masterpiece but not without its faults.

Swiss Cottage Library (373)
1963–1964
Avenue Road, NW3; tube: Swiss Cottage
Basil Spence, Bonnington and Collins

airy with fine materials and detailing. John McAslan and Partners completed a refurbishment in 2003.

Hayward Gallery (374)
1963–1968
South Bank, Waterloo Road, SE1;
tube: Waterloo
London County Council/Greater London Council, Special Works Group

Designed to show temporary exhibitions, the building has five galleries on two levels and three open sculpture courts, which have been little used. It is

The library was intended, along with a swimming pool, to be the first instalment of a central Civic Centre for a borough that was later abolished; the pool has been demolished so the library is all that remains. Rectangular with rounded ends it is three storeys and concrete framed. The ground floor, housing back of house facilities, is in stone and painted concrete with a continuous clerestory window. The upper floors are divided by closely spaced projecting pre-cast white concrete fins, which lend consistency to the façades; between the fins are either aluminium windows or black concrete infill panels. The top lit stair is in the centre of the plan, from which the lending and reference libraries in the apsidal ends are accessed. Both are galleried and top lit. All these spaces are light and

constructed of in-situ concrete with pre-cast concrete cladding panels in places. The concrete has weathered dreadfully and this, combined with the deliberate

use of uncompromisingly harsh or 'brutal' forms, make it a difficult building to like from the outside. The entrance at first floor level from the end of the bridge has also created problems with poor and unclear accessibility. The ground floor houses service spaces and is not at all kind to the embankment. Inside, the galleries are better than the exterior might suggest and are well suited to some kinds of exhibition, if not all. They are either top-lit or unlit with much exposed concrete. A glass foyer by Haworth Tompkins and a glass pavilion by artist Dan Graham have been added recently and help with the building's appearance and legibility.

Queen Elizabeth Hall (375)
1963–1968
South Bank, Waterloo Road, SE1;
tube: Waterloo
London County Council/Greater London
Council, Special Works Group

The venue has two halls: the Queen Elizabeth, seating 900, and the Purcell Room, seating 370. Both have single arrays of raked seating and are lined with acoustic perforated wooden panelling. They share with the Hayward (no. 374) the stained concrete, the awkward access, the unpleasant ground floor and the wilfully inelegant shape making. The foyer space, however, with its octagonal concrete mushroom columns is attractive in the currently fashionable 1960s retro manner. Likewise, the au-

ditoria are pleasant and seem to fulfil their function well. The pampered cultural elite should surely consider themselves fortunate to have their very own miniature, fantasy concrete jungle in which to play.

Commercial Union Building (376)
1963–1969
Leadenhall Street, EC3;
tube: Monument/Liverpool Street/Bank
Gollins, Melville and Ward

This was the first purist skyscraper in the Miesian manner in the City, although the later Bastian House is better. The twenty-five-storey tower is supported from its central core via large cantilevered steel trusses at the top and half way up from which the floor edges are hung. It is this that allows for the impressive column free, double height reception area at the base. The curtain walling is black with projecting verticals, flat and deeper horizontals and tinted glazing. It is a reasonable iteration of the Miesian model, which it follows closely, offering nothing that is unique. The tower was re-clad in 1992 after bomb damage. The smaller, adjacent P&O building was part of the same scheme, as was the most welcome little plaza with its trees.

223

Space House (377)
1964–1968
Kemble Street, WC2; tube: Holborn
Richard Seifert and Partners

The name of this piece of 1970s ersatz futurism could not be more appropriate. The circular tower sits on the back of a dull slab block on Kingsway, the two structures connected by a bridge. The tower is supported by a central concrete core and, around the edges at ground level, by chunky, two-storey, 'Y'-shaped columns. This shape seems to have been chosen as a result of the building's location at the junction of three quite narrow streets. The upper fifteen storeys are clad in pre-cast concrete panels similar to those on Centre Point (no. 361), though with thin black spandrel panels in this instance. The tower makes for a wonderfully incongruous and picturesque addition to the Victorian streetscape.

Lillington Gardens Estate (378)
1964–1972
Vauxhall Bridge Road, SW1;
tube: Pimlico
Darbourne and Darke

Unease with the social and architectural outcomes of high rise social housing schemes began to be felt fairly early on, though the penny took a while to drop in some quarters. Lillington Gardens is a direct response to this unease and was highly influential in suggesting an alternative. The aim was to attain similar densities while creating a more humane environment. In fact the scheme is not strictly low rise, rising to eight storeys in places with an average

of six. A series of blocks are arranged around leafy communal gardens. Access to the accommodation is via decks, but the plans and sections are manipulated to keep these to a minimum and they are wide enough for small front gardens in some cases. The predominant material is a rich red brown brick, which is well chosen but rather conspicuous in stuccoed Pimlico. Concrete slab edges are exposed and there are occasional outbreaks of slate hung cladding at high level, with flat roofs behind parapets. The development also includes shops and pubs with a listed Victorian church at the centre. There is no doubt that the estate has been a success and that the design has played some part in that, as have the high quality of the original build and the careful maintenance.

Brownfield Estate   (379)
1965–1967
St Leonard's Road, E14;
tube: Bromley-by-Bow
Ernö Goldfinger and Partners

The estate comprises three blocks: twenty-six-storey Balfron Tower, eleven-storey Carradale House and fifteen-storey Glenkerry House. They are all of in-situ concrete that has not weathered too badly, but can still look powerfully grim on a wet grey day. The blocks are deck access with a deck only needed, after manipulation of the plans and section, at every third floor. The infill between the concrete slabs and cross-walls is nearly all glass. Goldfinger employs the device later to be made

famous at Trellick Tower (see no. 385) of freestanding, highly articulated and expressive service towers connected to the accommodation with bridges. It is noticeable that Balfron Tower has not encouraged middle-class sophisti-cates to flock to the Poplar area in the way they have colonised its near twin, Trellick Tower, in sunny Notting Hill.

School of Engineering and Science, Regent Street Polytechnic   (380)
1965–1968
New Cavendish Street, W1;
tube: Regent's Park/Great Portland Street
Lyons, Israel and Elis

The school is a very substantial building, occupying the best part of a large city block. Some parts are eight storeys and some five. The cladding is repetitive with brown mullions and spandrel panels, though it does step in places. For relief, there are tall in-situ concrete stair and service cores with beak-like projections at high level. Employing the hoariest brutalist cliché, the building is entered off Cavendish street under the sloping concrete floor of a lecture theatre above; having ticked every other Brutalist box, why miss that one?

Barbican Estate (381)

1965–1973
Chamberlin, Powell and Bon

During the war, the Cripplegate Ward of the City was virtually completely demolished. After the success of Golden Lane, the Corporation decided it would redevelop the whole of the fourteen hectares site with housing and associated facilities. The development centres on three large interlinked courtyards; the central one is mostly filled with the Arts Centre and a Girls' School, while the flanking pair are lined with great slab blocks of flats up to ten storeys high. North of this are three triangular 43 storey towers; there are a few more slab blocks further north still beyond Beech Street. This street is buried in a tunnel and throughout the estate there are no cars, since the whole massive development is raised up on a podium in accordance with the City's then policy of separating people and vehicles. The architectural expression is above all massive; the blocks and towers are huge, the bush hammered concrete structure muscle bound. The slab edges/balconies are very strongly emphasised; filling in between them are hardwood glazed screens. The top of the slab blocks have a series of repetitive little vaults painted white while the towers have jagged, highly romantic terminations.

Somewhere in the drawn out building process the City revised its intention of letting the 2,113 flats to low paid City workers and sold them instead; it has been a great success with high demand for flats especially as second homes for City workers and Politicians. It undeniably has its pleasures; the suspended walkways between the giant Piranesian columns underneath some of the slab blocks are awe inspiring and the way the triangular towers appear like enormous flat cut-outs from some viewpoints is most intriguing. Where it fails is as an integrated urban district. It is notoriously difficult to find your way in and then navigate the walkways; so much so that the management were reduced to painted yellow lines on the floor to guide people around. Its great fault however is its lack of any kind of street life. There never seems to be anybody around, the thousands attending events at the Arts Centre leave immediately after viewing. It suits people who want to live quietly and anonymously in the city without having to be involved with it or their neighbours, a peculiar kind of urban life.

Gilbert House, Barbican Estate.

left: Defoe House, Shakespeare and Cromwell Towers, Barbican Estate.

**Institutes of Advanced Legal Studies
and Education** (382)
1965–1976
Bedford Way, WC1; tube: Russell Square
Denys Lasdun

At six and a half storeys and 236 metres in length, the building is a substantial intrusion into the Georgian city and rather a rude one. The relentless combination of bronze curtain walling and hulking concrete stairs is very big but not the least bit clever. It is not quite so unsympathetic on the west side, at the south end of which is a spur off the main north-south block which steps down dramatically, finishing with a highly sculptural concrete stair. This spur is only one of an intended five as if the building wasn't big enough as it is. Also at the south end is Lasdun's library extension for the School of African and Oriental Studies (1968–1973), a freestanding seven-storey pavilion that is much more in Lasdun's more usual highly articulated style.

**Tower Building, London
Metropolitan University** (383)
1964–1966
Holloway Road, N7;
tube: Holloway Road
*Greater London Council Architects
Department*

The Tower is a simple and direct building with a perverse appeal. At thirteen storeys it is much taller than anything nearby and clearly marks the presence of the university. Bands of in-situ concrete alternate with continuous windows, which wrap around the cantilevered corners. The core tower in the centre of the north side ascends to create a flat-topped pavilion on the roof. Until recently, it had a number of communication relays on the roof and resembled exactly an East European secret service facility keeping a sinister watch over the chaos and squalor of Holloway Road. It was extended brilliantly by Rick

Mather Architects between 1998 and 2000. Their slick, curved, nine-storey 'Technology Tower' is a perfect complement to the rugged quality of the older building.

Paddington Maintenance Depot

(384)

1966–1968
Harrow Road, W2;
tube: Warwick Avenue
Bicknell and Hamilton

The small complex housed workshops and associated support facilities for British Rail's truck maintenance team and has two components. The big workshop by the canal is a long single-storey rectangular block with rounded ends. It is rendered with a continuous clerestory window under a cranked, zinc clad, pitched roof. The roof, which shelters an impressive internal space, is supported by cranked concrete beams and currently houses Nissan's European Design Centre. The larger building, which housed smaller workshops and offices, is on the most extraordinary triangular site, completely surrounded by whirling roadways at all levels. At the fat end of the site, the building is four storeys with towers to each side for circulation and flues. The thin end is only two storeys but the whole is tied together by the continuous strip windows that zip around the radiused corners. Mosaic tiles adorn the walls while the windows, which sit proud of the walls, are in steel. The best interiors are the continuous cantilevered concrete stair and the ground floor workshop in the thin end of the wedge.

Cheltenham Estate

(385)

1966–1972
Golbourne Road, W10;
tube: Westbourne Park
Ernö Goldfinger and Partners

The estate comprises a seven-storey slab block, a thirty-one-storey tower and a massive free-standing circulation tower built in the corner made between them. This is connected to the blocks via bridges every third storey. The tower and blocks are all in bush hammered in-situ concrete and the infill between the cross walls and slabs is mostly glazing. Most levels have balconies. Unlike the very similar Balfron Tower (see no. 379), Trellick Tower is located right by the Westway and is therefore extremely prominent, made more so by being the tallest structure for miles around and very aggressively styled. Aided by all of this, it became the most famous tabloid

'Tower of Terror' of them all, but has somehow recently morphed into an icon of urban cool. The flats are now highly sought after, suggesting that people can adapt to anything.

Robin Hood Gardens (386)
1966–1974
Cotton Street, E14;
tube: Canary Wharf, DLR All Saints
Alison and Peter Smithson

The Smithsons elected to test the limits of human adaptation with this effort, which comprises two long cranked blocks of seven and ten storeys facing each other across a blasted hill. The outer faces are to busy roads and have narrow deck access. Regardless of orientation, these outer faces house the living spaces, while the kitchens and bedrooms are on the inside with narrow balconies. It is all made from raw pre-cast concrete units on the Swedish Sundh system, which, although well-proportioned, have weathered atrociously. A variety of functional and construction shortcomings have led to proposals for demolition. Ironically, after the Golden Lane competition, the self-publicising Smithsons continued to promote their entry with its 'streets in the sky' to the extent that one might, even now, imagine that they had won the competition. The self-effacing actual winners went on to build a lovely scheme, while the 'visionary' Smithsons went on to preside over this debacle.

Hyde Park Barracks (387)
1967–1970
Knightsbridge, SW7; tube: Knightsbridge
Basil Spence and Partners

It is perhaps inevitable that a thirty-three-storey tower on the edge of Hyde

Park in a very upmarket area would prove controversial, although it is a little surprising that it should remain so nearly forty years on. It is at least slender and the top is interestingly modelled, although the vast concrete fins are not as functional as they appear to be. The tower houses guardsmen's quarters, with squash courts in the roof ensemble. Continuous bands of windows alternate with ribbed and bush hammered pre-cast concrete spandrel panels. The low level buildings, in red brick with Corbusian concrete vaults, are fragmented and uncertain.

Czech and Slovak Embassies (388)
1968–1969
Notting Hill Gate, W8;
tube: Notting Hill Gate
Jan Šrámek, Jana Bočan, Karel
Štepánský and Robert Matthew

The Velvet Divorce necessitated some re-organisation in Kensington as well as at the heart of Europe. Czechoslovakia had two buildings, constructed as one project. On Notting Hill Gate was the seven-storey Czechoslovak Centre, while around the back was the much smaller four-storey embassy itself. The embassy is in pre-cast concrete with a flat roof, large windows and some cast in-situ elements. It is very severe and abstract. The larger building is also in pre-cast concrete panels but less severe and more commonplace, although there are some interesting set backs and cylindrical elements at high level. Both have weathered well and present a fascinating snapshot of 1960s Eastern European architecture. The Slovaks got the quality and the Czechs the quantity.

Apartment Building,
125 Park Road (389)
1968–1970
Park Road, NW8; tube: St John's Wood
Terry Farrell and Nicholas Grimshaw

It may not be obvious but this apartment block with its lightweight cladding and flexible layout was one of the precursors of 'High Tech'. The building has eleven storeys and the façade comprises bands of continuous aluminium windows alternating with corrugated aluminium sheeting. The ground floor is recessed, the corners curved and the edge of the roof is sloping glazing – it is very simple but elegantly done. The central concrete core was over-sized to allow for easy replacement of services and there are a variety of flat types which were left bare for maximum economy and flexibilty.

The flats were built on a co-ownership basis, which at the time attracted some government support. In this instance, the co-owners were a group of friends which included the young designers.

Brunswick Centre (390)
1968–1972
Brunswick Square, WC1;
tube: Russell Square
Patrick Hodgkinson

If you have ever wondered what Sant'Elia's hypothetical buildings with their stepped sections and bunched rec-

tangular towers would have been like, then the Brunswick Centre is the place to look. Two rows of vast, stepped, concrete 'A' frames run parallel with each other with two levels of parking and five levels of flats, the ranges punctuated with massive ventilation towers. The flats are entered from walkways inside the Piranasian 'A' frames. All the flats are necessarily single aspect with balconies and lean-to glass conservatories. The central space is lined with shops and there is an underground arthouse cinema. At the south-east corner, one of the 'A' frames is cut in half and the shops omitted to form an entrance from Brunswick Square. The development, which was meant to be even larger, was private but the local council took over the housing midway through the process. The retail part of the scheme has recently been revamped by Levitt Bernstein (2002–2006), and for the first time the concrete was painted as originally intended.

Museum of London (391)
1968–1976
London Wall, EC2;
tube: Barbican/St Paul's
Powell and Moya

It is unfortunate that this very worthwhile building and its contents have been somewhat isolated by their location in the City's now abandoned, high-level walkway network. The glazed entrance canopy is at high level on a bridge onto a roundabout, a large blue brick rotunda containing a sunken garden with charming little framed café buildings. Inside, the galleries are arranged in a set route

around two floors of a 'C'-shaped courtyard centred on Ironmongers Hall; the character of the different spaces along the route is deliberately varied. One letter-box style window is directed on a surviving segment of the City's Roman wall. The building is clad in white tiles with black tile trimming and black steel windows and in-situ concrete columns. As ever with Powell and Moya, it is reticent and modest but of a high quality. The bronze clad office tower Bastian House, to the east of the museum, was a commercial adjunct to the museum scheme and stands in mute reproach of the generations of inferior office buildings that rise and fall along London Wall.

Barbican Arts Centre (392)
1971–1985
Silk Street, EC2;
tube: Barbican/Moorgate
Chamberlin, Powell and Bon

Like the wider development, the arts centre is vast with a concert hall, theatre, studio theatre, library, art gallery, three cinemas, conservatory, three restaurants, bars and substantial foyer spaces. Also like the wider development, it is very easy to get lost. The complex makes a surprisingly small impact on the surrounding streets, being obscured by the rest of the estate. The main elevation looks south towards St Giles, Cripplegate (no. 25) over an open space with a lake. Arranged over five principle storeys and two basements, the arts centre has a coarser grain than the Barbican with bulky white tiled boxes and stumpy towers introduced into the mix of concrete structure and glazed infill. The interior too is on a grand scale, particularly the foyers, where the elephantine structure is at close quarters. Both the concert hall, with its timber linings, and the theatre are pleasant spaces. The latter is accessed via steps at the ends of the aisles which have individual doors operated automatically in unison – this can be the highlight of the evening's entertainment.

Alexandra and Ainsworth Estate (393)
1972–1978
Abbey Road, NW8; tube: Swiss Cottage
Camden Council Architects Department,
Neave Brown

The site is bounded to the north by a railway track, which determined the direction of the design. An eight-storey stepped blocked hugs the curve of the track, cantilevering out like the back of a grandstand, the north face of which contains minimal windows. In contrast, the south side is almost entirely of windows, with balconies and stairs up to the higher maisonettes. This block is faced across a pedestrian walkway by a four-storey block with two sets of maisonettes accessed from different sides. Behind this are communal landscaped gardens with three-storey houses on the further side. The construction throughout is in-situ concrete, which has not always weathered well, while glazed screens infill between slabs and sloping crosswalls, glass and concrete balconies. The estate is on a vast scale and certainly breathtaking, but is perhaps not the most

sensible way to build housing. It was a costly development and not all the bills are in yet.

National Westminster Tower (394)
1970–1981
Old Broad Street, EC2;
tube: Liverpool Street
Richard Seifert and Partners

At forty-two storeys and 183 metres, this was the city's first and, for a long time, only true skyscraper. The floors cantilever from the core and were the largest cantilevers ever at the time, but the arrangement severely limits floor plate size. Only boom time hubris and exhibitionism can account for the building of such an inefficient structure. The plan shape is based on three intertwining half hexagons, which bear a passing resemblance to the Nat West logo of the day. The core rises highest with the three sections of the plan stepping down two storeys at a time. It is clad in black glass between closely spaced stainless steel mullions, which sometimes catch the evening sun to good effect. The tower was re-clad after bomb damage in 1993 and the Bank did not move back in. A frightful steel and glass triple height lobby was added to the base of the tower in the late 1990s by GMW.

Inner Court Offices and Apartments (395)

1972
Old Church Street, SW3;
tube: South Kensington
Joseph Rykwert and Mark Livingston

This is a unique building, in that it is the only one known by famous architectural and urban theorist Rykwert. It is a small three-storey mews court behind Victorian buildings. The lower storey contains offices, while a ramp takes residents' cars up to a port on the first floor, which, along with the floor above, houses nine flats. It is all very compact and ingeniously planned, with much thought given to the positioning of windows in the confined court. The white rendered, flat-roofed forms recall 1930s Moderne and have an optimistic seaside feel.

Crédit Lyonnais (396)

1973–1977
Cannon Street, EC4;
tube: Mansion House
Whinney, Son and Austen Hall

A much-loved oddity, this office building sits on a long, thin, tapering triangular site. Predominantly of six storeys, it is reputedly the first building in the world to be clad entirely in glass-reinforced

cement. The panels are pointed arches on the ground floor, large tapering rectangles with rounded corners on the floors above. The top floor, absent in the south-west corner, has the same panels turned upside down as though the builder had made a mistake. The upper panels are a third the width of the ground floor ones except in the middle of the façades at the entrances where a wider bay extends the full height of the building with canted glazing. The whole façade leans out slightly which is most effective at the rounded ends. The panels are Portland stone coloured with black string course marking the slab edges. The building has weathered marvellously.

Banque Nationale de Paris (397)

1974–1978
King William Street, EC4;
tube: Monument/Bank
Fitzroy Robinson and Partners

A very superior commercial building of the time, the bank is in very solid-looking red granite. Large round columns at the ends and middle create an abstract classical framework with the projecting fifth floor, there is a recessed attic above that. Within the implied giant order is a finer division of windows with projecting granite mullions. The storeys jetty out very slightly as they ascend. It is the solid and sensible building you would expect a bank to occupy, and most unlike that of their frivolous Lyonnais confrères (no. 396).

**International Lutheran
Student Centre** (398)
*1974–1979
Thanet Street, WC1;
tube: Kings Cross St Pancras
Maguire and Murray*

The centre was built by the Lutheran Council of Great Britain to provide shelter for youthful Lutherans in the wicked city. The site runs between Thanet and Sandwich Streets, with a façade of six storeys in warm red brown brick to each. The lower storeys have a series of square brick and oak oriel windows with concrete lintols, which run up the façade to the continuous glazed oak attic storey. It is homely and modest in the nicest possible way. As well as student bedrooms, the centre has some communal spaces including a restful little chapel in the half basement, lit by low-level lunettes.

Crown Reach Apartment Building
(399)
*1976–1983
Grosvenor Road, SW1; tube: Pimlico
Nicholas Lacey, Maguire and Murray*

The wonderful opportunities presented by the Thames for residential development have nearly always been squandered. Crown Reach is one of very few that bears looking at, which certainly cannot be said of its partner on the bank opposite. The plan on the bank side is a long sweeping curve with straight lugs on the end, while the river side keeps in touch with the curve in a series of steps. The middle of the curve goes down to one storey on the bank side but rises to eight at the ends on the river side. All of this is cleverly

accommodated under one steep sweeping roof plane, clad in lead. The walls are in purple brick, hard with few openings to the road and lively with windows and balconies to the river.

Danish Embassy (400)
*1976–1977
Sloane Street, SW1; tube: Knightsbridge
Arne Jacobsen, Dissing and Weitling*

The thrill and honour of having a Jacobsen building in the city are only slightly mitigated by it being perhaps not one of his best, although there are some lovely bits. The ground floor is recessed and made in dark, rusticated, pre-cast concrete with some abstract reliefs; above that there are five bays and three storeys expressed as projecting black aluminium pods with rounded corners. The two recessed storeys above seem not to fit this narrative and appear an after thought, which can perhaps be attributed to Jacobsen having died by the time construction started. The mew's row of dwellings to the rear, with just a single level of pods, do not suffer this disjunction and are very handsome.

"Crisis, what crisis?" (401)

Sun Newspaper 'paraphrasing' James Callaghan, Prime Minister (*1912, †2005)

Post war optimism hit the buffers in the 1970s. The 1972 oil shock hit an ailing economy bringing a three day working week for many, roaring inflation and a very nasty property crash. The malaise culminated in the 1978 'winter of discontent' when rubbish went uncollected and the dead unburied. London effectively de-industrialised in this period. The Thatcher government's attempts to deal with these ills brought high unemployment and societal conflict; the building industry had a tough time. Things improved socially and economically in the early 1990s and after fifty years of decline London's population started to grow again. In the current turmoil, the decade between 1995 and 2005 look like very good years.

The architectural ground was also moving; public dissatisfaction with postwar architecture, Brutalism particularly, brought some new thinking. Some sought to turn their backs on the whole Modernist project, looking instead to classical or Vernacular buildings. Others tried to make Modernism more attractive by designing less unpleasant modern buildings, an extraordinary idea! Neo-Vernacular always struggled in urban London and what little there is looks a little foolish. Postmodernists seemed on safer ground in a classical city and there are some successful small and highly wrought buildings in this manner such as John Outram's Pumping Station (no. 409). Less satisfactory are larger buildings where the constructional language is stretched very thin and the buildings start to resemble cartoons of the original models; the 'Gothic' Minster Court (no. 412) is amusing at least, but living in a city-sized Disneyworld would be no laughing matter. The architect working in this style taken most seriously was James Stirling; his Deco-classical Tate Gallery extension (no. 237) and No.1 Poultry (no. 432) have merits but do not seem as clever now as we were led to believe.

Among less repentant Modernists a prominent strand was what became known as Hi-Tech. Demonstrative structure and technology were major pre-occupations. Both Richard Rogers and Norman Foster scored their first big successes outside of

Millennium Dome and Canary Wharf.

Britain with The Hong Kong and Shanghai Bank and the Pompidou Centre respectively. The first great Hi-Tech structure in London is Rogers' Lloyd's headquarters building (no. 402) which still startles. By the time Foster got to work in the capital his office was moving away from demonstrative 'techyness' to a highly refined and sleek reticence; this works best in contrast with existing buildings as at the Royal Academy of Art (no. 181). Other notable structures by Foster include the Millennium Bridge (no. 446) and 30 St Mary Axe (no. 468). Michael Hopkins built less in London; most noticeably the wonderfully cheerful Mound Stand (no. 406) and the forgettable Portcullis House (no. 447). If the pioneers of the style had moved away from overt technological display Future Systems could be relied upon for glimpses of the coming space age; the Media Centre at Lord's (no. 433) is one of the most remarkable buildings of the era.

Most contemporary architects are less technologically fixated; more typical is the humane and sensual Modernism of practices like Dixon Jones who remodelled the Opera House (no. 179), MacCormac Jamieson Prichard (no. 281) and Eric Parry (nos. 465, 485). Younger practices working in a similar vein are Tony Fretton who designed the much admired Lisson Gallery (no. 422), Caruso St. John (no. 195) and Haworth Tompkins (nos. 223, 478, 455). Also young but with a more minimalist sensibility are David Adjaye (nos. 474, 490) and M R J Rundell (nos. 457, 483).

The main zone of expansion was in Docklands, where the docks themselves had been closing since the 1960s. A Development Corporation was set up to oversee the development of this large, very run down area. Much of the new building is housing (nos. 405, 418) and most of it is disappointing. On the Isle of Dogs a new commercial district was created and work at the Royal Docks further east is ongoing. Most of the architecture at Canary Wharf is poor if flashy (nos. 416, 429 and 375). Both the Docklands Railway (no. 410) and the Jubilee Line extension serve Canary Wharf. The stations of the latter were each designed by different, prominent architects who produced some fine new stations (nos. 434–439).

Lloyd's of London (402)
1978–1986
Leadenhall Street, EC3;
tube: Monument/Bank
Richard Rogers Partnership

Even after twenty-four years, it still seems surprising that such a conservative organisation as Lloyds commissioned such a radical headquarters for themselves.

Essentially just offices, there are thirteen floors of these arranged around a central atrium with a barrel-vaulted glazed roof. There is some stepping down of the levels on the south side exposing the atrium. Working from the premise that maximum flexibility required uninterrupted floor plates, and that services are the most quickly replaced parts of a building and should therefore be easily accessible, Rogers came up with a solution whereby all services – stairs, lifts, toilets, vents and so on – are arrayed on the outside of the building. This has the additional advantage of adding a vast amount of visual interest that could not be accused of being decoration. It is also staggeringly expensive and not hugely practical. It did, however, yield an utterly unique and iconic building, where the services, the beautiful concrete frame and the slick glazing have visual interest to the point of being overwhelming in the narrow streets. The internal spaces around the atrium are nearly as dazzling. Stunning as it is, no one, not even Rogers, has ever sought to repeat the experiment.

British Library (403)
1978–1997
Euston Road, NW1;
tube: Kings Cross St Pancras
Colin St John Wilson

The Library, which was only spun off from the British Museum in 1973, has colossal holdings running into the tens of millions, from the most banal self-help book to ancient, priceless illuminated manuscripts. It is then no great surprise that the building is also huge and the biggest public building constructed in Britain in the 20th century. No one doubts Wilson's achievement in completing such a behemoth with an endlessly vacillating government client. No one doubts either that much of the interior is dignified and interesting. The exterior, however, is a great disappointment. It is in brick with red aluminium windows, slab and roof edges, green aluminium louvres and huge slate pitched roofs. It resembles an out of town supermarket on steroids. The model was the humane modernism of Alvar Aalto but it cannot support the massive inflation of scale. The piazza off Euston Road at the entrance to the Library is, as things stand, horribly lifeless.

Queen Elizabeth II Conference Centre (404)
1981–1986
Broad Sanctuary, SW1;
tube: Westminster
Powell and Moya

Such a large building directly opposite Westminster Abbey was always going to be a tricky assignment for the architects and it is fortunate that Powell and Moya naturally tended to restraint and self-effacement. The floor plates increase in

size with each storey up to the third, after which they recede with each storey until the highest, seventh, floor. The third floor, which houses the principle exhibition space, is expressed as a continuous louvred window with white concrete above and below, the lower hung from the upper with stainless steel rods. Elsewhere, there is more exposed concrete, black steel windows and much lead cladding. The interior, which accommodates numerous spaces for lectures, exhibitions and meetings, is generally considered workmanlike rather than inspired, but there are, of course, excellent views.

Horsleydown Square (405)
1983–1985
Shad Thames, SE1; tube: London Bridge
Wickham and Associates

A vivacious, Dutch inspired, mixed use development, the complex comprises retail at ground level with four floors of residential above and car parking beneath. There are four blocks arranged around a pedestrian only piazza. The exposed concrete frame is infilled with brick and rendered panels, and many balconies, oriel windows and rounded corner turrets leave it just the right side of cluttered. Shad Thames has a large and pleasant Victorian brewery at its west end and atmospheric warehousing with steel bridges of the same period to the east.

Mound Stand (406)
1985–1987
St John's Wood Road, NW8;
tube: St John's Wood
Michael Hopkins and Partners

The Marylebone Cricket Club, like Lloyd's of London (no. 402), seem a surprising patron of very Modernist architecture, renowned as they are for their conservatism, yet such has proved repeatedly the

case. Here, Hopkins chose to retain and extend the existing arched brick wall, which contrasts beautifully with the high tech metal and glass block upper parts of the stand poking out over the wall. The topmost tier is roofed with eleven tensile canopies in white PVC fabric, supported ingeniously from six steel columns. In some indefinable way, the design aligns itself exactly with the ethos of sunny days and cricket. Grimshaw Architects' Grand Stand opposite, completed in 1998, is impressive but by no means as close to the spirit of cricket.

Sainsbury's Supermarket and Houses (407)

1985–1988
Camden Road, NW1; tube: Camden Town
Grimshaw Architects

This is a good example of how a super-market, often a disruptive building type, can be successfully integrated into an inner urban area. The parking problem was solved by a moving ramp, which transports the shopping trolleys down to the shoppers' cars parked underground. The service yard is obscured by a row of work-shops to Kentish Town Road and a row of self-consciously futuristic, aluminium clad, three-storey houses facing the canal. The supermarket itself presents a metal clad, industrial face with a great show of structure, none of which is displayed inside the fairly conventional 'Sainsbury' interior. Most strangely, a large void in the building's section is given its own window the full length of the building, perhaps inviting the passing flâneure to speculate on the emptiness of modern consumer culture.

Broadgate (408)

1985–1991
Liverpool Street, EC2;
tube: Liverpool Street/Moorgate
Arup Associates;
Skidmore, Owings and Merrill

The use of Broad Street Station, immediately adjacent to Liverpool Street Station, was gradually phased out after the war and its final demolition left a large and lucrative development site on the northern fringe of the City. Arup Associates were responsible for the first buildings on Wilson and Sun Streets. These seven-storey offices clad in bronze coloured aluminium in a restrained high-tech style remain the best part of the development. The same company were retained for the following phases immediately to the east. These are slightly taller and have their aluminium cladding covered with elaborate and fussy granite screens hung on the façades, although the pattern of the blocks, surrounded by pedestrian passages and piazzas, is still fine grained and attractive. This pattern was abandoned for the later phases north of the Liverpool Street Station and along Bishopsgate, for which Skidmore, Owings and Merrill designed some disgusting ten-storey hulks in a vaguely classical idiom.

AFTER MODERNISM

Storm Water Pumping Station (409)
1987–1988
Stewart Street, E14;
tube: Canary Wharf, DLR: South Quay
John Outram

Outram's idiosyncratic design approach is to construct complex cosmological narratives for his buildings to articulate, thankfully, it is not necessary to understand any of that to enjoy his quirky and colourful creations. This little shed, or 'Temple of Storms', houses automated water-handling gear, much of it below ground, and is only ever peopled for maintenance purposes. The walls are of polychromatic brick with pre-cast concrete dressings and attached bundled columns to the flank walls supporting brackets under the overhanging pitched

roof. The gable elevations have massive hollow circular brick columns with flamboyant coloured concrete capitals. The metal clad tympana have fans in the form of giant jet turbines. Rest assured, it all means something!

Canary Wharf DLR Station (410)
1987–1991
Cabot Place, E14;
tube and DLR: Canary Wharf
César Pelli and Associates

With its unattractive buildings, corporate atmosphere and toy trains, it is tempting to entirely dismiss Canary Wharf along with its station, which is undoubtedly a modern take on a Victorian train shed.

However, on second glance, the little glazed elliptical shed with its tubular trusses has few overt historicisms and is pleasant and airy. It is even quite exciting pulling into the station at high level between the looming tombstone office blocks, even if the train is only a toy.

Milton Gate Offices (411)
1987–1991
Chiswell Street, EC2; tube: Moorgate
Denys Lasdun, Peter Softley
and Associates

An early instance in the city of a triple-skinned, glazed building with a ventilated cavity, the offices, despite their squat inelegance, have an emerald-like quality bestowed by the unframed outer

skin, which is of very green glass with many facets. The glazed façade is seven storeys high with raised turrets at the corners. Above this is a steeply pitched, aluminium clad roofscape with a cylindrical drum housing plant. It is all a little peculiar. The entrance was originally in the north-east corner marked by a blue brick column. Internally, the offices are arranged around an atrium. The building was recently refurbished by Squire and Partners, who moved the entrance and glazed in the corner among other changes.

Minster Court Offices (412)
1987–1991
Mincing Lane, EC3; tube: Monument
GMW Architects

Known in architectural circles as Munster Court, in affectionate memory of the 1960s Hollywood Gothick television series 'The Munsters'. Minster Court is the funniest building in the City. There are three large office blocks of up to thirteen storeys arranged around a shopping parade arcaded with a large Victorian style glazed canopy. The blocks themselves are clad in reddish granite and grey glass in a Disney Gothic style, with a frenzy of gables and pinnacles. More amusing than the intrinsically comic appearance of the buildings is trying to imagine the conversations amongst the design team and with sceptical outsiders. Someone, amazingly, most have been able to keep a straight face.

The Globe Theatre (413)
1987–1997
Bankside, SE1; tube: London Bridge
Pentagram Design

Rebuilding a structure demolished in 1642 that had only ever existed for forty-three years may seem quixotic. Such is

the cult of Shakespeare in Britain however, that it was achieved by actor and director Sam Wanamaker. The site is approximately 230 metres east of where the original is thought to have stood and is as close to the original design as modern imperfect knowledge allows. The plan shape is a dodecahedron, just over thirty metres across. There are three levels of galleries on the perimeter around the open yard and the raised stage has its own gabled roof. The framing is green oak with lime plaster infill on oak lath and staves, while the roof is water reed thatch. Quixotic or not, the building offers a unique and atmospheric theatrical experience, weather permitting.

Design Museum (414)
1988–1989
Maguire Street, SE1; tube: Bermondsey
Conran Roche

The Design Museum is a private museum, whose founding and functioning has been funded by a variety of design based companies, amongst which Habitat founder, Terence Conran, is a principle figure. The museum shows mainly temporary exhibitions but there is a small permanent collection of 'classic' designs.

There was a limit to what could be done with a very rough 1930s industrial building on a tight budget. What was done was to create a reasonably stylish approximation of 1930s white modernism with strip windows and minimal details. The ground floor houses a foyer, café and bookshop, above are a terraced restaurant and temporary exhibition space. The airy main exhibition space is at second floor level.

Imagination Offices   (415)
1988–1989
Store Street, WC1; tube: Goodge Street/
Tottenham Court Road
Herron Associates

Imagination are an advertising group who wanted something striking and cool for their London Head Offices. Albert Place with its crescent at either end was laid out in 1810, although no buildings from that era survive. The south crescent is occupied by a pleasant red brick Edwardian building – this, and the building behind it, are the Imagination offices. Herron created a covered six-storey atrium in the space between the two. This space, which is crossed with lightweight steel bridges, and the

rear building are covered in a knobbly tensile fabric roof on a lightweight steel structure. It is as striking and cool as even the most hyperactive ad-man could wish for.

245

No. 1 Canada Square Offices (416)

1988–1991
César Pelli and Associates

At 244m and with fifty floors, No.1 Canada Square is the tallest building on the island, though some taller are in the works. Pelli apparently kept it simple to render it 'elemental'. Square on plan with slight recessions at the corners and top; it terminates in a pyramidal roof the top part of which is glazed. Cladding is a polished stainless steel rain screen with a regular grid of rectangular windows; the material was chosen so that it might reflect the shifting patterns of the English weather; Londoners were suitably impressed with this contextual gesture. The Foyer lobby spaces are the usual corporate mix of marble and glass and 'art'. It is difficult to imagine how this building could have been dumber. The consolation is that it doesn't ruin a bit of the City as skyscrapers generally do when they hit the ground; there is nothing at Canary Wharf to ruin. The Isle of Dogs stands to the east of the City on a loop of the Thames which, until the early 19th Century, was little more than a marshy waste. It was drained and the first dock, West India Docks, was constructed here in 1802; more followed as the Century wore on together with associated industry. Thus it was a tough working district little visited by those who didn't have business there. The Island was devastated during the Blitz as the German bombing campaign was heavily focused on the Docks. After the war industry gradually moved away to better connected places and the dock traffic declined as trade moved to larger ships that couldn't fit in the old docks; the Docks finally closed in 1980. The whole of London's Docklands were in an appalling state after the long decline and were now without a raison d'etre. The government established the London Docklands Development Corporation in 1981, vesting in it ownership of the land and planning authority, and tasking it to attract new industry to the old docks. Progress was slow until it was realised

that on the Isle of Dogs at least, close to the City, then offices if not industry might be tempted to move there. This could only be achieved with improved transport links and to this end was built first the low budget Docklands Light Railway and, crucially, saw to it that the Jubilee Line Extension passed through. It was this connection that persuaded Canadian Developer Olympia and York to undertake to build a huge new office district on the northern part of the Island. After some anxious moments during the 1990s recession Canary Wharf, as it was named, has been a runaway 'success' with 100,000's of square metres of office space constructed and let; further expansions are planned. The overwhelming bulk of it is architecturally undistinguished, the mere translation of economic calculation into built form. Despite claims to the contrary the district is lifeless and characterless, utterly Americanised and corporate. It is surprising but some people do appear to genuinely enjoy this ambience; it will be fascinating to see what kind of a society that will bring in its wake.

No. 1 Canada Square.

Canary Wharf Towers.

St Paul's, Harringay (417)
1988–1993
Wightman Road, N4;
tube: Finsbury Park
Inskip and Jenkins

The Victorian church burnt down in 1984, thus presenting Inskip and Jenkins with the unusual opportunity to build a modern church in London. They certainly rose to the occasion with this small but powerful and monumental building, which reads externally as a red brick box topped by a floating zinc triangle roof. The walls have white concrete bands, copings and window surrounds. The gables are glazed, the west one projects boldly out over the entrance which appears as a slot between two triangular brick masses. Inside the

main space is simple high box of painted brickwork, chaste but made numinous by the clever natural lighting. The vestry and other facilities are located underneath the east end, taking advantage of the fall across the site. The architects also designed the vicarage next door to the church.

David Mellor Showroom, Offices and Flat (418)
1989–1991
Shad Thames, SE1; tube: Bermondsey
Michael Hopkins & Partners

Built for the designer and cutler David Mellor, this six-storey building is admirably simple and tough and entirely at home in its robust, canal-side location. The structure is exposed concrete slabs and columns, infilled with glazing front and back and with lead panels on a steels substructure to the flanks. The stair towers at each end are in pre-fabricated steel unit. The plate glass, recessed

ground floor houses the showroom, which is now Terence Conran's, while the top two floors were Mellor's London home with his company offices on the floors below.

Independent Television News (ITN) Building (419)
1989–1992
Gray's Inn Road, WC1;
tube: Chancery Lane
Foster and Partners

Accommodating offices and studios for a large television news agency, this was Foster's first substantial building in London. There is a colonnade to Gray's Inn Road with double height concrete columns, above which are four storeys of slick frameless glass façade, although the transparency of this tends to be mitigated by most of the blinds being down most of the time. A further two storeys

are set back from the road. There is more glass to the rear along with some large louvred aluminium clad service towers. The concrete floor plates are arranged around a large spectacular atrium with a huge obscured glass window at the south end outlining minimalist bridges across the chasm. Everything is glass, white, grey or silver, a recipe to become very familiar.

The Ark, Office Building   (420)
1989–1992
Talgarth Road, W6; tube: Hammersmith
Ralph Erskine, Rock Townsend

The only building in London by celebrated architect and Swedish domiciled expat Erskine, the native returned at the behest of Swedish developers. Erskine employed his trademark organic forms to create what looks like a vast

ship run aground by the terrible road spaghetti where Hammersmith used to be. The profile of the building gradually bows outwards as it ascends, with eight storeys on the north side and six on the south. Above this is a recessed storey under a large curved sloping roof. A strange observation tower pops up through the middle of the roof. There is some brickwork at low levels but the façade is mostly striped in greenish and black glass and copper bands. The interior was originally freely arranged around a large open atrium with many bridges and a tower in the middle. A refit by DN-A (2006–2008) has seen much of this either filled-in or glazed-in to produce a far drearier, more lettable, set of floor plates.

Alban Gate Offices   (421)
1990–1992
London Wall, EC2; tube: Moorgate
Terry Farrell and Partners

The site is 'L'-shaped with the lower part over the junction of London Wall and Wood Street. The architects chose to express the shape as two separate eighteen-storey towers joined at the corner. The ends are alternating strips of glazing and beige cladding that start to step back towards the top, while the fully glazed central sections rise to segmental vaulted curved roofs. It is most successful from those viewpoints where it looks like two towers, and less successful where it looks like a pair of awkwardly conjoined twins. The structural gymnastics where the south tower straddles the road are exciting and embellished with some tongue-in-cheek Hi-Tech Deco gymnastics.

Lisson Gallery (422)
1991–1992
Bell Street, NW1; tube: Edgware Road
Tony Fretton Architects

The gallery, infilling in a row of terraces, is a simple little building that somehow seems to add up to more than its parts. The lowered ground and first floor are fully glazed with sliding windows, while the floor above is rendered with a recessed panel and the top floor has a single offset window with aluminium cladding to the side. All of this is very subtly layered and lapped to create much more interest and elegance than a description might suggest. There is a

single well-lit gallery space on each of the four floors. Fretton had previously converted a house in Lisson Street to serve as the gallery, this now forms the rear part of the current gallery at first and second floor levels.

Channel 4 Headquarters (423)
1991–1994
Horseferry Road, SW1;
tube: St James's Park
Richard Rogers Partnership

Channel 4 primarily commissions external work so the building houses mostly offices, although there is a studio, a post-production suite and a screening room in the basement. The site is on a corner, where there is a concave curved block housing the entrance fronted by a four-storey frameless glass screen, behind which are bridges connecting the two wings of offices. Either side of the screen

are meeting rooms, stairs and a bank of lifts, all highly articulated in a manner similar to the Partnership's Lloyd's building (no. 402). The two rectangular office wings are plainer, with the concrete frame clad in a regular curtain wall with glass and metal infill panels. The columns are exposed at ground level and a fourth floor is set back from the road behind a terrace. The entrance has to be approached via a bridge spanning melodramatically over the glass roof of the basement screening room lobby.

BAPS Shri Swaminarayan Mandir (424)
1992–1995
Brentfield Road, NW10;
tube: Neasdon/Stonebridge Park
C. B. Sompura

To describe this fairytale Gujarati Temple as unexpected in the ordinary suburb of Neasden is an understatement at the very least. The domed main space of the Mandir is raised at first floor level and approached by a long flight of ceremo-

nial stairs and a domed porch. Additional domes and pinnacles ornament the façade and roof. All of the stone, which was quarried in Italy, Bulgaria and India, was intricately carved in India and shipped to Britain for assembly on site. Since the inclusion of metal in the construction is not permitted for religious reasons, all of the stone is load bearing. Both the edifice and its story are extraordinary. Behind the Mandir is the much larger Haveli, or meeting house and cultural centre, which makes extensive use of ornately carved hardwood.

Turquoise Island Public Toilets and Flower Shop (425)
1993
Westbourne Grove, W2;
tube: Royal Oak/Bayswater
Campbell, Zogolovitch, Wilkinson and Gough

Piers Gough is noted for the light-hearted humour of his designs. Given that he normally works for developers, the joke can sometimes wear as thin as the budget and planning guidance are stretched. In this instance, however,

Gough achieved exactly the right tone. Locals unhappy with the council's plans for automated pod toilets prevailed to get this charming little building instead. Situated at the broad end of a long tapering island in the road, the toilets have turquoise glazed brick walls and no windows. The walls step down to form a plinth for the frameless glazing of the flower kiosk. When the space becomes too thin, the plinth continues to the apex, acting as outdoor display. There is a Guimard style opalescent glass canopy around the long sides and a clock at the back.

Fifth Floor Harvey Nichols (426)
1993
Knightsbridge, SW1; tube: Knightsbridge
Wickham and Associates

251

For all its social pretensions, the architecture at the Harvey Nichols Department Store had been unambitious until the construction of the fifth floor restaurants, bar and food hall. Little can be seen from outside since the new areas are enclosed on three sides by the existing buildings, it is only to the east that a stepped, fully glazed wall behind a terrace can be made out amongst the Edwardian turrets. Inside is a jolly and airy space under a lofty sawtooth roof. The upper parts of the pitches are glazed and the lower parts clad in a yellow board. The restaurant itself is an oval room adjacent to the main space with a translucent suspended ceiling.

Hauer-King House (427)
1993–1994
Douglas Road, N1;
tube: Highbury and Islington
Future Systems

One of the first actual buildings completed by the high tech fundamentalists Future Systems, the Hauer-King House occupies a sliver of a site in a terrace between two roads. The house has three and a half storeys to the road and four to the garden. The lower part of the road eleva-

tion is glass block with sloping glazing at the top. The rear elevation is all sloping frameless glazing with full width glass doors at the bottom. It is understood that the trees on the site are to provide shade and privacy, though presumably not any insulation. The inside has enclosed service pods and stairs between the various

living platforms. The future with all its studded rubber flooring had arrived at last!

Palm Housing Co-operative (428)
1993–1994
Broadwall, SE1; tube: Waterloo
Lifschutz Davidson Sandilands

The client for this project was Coin Street Community Builders, who had formed to protect their neighbourhood from property developers in the 1980s. A row

of three-storey houses with four-storey blocks to the ends is terminated on the north side facing the river with a slender nine-storey tower of apartments. The materials are red brick and Iroko boarding with extensive glazing, the roofs are metal and there are prominent shiny silver flues. The houses face west over Bernie Spain Gardens, which was another Coin Street development. It is evidently a wonderful place to live and an achievement for client and architect alike.

Floating Footbridge (429)
1994–1996
West India Quay, E14;
tube: Canary Wharf
Future Systems

Developers cannot seem to get enough of footbridges; the fat the development, the more bridges required and the more absurd they have to be. This one is part of the very fat Canary Wharf development and spans the West India Import Dock. There is a very thin metal deck in a gentle arc across the ninety metres be-

far only one has been reused. The primary structure, a large circular section on the west side, is cable-stayed with an inclined tubular central mast. The bridge can pivot about this centre point to allow boats to pass. The deck is of oak and the guarding is grey painted steelwork. Jan Bobrowski and Partners were the engineers.

tween the quays, supported by four sets of 'X'-shaped props standing on large floats. The balustrade is formed of wires between simple steel uprights. The metalwork is all painted an electric lime green, a very popular colour in the future apparently. The central section can be lifted up to allow boats to pass. It looks its best at night when the unsightly floats are not illuminated. The engineers were Anthony Hunt Associates.

South Quay Footbridge (430)
1994–1997
South Quay Plaza, E14;
tube: Canary Wharf
Wilkinson Eyre Architects

The boomerang bridge, as it is sometimes known, was initially 'S'-shaped and twice the length. It was part of the original brief of the competition, however, that the bridge would have to change format in this way to accommodate the overall development programme. The longer version had two identical boomerang shapes that could be reused individually when the south dock had been narrowed; so

Abbey Mills Pumping Station (431)
1994–1997
Abbey Lane, E15; tube: West Ham
Allies and Morrison

Despite its central role in the unglamorous business of pumping sewage, this is one of Allies and Morrison's more charismatic buildings. It sits alone and

enigmatic out in the flat landscape of the Lea Valley. A finely articulated and well-proportioned shed, it has a steel structure and silver and grey aluminium cladding. It is only very sparsely inhabited by people and its single volume interior is mostly filled with machinery, as much below ground as above.

No. 1 Poultry Offices (432)
1994–1998
Poultry, EC2; tube: Bank
Stirling Wilford and Associates

A development with a tortuous gestation and doubly controversial, the offices were built on a site occupied by pleasant if unexceptional Victorian buildings. The developer's father had received planning permission in the 1960s for a tower by Mies van der Rohe, one of his last designs. The son, Peter Palumbo, however, turned to Stirling to design this flamboyant but

253

cumbersome, six-storey, striped postmodernist fancy with its wealth of inventive, colourful and clunky detailing. Stirling died in 1992 before construction com-

menced. For all its faults it offers features to the city most office buildings do not, including shops, a convenient shortcut across the site, a vastly improved entrance to Bank tube station, a dramatic staircase entrance at the building's prow and, best of all, a fantastic roof garden and restaurant overlooking the City, accessed via a glass lift in the central courtyard.

Lord's Cricket Ground Media Centre (433)

1995–1998
St John's Wood Road, NW8;
tube: St John's Wood
Future Systems

The Media Centre is a building that astonishes in many different ways. Visually, it is extraordinary and otherworldly; a huge

smooth, seamless, white elliptical capsule on two concrete legs that raise it fifteen metres and up over the stand in front. The accommodation inside is for journalists and broadcasters to watch the cricket, which they do through a two-storey frameless glass window. Print journalists are accommodated on the stepped lower level with broadcasting boxes above and the requisite journalistic refreshment facilities behind. The structure of the capsule is a semi monocoque with an aluminium skin welded to aluminium ribs and spars. The preassembled sections were lifted into place by cranes and welded together insitu by boat builders. The interior is not quite so futuristic, resembling more a 1960s filmic idea of the future. The building was very very expensive.

Westminster Underground Station (434)

1995–1998
Bridge Street, SW1; tube: Westminster
Michael Hopkins and Partners

Not unique in its degree of difficulty but certainly one of the harder of the Jubilee Line stations to execute, Westminster Station had to be constructed underneath the continuously running 19th-century District and Circle lines, underneath Portcullis House (no. 447) and right by the Thames. The ticket hall at half basement level in Portcullis House has a beautifully elegant, but bulky, concrete structure. This gives way to the escalator hall, a thirty-metre deep, concrete box full of concrete structure, escalators and stairs, some of which are enclosed in steel tubes for fire protection. It is impressive in the Piranasian manner, though you may wonder if your colour vision has been temporarily impaired.

Southwark Underground Station (435)

1995–1999
The Cut, SE1; tube: Southwark
MJP Architects

Situated on a corner site, the exterior of the building is a single-storey riff on the Holden station theme with descending steps under a double canopy arrangement, one concrete and one glass, to a circular ticket hall with a glass block drum above. The structure of all this was designed to tolerate an over-building if ever required. From the ticket hall, escalators lead down to the impressive intermediate concourse, a deep half elliptical cone lit with a huge roof light. The curving wall is lined with patterned blue glass by artist Alex Beleschenko. The steel lined, lower concourse hints again at the 1930s with its illuminated beacons at each end. There is a connection to the overground station, Waterloo East, for which the same architects designed a pleasant new ticket hall and platform canopies.

Bermondsey Underground Station (436)

1995–1999
Jamaica Road, SE16; tube: Bermondsey
Ian Ritchie Architects

From the street, the station appears as a modest, elegantly detailed, single-storey, steel framed building. This gives access to a concourse with a curved translucent roof, which in turn leads to the escalator hall, another deep concrete box lit from above. In contrast to Westminster Underground Station (no. 434), this is kept as clean and simple as possible, emphasising its sheerness. At the bottom is some enjoyably tough and bewildering concrete architecture.

Canada Water Transport Interchange (437)

1995–1999
Surrey Quays Road, SE16;
tube: Canada Water
Jubilee Line Extension Architects,
Eva Jiricná Architects

The interchange comprises two elements, a Jubilee Line Extension tube station by the in-house team and a bus station by Jiricná. The tube station is a fairly literal translation of a Holden drum into glass with a projecting silver metal flat roof. This creates a light and

255

airy space and curved glass always looks swish. The bus station is like a long bird with a central body of a glazed tubular truss with two curved wings supported by five central columns and suspension members. One wing is cut short to accommodate the tube station, the central truss cantilevers beyond to support the remaining wing.

North Greenwich Underground Station (438)
1995–1999
Edmund Halley Way, SE10;
tube: North Greenwich
Alsop and Störmer

This is one of the most vivid of the Jubilee Line Extension stations, due at least in part to the extensive use of an intense blue glass mosaic tile. The escalator descends into a vast, murky, concrete box divided by a line of large columns in 'V's, covered in mosaic. The concourse runs through this box at high level with views down to the platforms. Apart from providing spatial drama, this arrangement allows passengers to see where they are going, a key ambition for the new stations. Further escalators lead

down to the platforms. Strangely, the responsibility for the bus interchange on top of the station was handed to Foster and Partners (1998–1999) and the contrast between the intensity of Alsop's section and Foster's anodyne wing-shaped realm is abrupt and striking. It seems a shame, as Alsop would surely have provided a more animated counterpart to his station.

Canary Wharf Underground Station (439)
Upper Bank Street, E14;
tube: Canary Wharf
Foster and Partners

The construction of the station was partially funded by the Canary Wharf developers and it has been built on the same gargantuan scale as the rest of the place. It is a busy station, although not nearly the busiest, and no other on the entire network is on this scale. It seems too big for the activities it houses. The double concourse is over 200 metres long and divided by a row of concrete columns down the centre, which support a curved concrete soffit. The entrances at each end of the concourse – vast, curved, glass blisters on steel arches springing from concrete upstands – are, however, truly magnificent. Ascending the escalators has a truly epic feel.

Millennium Dome (440)
1996–1999
Millennium Way, SE10;
tube: North Greenwich
Richard Rogers Partnership

Burdened with this embarrassment and disgrace of a building, the nation was finally relieved of its humiliation when the old Millennium Dome was re-opened as an arena and general commercial operation in 2007. The structure itself is reasonably elegant with a circular footprint 365 metres in diameter. The glass fibre fabric dome is hung from cables supported by twelve bright yellow Skylon-like tubular columns; the circulation cores are likewise fairly handsome and highly articu-

lated in the Rogers style. The refit, however, is an orgy of corporate vulgarity and it is hard to envisage a less atmospheric music venue.

The Lux   (441)
1996–1997
Hoxton Square, N1; tube: Old Street
MacCreanor Lavington Architects

MacCreanor and Lavington's strong connections with the Netherlands are clearly apparent in this rational and

undemonstrative mixed development. It originally housed gallery space, a cinema, teaching rooms and offices for the British Film Institute, as well as a bar, restaurant and some space for rent. The film people subsequently moved out and the cinema now functions as a performance space. Reflecting the multiplicity of users, the building is expressed as a pair, one of four bays and five storeys,

the other three bays and four storeys. Both have the same simple repetitive grid of large windows in blue brick. The interiors are light and airy and the long sunken bar offers an unusual view of the battered and unlovely but fashionable streets of Hoxton.

Sadler's Wells Theatre   (442)
1996–1998
Rosebery Avenue, EC1; tube: Angel
Nicholas Hare Architects, Renton
Howard Wood Levin

There has been a theatre on this site since 1683 and the current building is the sixth. The project was one of the very first to be lottery funded and the associated funding criteria demanded that the project be completed within a very short time, which is noticeable in some rough edges. The principle façades are in brick, seemingly of great thickness, and there is a full four-storey frameless glass screen between the massive brick planes to the entrance and foyers. The fly tower is expressed as a large, metal clad cube. Flying dog-leg stairs in the foyers provide

257

some excitement as well as access to the two auditorium balconies. The 1,500-seat auditorium is wide and can accommodate a broad diversity of dance performances, with which Sadler's Wells has become increasingly associated in recent times. The auditorium is not lavish but reasonably appealing.

Office Building, Wood Street (443)
1997–1999
Wood Street, EC2;
tube: St Paul's/Moorgate
Foster and Partners

This was one of a pair built simultaneously on adjacent sites by two of the city's most renowned architects, which led inevitably to some press nonsense about a 'battle of the giants'. Ignoring that, it is interesting to see how their approaches to the same problem and environment differ. The Wood Street façade of Foster's building, perhaps due to planner pressure, is restrained and abstract. A six-storey chequerboard pattern with alternating pinkish granite and frameless glass mutates into a barrel-vaulted top, where the panels become diamond shaped. The whole is simply a smooth patterned skin. A typical City passageway through the building leads to a tiny little court around a tree. On this side, the building is a super slick, 1960s futurist, curved and inclined curtain wall over an arcade of suspiciously large raking columns and is as much fun as the street façade is tedious.

Daiwa Securities Office (444)
1997–1999
Wood Street, EC2;
tube: St Paul's/Moorgate
Richard Rogers Partnership

Rogers was at a disadvantage from the outset as this building is far larger than Foster's (no. 443). Whereas Foster hides everything under seamless skins, Rogers seeks to express every bit of the programme in architecturally distinct pieces, despite the sad fact that offices do not have too much to express. The office floor plates are therefore expressed as three glass and steel faced blocks in eight to ten storeys to Wood Street and fourteen and eighteen storeys to London Wall. The lobbies or foyers in between are fully glazed and the stairs and lifts accentuated in prominently expressed glazed towers. This all provides some initial visual interest, but after reflecting on the banality of what is being expressed, the building's complexity seems to lose any significance it might have had.

Millennium Wheel (445)
1997–2000
South Bank, SE1;
tube: Embankment/Waterloo
Marks Barfield Architects

It certainly reveals something, not good, about the state of Britain that this self-evidently excellent idea met with the resistance it did. The Millennium Wheel was the brainchild of its architects and it was their staunch determination that eventually overcame the opposition from the establishment to find funding. Perhaps the fact that it was ultimately achieved does, in the end, reveal something positive about Britain. The structural prin-

ciples follow exactly those of a bicycle wheel, yet it still seems impossible that those slender pieces of wire can keep the tubular wheel (122 metres in diameter) and its thirty-two ovoid viewing pods in the air, and that is before considering the single-sided support and the tension in its tie-backs. The Wheel is certainly the best addition to the London skyline since the GPO Tower (no. 365). Permission has in fact only been granted for temporary installation, but the attraction's continuing popularity should see it survive for a while yet.

Millennium Bridge (446)
1998–2000
Peter's Hill/Bankside Walk, EC4/SE1;
tube: St Paul's
Foster and Partners

The British love a good fiasco and the sight of the new footbridge swaying violently on opening day was certainly entertaining, as was the unseemly bout of accusations that followed. The installation of an active damping system has restricted the movement to an acceptable amount. The damping may spoil the purity of the idea of the bridge, but the resultant structure is undeniably elegant and wonderfully slender. There are two 'Y'-shaped, intermediate supports near the banks followed by a very shallow steel suspension structure and a very slender arched deck. The deck is stainless steel with a steel balustrade on curved uprights. The landing on the south side is disappointingly convoluted. Ove Arup and Partners were the beleaguered engineers.

Portcullis House (447)
1998–2001
Bridge Street, SW1; tube: Westminster
Michael Hopkins Architects

Something went awry with this project between the planning and construction stages. The competition-winning drawings showed an alluring contrast between a heavy masonry structure and delicate filigree-like Oriel windows, inspired, it was claimed, by Peter Ellis' wonderful Oriel Chambers in Liverpool. The heaviness remains but is unleavened by any delicacy. Whatever bureaucratic, technical or legislatory coils were responsible, the MPs' offices as built are fairly joyless. They are five storeys with masonry piers and Oriel windows as promised, but the masonry is too smooth and the oriels too opaque for the contrast to be successful.

259

There is a steeply pitched, aluminium bronze roof above with prominent ventilation chimneys. It is planned around a rectangular central courtyard, which is sited above the Westminster tube station ticket hall (no. 434) and has an interesting vaulted glass roof with a timber and steel diagrid structure. The building's design life was 200 years, materials are correspondingly robust and prices correspondingly high.

Peckham Library (448)
1999
Peckham Hill Street, SE15;
train: Peckham Library
Alsop and Störmer

Gimmicky and flashy, the library perhaps offers neglected Peckham the cheap glamour it needed. It is in the form of an inverted 'L', the overhanging upper part of which is supported by thin steel columns at erratic angles forming a sheltered public space underneath.

The vertical leg of the 'L' is clad front and back with highly coloured curtain walling; the cladding is otherwise copper sheet with small window openings. The vertical leg houses meeting rooms, offices and a learning centre. The principal reading room is in the horizontal leg of the 'L' at fourth floor level. Double height, the room contains three pods raised on stilts which penetrate the flat roof to allow high level lighting; the central pod has an absurd orange tongue for a roof. The elevated reading room allows for good views out beyond grey, old Peckham.

British Film Institute London Imax (449)
1998–1999
Waterloo Road, SE1; tube: Waterloo
Avery Associates Architects

The site was the meeting place of a number of underground pedestrian walkways in what still is an unpleasant, road dominated area. The Imax is a brilliant use of what was an unsightly and scary area of essentially wasted space. The building is circular, following the shape of the old roundabout, while the auditorium inside is rectangular with ancillary functions filling the interstices. The raked seating faces a screen twenty metres high and twenty-six metres wide. The drum is surrounded by a circular gallery with a wall of frameless glass. Intended for temporary art exhibitions, the wall intially displayed a mural by Howard Hodgkin, but the space is now used for advertising, sadly. The pedestrian walkways at low level around the drum have been covered in vegetation on a network of wires and the lighting vastly improved, making the area slightly less scary at night than it used to be.

Dalston Road Estate (450)
1998–1999
Dalston Road, E8;
tube: Dalston Junction,
train: Dalston Kingsland
Allford Hall Monaghan Morris

The Peabody Trust has long had a reputation for being one of the best social landlords in the city and they have lately started to commission innovative new housing from younger architects. This scheme of twenty-four flats over ground floor retail units is one of the best of

these. It is very simply arranged with the flats stacked between crosswalls and generously glazed to the south onto balconies. The light and dark blue render chequered super graphic looks fresh and optimistic, at least on a sunny day.

London City Hall (451)
1999–2002
The Queen's Walk, SE1;
tube: London Bridge
Foster and Partners

County Hall, the old seat of London governance, was sold by Mrs Thatcher to a Japanese developer. So when the role of Mayor of the City was reconstituted, the taxpayers had to pay out for a new home. The ten-storey building, clad in glass with grey infill panels, is apparently in the shape of a modified sphere, though it looks more like a subsiding grey blancmange. Internally, the spaces are arranged around the path of a spiral ramp that passes all the way through the building. The spaces onto the ramp have

glazed walls, which was intended to demonstrate the openness and transparency of the City's democracy. Unfortunately, the ramp passes through the Council Chamber and is closed off to prevent sittings being disturbed. It is all very silly and has been further tarnished in people's minds by less than impressive incumbents.

The Queen's Gallery (452)
1999–2002
Buckingham Gate, SW1; tube: Victoria
John Simpson and Partners

The Prince of Wales' enthusiasm for 'traditional' architecture is well known and no doubt explains the selection of Simpson, a leading 'modern classical' architect, for the design of the gallery, which is used to display temporary exhibitions of parts of the Royal Collection. It incorporates individual galleries built earlier by Pennethorne and Nash and replaces a 1963 extension. Externally, it is quite modest at only two storeys in Portland and Bath stones and most of it is hidden behind the Palace walls, though a pedimented Ionic gable peeks over. The most insistent part, the Doric entrance porch, is the least successful part. The double height entrance hall with its glazed roof is quite impressive, but the fussy stair hall less so and the top-lit galleries are unexceptional. The style is Greek with references to Schinkel and Soane and, like much of this sort of work, it has a rather stiff academic feel to it.

Sir Norman Foster
*1935 in Manchester (453)

Foster was born in modest circumstances in Manchester. After national service and clerical work he studied architecture at Manchester University where he won a scholarship to Yale University. There he met Richard Rogers and they established Team 4, a short-lived partnership back in Britain. Team 4's and later Foster Associates' early projects tended to be lightweight and inexpensive with an overtly industrial high-tech aesthetic. The 1970s and early 1980s saw a string of technologically innovative and increasingly slick projects. The IBM Pilot Head Office in Portsmouth, Willis Faber and Dumas Head Offices in Ipswich and the Renault Distribution Centre in Swindon all garnered increasing international interest and acclaim.

Surprisingly, these admired but modest projects led to one of the commissions of the era. The headquarters of the Hong Kong and Shanghai Bank in Hong Kong are forty-four storeys high and cost in excess of £400 million – quite a coup for a practice whose biggest building previously was only three storeys with less than a twentieth of the budget. The

Bank remains the office's greatest triumph, the most refined and exciting skyscraper ever built. The Bank reinforced Foster's reputation for innovation and confirmed that no job was too large, too complex or too expensive. Other important projects around this time include Stansted Airport on London's northwest fringe and the Médiathèque in Nîmes. A project for a new BBC Radio Centre in Langham Place was abandoned in 1985, so London had to wait until 1990 for its first extant Foster buildings when two were completed: Foster's own offices by Albert Bridge and the ITN Headquarters (no. 419). Both buildings are of elegantly proportioned glass and aluminium boxes, minimally but slickly detailed. They are much sleeker than the older high-tech buildings, reflecting larger budgets and improvements in the technologies (driven by Foster's office in some instances), but not as technologically and structurally expressive as their earlier work.

Foster's first non-office building in London was the much liked and admired Sackler Galleries at the Royal Academy of Arts (no. 181). Much of its appeal is in the contrast between the old and new fabric. By the time the Sackler was completed in the mid 1980s Foster had become the world's premier 'starchitect', a global brand with ever more, ever larger commissions all over the world. It is beyond the scope of this brief description even to list all these projects. Some of the better known highlights include Hong Kong Airport, the Duxford American Air Museum, the Commerzbank Tower in Frankfurt, the Berlin Reichstag and the Millau Viaduct over the River Tarn in southern France. Current work ranges from a yacht to a Spaceport and from Buenos Aires to Astana.

With respect to London, Foster and Partners have certainly made up for their slow start with an array of projects that can be divided into the 'specials' and the 'not so specials'. The specials are nearly always public, smaller and structurally ambitious with simple, striking, easily understood forms. Examples would be the Millennium Bridge (no. 446), the British Museum Great Court (no. 143), Canary Wharf tube station (no. 439) and the 'Gherkin' office building (no. 468). Wembley Stadium (no. 479) and City Hall (no. 451) are perhaps half specials.

The 'not so special' projects are usually privately funded, large and simplistically modelled. They are many and multiplying. Some of the least attractive are Albion Square at Spitalfields, the Sainsbury Headquarters building at Holborn Circus and, by far the worst and the biggest, the 'More London' development on the Southbank opposite the Tower of London. In schemes like these the lack of detail and texture is unrelieved by any interesting form or structure; the endless acreage of shiny, expensive curtain walling is mind-numbing and dispiriting in its banality. These soulless corporate monotonies are not worthy of London or its citizens. If the images of the future Walbrook development are to be believed then there is worse still to come.

There is no doubting Foster's influence on the design and technology of architecture during the last four decades; it probably exceeds that of any other single architect. Many fine buildings have been produced and legions of imitators spawned. Unfortunately, Foster and Partners are currently leaving a mixed legacy in their home city.

30 St Mary Axe.

is recessed and clad in terne coated steel. The inner façades to the square are softer and more varied with much timber board-

ing and steel balconies. In 2007, the architects completed a Neighbourhood Centre on the fourth side of the garden. This has five storeys housing education facilities, offices and a café. It is a pleasant building, utilising the currently fashionable unaligned windows and bright yellow.

Blue House (454)
2000
Garner Street, E2; tube: Bethnal Green
FAT

FAT, with their interest in pattern and symbols, forge a fairly lonely path in the world of design, but this makes them no less interesting. This small, three-storey building ingeniously squeezes in a two-bedroom house, a one-bedroom flat and an office, along with interesting spaces and plenty of light. It is clad in baby blue, plastic tongue and grooved boards with darker blue windows. The street façade boasts a cutout of a child's drawing of a house impressed upon a sort of abstract 'office block', while the garden and parapet walls are cut into other fanciful shapes. It is all good clean fun.

Iroko Housing Co-operative (455)
2000–2001
Stamford Street, SE1; tube: Waterloo
Haworth Tompkins Architects

A further development by Coin Street Community Builders (see no. 428), this is an attractive housing development around three sides of a landscaped garden. The garden is the roof of a large underground car park and the four and five-storey blocks accommodate fifty-nine houses and flats. The outer façades to the streets are in red brick with repetitive large horizontal openings with grey aluminium windows; the top storey

Bankside Lofts Apartment Building (456)
2000–2001
Hopton Street, SE1; tube: Southwark
Campbell Zogolovitch Wilkinson Gough

Of the very many commercial housing developments over recent years, this is one of the very few to make some kind of contribution beyond function and profit. The project partially involved converting

some existing buildings to 'lofts', one of which was a fairly functional 1950s industrial building curved around the end of the street. The new building extended this and stepped it up at intervals from six to sixteen storeys creating a double spiral. Outside is an orange yellow wall with regular, very large rectangular windows, while the white interior walls of the apartments open onto terraces on the added floors. It is a picturesque and popular addition to the skyline.

White Cube Gallery (457)
2000–2002
Hoxton Square, N1; tube: Old Street
M. R. J. Rundell and Associates

Artists began living in dilapidated Hoxton in the early 1980s and by a decade later, bars and clubs had started to arrive. It was only a matter of time before a West End gallery appeared. The White

Cube moved into a disused, two-storey print shop in 2000 with a top-lit gallery at first floor level and a basement gallery. In 2002, the two upper storeys of offices and stores were added and clad in fully glazed, prefabricated units. The white painted flank wall was briefly the canvas for one of Banksy's most famous stencils, his maid, which was mysteriously and very quickly painted over. Hoxton and Shoreditch have been favoured Banksy stamping and stenciling grounds.

Royal Academy of Music, Concert Hall and Museum (458)
2000–2002
Marylebone Road, NW1;
tube: Baker Street/Regent's Park
John McAslan and Partners

The principle Academy building is a large, red brick Edwardian pile, but they have been occupying parts of Nash's York Gate building since the 1920s. Most of the original interiors were lost during the war. More recently, the Academy purchased the entire building and refurbished it for use as teaching and practice rooms, as well as to house their library and museum. Between the two buildings, they have built a delightful timber lined recital room. The hall is sunken so that only the lead covered, barrel-vaulted roof and its fully glazed gable are visible. Apart from it being pretty in itself, there is added interest in looking down at a room from an unusual and unexpected vantage point.

Hampden Gurney CE Primary School (459)
2000–2002
Nutford Place, W1; tube: Edgware Road
Building Design Partnership

Much of the post-war school building fabric is reaching the end of its design life, so recent years have seen a spate of urban school building, of which Hampden Gurney was one of the earliest. It occupies a corner site and is nearly a quadrant of a circle on plan. The ground floor accommodates a nursery school with the primary school on the three floors above and, recalling the old Board schools, the roof serves as a playground with a tensile fabric roof cover. There are deep balconies with high glass balustrades forming play balconies at the upper levels. A semi basement houses a hall and a music room. The stair towers at the ends of the curve and the plinth are in buff brick and the cladding is otherwise glass with dark metal trim. Hampden Gurney transformed the image of the urban school in London, offering something glossy, futuristic and entirely unprecedented.

Laban Centre (460)
2000–2002
Creekside, SE8; tube: New Cross,
train: Deptford
Herzog and de Meuron

The Laban is one of Britain's leading modern dance colleges. Their new building by Swiss pair Herzog and de Meuron is an irregular three-storey rectangular box on the banks of Deptford Creek. Formed as a long, gentle, concave curve, the entrance elevation is the most irregular and the entrance itself aligns exactly with St Paul's Deptford (no. 78). The box is clad almost seamlessly in translucent polycarbonate cladding with frameless windows and, where it

is not required to let in light, the polycarbonate is backed by a collage of delicate colours. The cladding lends the building an ethereal shimmering quality, as if its exact location is not quite fixed. Inside, the principle space is the 300-seat theatre, accompanied by thirteen dance studios, a library, health centre, café, bar and ancillary spaces. This is all arranged around a series of colourful tapering corridors and light wells, the wall space adorned with pop art murals by Michael Craig-Martin. If the exterior is a little otherworldly, the interior is more earthbound with the vitality and pizzazz expected of a dance school.

Hong Kong and Shanghai Bank (HSBC) UK Headquarters (461)
2000–2003
Canada Square, E14;
tube: Canary Wharf
Foster and Partners

Neither as tall as No. 1 Canada (no. 416) nor, disappointingly, as interesting as Foster's Hong Kong Headquarters for the same Bank, the structure is forty-two storeys and 200 metres high and cost more than one billion pounds. Square on plan with curved corners and a central core, it is clad in almost seamless glass with obscured strips at the floors and in a band around the top, which forms the field for an enormous 'HSBC' logo. The lobby space reaches twenty-eight metres in height but barely leaves the ground in terms of interest generated. It features a 'History Wall' installation by Thomas Heatherwick.

Paddington Basin Development (462)
2000 onwards
South Wharf Road, W2;
tube: Paddington
Richard Rogers Partnership

The industrial areas around Paddington Canal Basin and Railway Station had become so dilapidated and under utilised that some form of regeneration was essential. The Rogers master plan does not look unsound as a plan, but the built reality is most disappointing – it is all too big, most of the sections are individually ugly, the buildings have

ludicrous names and yet another vast chunk of the City has been corporatised and sanitised. Rogers' thirteen-storey office building for Marks and Spencer is the best of them. It is in his trademark style with all the elements articulated, yellow steelwork and lots of glass, some of which, in a new move from Rogers, has timber shading. The less said about the rest of the buildings the better.

Fawcett Women's Library (463)
2001–2002
Old Castle Street, E1; tube: Aldgate East
Wright and Wright

The library is an offshoot of a women's rights campaigning organisation, the Fawcett Society, whose records and library were put into the keeping of what is now the London Metropolitan University. The architects were obliged to retain the two-storey brick wall of an old washhouse, which they utilised to form the entrance façade to the east and to enclose a pretty courtyard to the north. Within the walls is a sober, likeable four-storey brick box with a further recessed attic storey. The gap between this and the old wall on the east side is filled with confused, copper clad volumes. A double height exhibition hall forms the main public space along with a seminar room, which rather clogs up the central area. Much more pleasant is the distinctly Scandinavian and most restful second floor library reading room.

267

Fashion and Textile Museum (464)
2001–2002
Bermondsey Street, SE1;
tube: London Bridge
Legorreta and Legorreta, Alan Camp

Founded by British fashion giant Zandra Rhodes for educational purposes, the building houses teaching areas as well as the large, two-storey gallery space that is the heart of the building. Its designer and character could not be more surprising in Bermondsey. Legorreta is a pupil and disciple of the legendary Mexican architect, Luis Barragan, and well known in his own right. The gallery is the conversion of a 1950s garage; a simple two-storey, flat roofed, rendered structure well suited to the application of the intense colours used by Legorreta. As well as recalling Barragan, it has a definite Deco feel, the Deco of Miami rather than rainy London. A rooftop extension containing residential accommodation helped to pay for the museum, which was denied government funding.

Office Building. 30 Finsbury Square (465)
2001–2003
Finsbury Square, EC2; tube: Moorgate
Eric Parry Architects

It reveals something about the general standard of office building design that this building should have caused such a stir. It is undoubtedly visually interesting and offers a real relief sitting, as it does, in one of the capital's least lovely squares. It is clad in a stainless steel and glass curtain wall behind a seven-storey,

bulky exo-skeleton of Portland stone. What is unique about this is that it is fully load bearing and that the piers on each level do not align but are shifted slightly for visual effect. There is a two-storey, recessed, glazed attic behind a spindly steel framework. It is effective, intriguing and well-proportioned, but also wilful and irrational. The interior, which was fitted

out by a different firm of architects, is organised around an impressive, full height atrium approached via a deliberately constrained entrance space.

Paternoster Square (466)
2001–2003
St Paul's Churchyard, EC4;
tube: St Pauls
Whitfield and Partners

The area immediately north of the cathedral was destroyed during the war and rebuilt in the years following it. By the late 1980s, that scheme was outdated as offices and looking neglected and its owners no doubt also sensed the possibility of a denser scheme. Between 1987 and 2001 a series of masterplaners were approached and their schemes rejected and it is therefore unsurprising that the final result pleases few. Whitfield proposed a series of blocks divided by narrow alleys and arranged around a small square centred on Wren's Cathedral Chapter House. Around the Square, Whitfield stipulated a classical arcade to be adopted by every building. Despite the involvement of some reputable architects, it is not a great success. Apart from the fact that none

AFTER MODERNISM

of the architects involved did their best work, there is only office and retail use, the buildings are too high and it is all too corporate. Perhaps surprisingly, the most attractive building is by Whitfield and Sidell Gibson; their red brick Paternoster House lies off the Square to the east.

Hungerford Pedestrian Bridges (467)
2001–2003
Victoria Embankment, WC2;
tube: Embankment
Lifschutz Davidson Sandilands

Various ad hoc pedestrian walkways have been fitted onto the side of John Hawkshaw's 1864 wrought iron, lattice, girder railway bridge. The last iteration of these was narrow and, by the mid 1990s, squalid. Lifschutz Davidson Sandilands won a 1996 competition for the bridge concept, although they did not complete the detail design. It comprises two cable-stay bridges, one either side of the old bridge and supported from inclined masts braced back to the existing bridge piers. The technical challenges were formidable, from having to keep the railway line open to the possibility of unexploded ordnance in the river bed

adjacent to a tube line. The new four-metre wide walkways are vastly superior to the old one, but the complex structure with its fourteen different masts has a cluttered, confusing appearance and the builder's detailing is by no means suave.

Swiss Re Office Building   (468)
2001–2004
St Mary Axe, EC3; tube: Liverpool Street
Foster and Partners

A combination of a unique planning circumstance and boom time hubris was to work greatly to London's advantage. Very rarely does it make financial sense to build such slender towers, notwithstanding their skyline benefits. The forty-storey tower is 180 metres high with a central core and a triangulated, lattice-like steel frame to the perimeter. Triangular panels of clear and grey glass clad the façade in a spiralling pattern. The plan has six perimeter voids, which also spiral around the circumference aiding ventilation and contact between floors. Some of the interiors are very dramatic in their combination of large structure, spatial complexity and

stunning views, although the best part of the design is perhaps the building's landing, located in a little plaza. The building's small plan area and slender profile mean that it does not ruin the area around its base, like many skyscrapers, but actually enhances its location.

Allies and Morrison Office Building (469)

2002–2003
Southwark Street, SE1; tube: Southwark
Allies and Morrison

A good example of a simple but elegant infill office building, Allies and Morrison's structure renews the city without violating its texture. The ground floor, which also houses a café, is fully glazed and recessed behind exposed concrete columns. The three storeys above are clad in very minimal frameless glass, while the concrete frame and yellow shutters add texture and interest. A recessed attic storey above is framed with a steel pergola and the irregular rear elevation is rendered with punched windows. The interior is very cool with the concrete frame and slabs simply detailed, characteristically slick stairs and balustrades and a small but effective atrium. Having produced such an urbane building, it is hard to imagine their thoughts on looking out at the ghastly Bankside 123 across the road, for which they alone are unfortuantely responsible.

Paddington Basin Footbridges (470)

2002–2004
South Wharf Road, W2;
tube: Paddington
Langlands and Bell, Marcus Taylor,
Thomas Heatherwick

The developers' love of footbridges is touching and seems eternal. The unique selling point here was to have them designed by artists and a designer rather than dreary architects. Langlands and Bell's bridge is very simple with minimal glass balustrades and is divided by a translucent, steel framed screen wall with a large opening in the middle. The wall is illuminated from within, to good effect at night. Marcus Taylor's Helix Bridge is an ingenious, stainless steel framed, blue and clear glass tube, which retracts into the quayside with a corkscrew action. Thomas Heatherwick's Rolling Bridge is also retractable; the articulated steel frame curls back on itself to stand by the

canal as an octagonal wheel. All things considered, it seems those artist fellows and their engineering chums did not do such a bad job.

Graduate Centre (471)

2002–2004
Holloway Road, N7;
tube: Holloway Road
Studio Daniel Libeskind

The motivation behind this project seems to have been a wish on the part of London Metropolitan University to impose their presence upon the visual chaos that is the Holloway Road. The small building houses a lecture theatre, seminar and IT rooms and 'social' spaces. The com-

position is of three rectangular concrete boxes thrown together at different angles and inclinations. These forms are clad in stainless steel sheeting carved up with large jagged windows. The interiors are surprisingly conventional, apart from their strange angles. When he completed his acclaimed Jewish Museum in Berlin, Libeskind explained that the fractious, aggressive shapes and angles were meant to speak of the alienation and dislocation of the victims of the holocaust. Can the same logic possibly apply to the Holloway Road development? Or is it just meaningless shape-making?

Mossbourne Community Academy (472)

2002–2004
Downs Park Road, E5;
train: Hackney Downs/Hackney Central
Richard Rogers Partnership

Mossbourne was one of the first generation of new 'community academies', or schools as they used to be known. The site is unfortunate, located in an angle between two railway lines. The building is 'L'-shaped and lies parallel to the railways, which are faced with massive blank masonry diaphragm walls painted the brightest possible blue. Inside of this

are triple height, top-lit circulation spaces with the classrooms and other rooms organised over three floors. The structure is a glulam timber frame, which is the prevalent feature of the galleried colonnade in the centre. Glazing occupies most of the infill, apart from the gym and other solid façades where the walls are rendered a bright yellow. The internal spaces are light and airy and the school is a pleasant place to be.

Vauxhall Cross Transport Interchange (473)

2002–2005
Wandsworth Road, SW11; tube: Vauxhall
Arup Associates

Vauxhall Cross is possibly the saddest and unluckiest part of London; along with an overground railway line carried on brick arches, it is the meeting place of seven major roads arranged as a type of super roundabout race track. It has been further blighted by Terry Farrell's ludicrous monster for MI6 and Broadway Malyan's St George Wharf, a fancied competitor in the 'worst ever London building' contest. In the midst of this witches brew is Arup Associates' lively little bus station comprising a pair of long undulating canopies with silver eaves and soffits. The canopies, which are supported on raking columns, flies off at the east end into two huge cantilevers. At this end are the corrugated, silver siding clad offices, presumably evoking greyhound buses, although few of these have found their way over Vauxhall Bridge.

Whitechapel Idea Store (474)
2003–2004
Whitechapel Road, E1;
tube: Whitechapel
Adjaye Associates

An 'Idea Store' is a library with computer facilities for people who dislike scary-sounding old names. The library block itself is five storeys with concrete slabs and frame. The simple envelope is clad entirely in a glass, aluminium and timber curtain wall with slender coloured panels evoking the stripped awnings of the nearby market stalls, as well as books on a shelf. A lower block to the rear accommodates a dance studio and treatment centre. The ground floor is accessed directly from the street and the upper floors via escalators open to the street and situated in a gap between a double façade. This is an exciting space and a direct means of expressing openness. The other spaces are light and cheery and, best of all, well used. Like the borough's other new libraries, the Whitechapel Idea Store has experienced a dramatic increase in use compared to the library it replaced. Adjaye Associates have completed a similar building on East India Dock Road in Poplar.

Ben Pimlott Building, Goldsmiths College (475)
2003–2004
New Cross Road, SE14;
tube: New Cross/New Cross Gate
Alsop Architects

Goldsmiths is a leading art school and this new building provided additional studio space, particularly for digital arts. It is a large seven-storey rectangular box with a two-storey chunk removed at the top of the west end creating a terrace. The long north face is entirely clad in a glass and aluminium curtain wall. The other walls are clad in standing seam aluminium sheeting with small punched windows. This modest base is enlivened on the south side with an expressive external escape staircase and bits of 'scribble' designed by the architect in aluminium and stuck on the building wherever it becomes monotonous. The terrace is surrounded by something similar but three dimensional, nine metres high

and in steel. The flexible interiors are of no great interest, though the building's position on the hill gives it spectacular views of the city to the north.

Unicorn Theatre (476)
2003–2005
Tooley Street, SE1; tube: London Bridge
Keith Williams Architects

This theatre is a very enjoyable little building that looks even better for its setting in the corporate sludge of the 'More London Development' behind. About five storeys high, the exterior is a highly modelled, cubist composition with elements in blue brick, render, copper sheeting and blue mosaic along with large glazed areas. The

larger of the two auditoria is clad in copper and sits over the foyer space and the studio theatre. The former seats 340 in a roughly square volume, with semi-circular seating and galleries; the balcony fronts and side walls have dark slatted timber linings. The studio has a thrust stage and seats 120. The foyer spaces and circulation are spatially intriguing, exciting and interestingly lit.

School of Slavonic and
East European Studies (477)
2003–2005
Taviton Street, WC1; tube: Euston Square
Short and Associates

This school is the largest single centre for the study of Eastern European languages and culture in Britain and houses classrooms, offices and a considerable library. The architects pay little attention to the vagaries of architectural fashion, but have

a long-standing fixation with environmental issues and traditional forms of construction. As infilling in a Georgian street, the site is very cramped. The four-storey street façade is in brick with windows arched except for the row at the top under a continuous pre-cast concrete frieze. The windows either side of the central entrance step up to reflect stairs behind. The overall effect is reminiscent of Eastern European Expressionist architecture, which may seem appropriate, although all of this architect's buildings have a similar feel. Behind the flat front the building takes the form of a semi-circle around a glazed triangular atrium. The atrium and the prominent chimneys are elements of the complex natural ventilation system.

Young Vic Theatre (478)
2003–2006
The Cut, SE1; tube: Southwark
Haworth Tompkins Architects

The new building replaces a famous 'temporary' building of the 1960s, which, well past its design life, had become severely dilapidated. As the name suggests, the theatre is focused on youth and the new building has a distinctly cheerful, ad hoc student's union feel about it. The new theatre retains the old irregular octagonal auditorium, which is clad in modish metal lathing and a tiled butcher's shop, which now serves as a reception space. Two new studios to the west of the foyer are clad in dark brick laid at angles to create a textured surface. The same architects recently refurbished Lyons, Israel and Ellis' 1957 brutalist theatre workshop building further west along The Cut, which looks much better for the work.

Dixon Jones Architects

Naill McLaughlin

David Chipperfield

Michael Hopkins

Foreign Office Architects

David Adjaye

Norman Foster

Richard Rogers

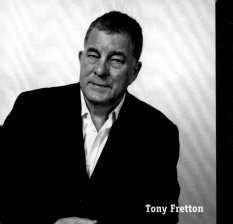

Tony Fretton

Richard McCormac

Nick Grimshaw

Caruso St John Architects

Zaha Hadid

Chris Wilkinson

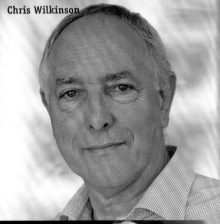

Harworth Tompkins Architects

Eva Jiricna

Wembley Stadium (479)
2003–2007
Olympic Way, HA9;
tube: Wembley Central/Wembley Park
Foster and Partners, HOK Sport

The bowl of the stadium is magnificent and contributes to an excellent match-day experience. Compared to most other British stadiums, it is highly successful in moving 90,000 people in and out and keeping them fed and watered. The concourses for the cheap seats are spartan, tough and partially open to the air, which is all as it should be. The upper concourses to the more expensive seats are bland and corporate, like an airport lounge, which is very much not as it should be. The external architectural treatment is likewise lacking in character, except for the notorious and embarrassing arch.

Victoria Miro Gallery (480)
2004–2006
Wharf Road, N1; tube: Old Street
Claudio Silvestrin Architects,
Michael Drain Architects

The existing furniture factory was converted by Trevor Horne Architects in 2000 in a pleasant renovation that retained much of the structure and fabric. Michael Drain Architects converted further industrial premises to the rear to accommodate the Parasol Unit, foundation for contemporary art. Finally, the rooftop extension is a six-metre high gallery, with small mezzanines, positioned on the top of a three-storey, Victorian brick industrial building. The new building's geometry is slightly skewed with respect to the old building, emphasizing the almost surreal impression of the one simply being dropped on top of the other. The new gallery is approached by a very long, very narrow staircase of six flights and seventy-two treads. Another similar stair abuts the atrium, around which the top three floors are arranged, thereby creating a deceptively complex small space. Huge windows allow wonderful views of rooftop and sky.

Emirates Stadium (481)
2004–2006
Ashburton Grove, N19;
tube: Holloway Road
HOK Sport

The Emirates is better integrated with its location than Wembley with some echo of old-style stadiums nestling in amongst the housing of the people who support the team. Otherwise, it shares Wembley's strengths and weaknesses. Inside, the stadium looks wonderful on matchday and functions well; outside, the cladding is unexciting and characterless, though the floating roof above is satisfying and its structure feels both proportionate and

rational. Some of the concourses are completely enclosed, which is unpleasant and oppressive.

Classroom of the Future   (482)
2005–2006
Various locations, currently at Haver-stock School, Haverstock Hill, NW1;
tube: Chalk Farm
Gollifer Langston Architects

A number of classrooms were commissioned as part of the government's investigation into the design of future educational spaces and this contribution from Gollifer Langston was the most charismatic. If the concept was somewhat weak and the mode of transportation on the back of a truck somewhat less than futuristic, at least the object itself is beautiful. It is an almost square aluminium tube with sides inclining inwards slightly and rounded corners. The classroom levels itself on steel legs and expands outwards to the sides. The pretty top-lit interior is wood lined and carries an array of the most up-to-date IT equipment and teaching aids. The engineers were Michael Hadi Associates.

White Cube Gallery   (483)
2005–2006
Mason's Yard, Duke Street, SW1;
tube: Green Park
MRJ Rundell and Associates

Built on a landlocked site previously occupied by a electrical substation, the gallery is accessed via arched passages.

To achieve the accommodation required on a very cramped site, an eight-metre basement was dug to form a double height gallery, top-lit via glazed slots in the pavement surface. The ground floor, which also houses a gallery space, is of in-situ concrete and glass. The two floors above are rendered with long slot windows under a recessed glass attic storey. Every superfluous detail has been eradicated for an ultra-minimalist effect.

Peter Harrison Planetarium   (484)
2005–2007
Blackheath Avenue, Greenwich Park, SE10;
train and DLR: Greenwich
Allies and Morrison

The project involved the restoration of and alterations to William Crisp's 1899 South Building, including the insertion of an impressive three-storey helical stair in steel. The new 118-seat planetarium and foyer are adjacent and mostly underground. The hemisphere of the planetarium is housed in an inclined cone, which rises above the paved terrace. Inclined at 51.5°, the latitude of Greenwich, the cone is situated on the prime merid-

ian. The truncated face is clad in frameless glass, while the curved faces, which were formed in concrete, are clad in bronze strips welded on site to form a seamless platonic solid, except for a joint on the prime meridian line. This impressive piece of expensive craftsmanship can sometimes be a little too hot to handle.

Office Building,
5 Aldermanbury Square (485)
2005–2007
Aldermanbury Square, EC2;
tube: Moorgate
Eric Parry Architects

in stainless steel with the expression of alternating slabs suppressed to form double height bays. There is a deep recession on the north and south sides creating the effect of two slender towers, while the other façades curve inward slightly as they ascend. There is some indefinable affinity with the nearby Wood Street Police Station tower (no. 370). To the east of the tower a new, genuinely attractive, public space was created, which continues under part of the building to form a public route between Wood Street and Aldermanbury Square.

Gorilla House, London Zoo (486)
2005–2007
Regent's Park, Prince Albert Road, NW1;
tube: Regent's Park/Camden Town
Proctor and Matthews

This is the best of recent City office buildings by a considerable margin. The steel frame is located in front of the glazing of the eighteen-storey tower and is clad

AFTER MODERNISM

This was a replacement for the iconic Tecton Gorilla House (no. 317), which, whatever its architectural virtues, was never well suited for housing gorillas. The Tecton building was first superceded, in 1973, by John Toovey's Sobell Pavilion, parts of which are incorporated in the new scheme. The gorillas occupy a moated 'island', in the north-east corner of which is the enclosure. The principle feature is a high-roofed walkway, glazed with forty-millimetre-thick glass to the 'island' and supported by bamboo columns. Its plywood linings are cut with textile patterns from the gorilla's African homeland region. There is also a new glazed day gym, private sleeping area and education room. If the creatures must be kept in a zoo, at least this does not feel like such a bad environment.

Kings Place (487)
2005–2008
York Way, N1;
tube: Kings Cross St Pancras
Dixon Jones Architects

Kings Place is an unusual development in that alongside the standard offices, retail space and restaurants, there are two concert halls and an exhibition space; these reflect nothing more the private enthusiasms and public spiritedness of the developer, who is himself an unusual man. The site is next to a small canal basin in what used to be the wilderness behind Kings Cross Station. The building comprises one six-storey, 'L'-shaped block with an eight-storey drum between the arms of the 'L' with a public atrium space in the interstices. The facades are generally large windows in stone clad walls. To York Way this changes, for no very obvious reason, to a slick undulating frameless glass curtain wall over exposed columns. Internally, the atrium is somewhat clinical, but the oak-lined concert halls are attractive.

Broadgate Tower (488)
2005–2008
Primrose Street, EC2; tube: Liverpool Street
Skidmore, Owings and Merrill

The thirty-three-storey tower sits besides a thirteen-storey hulk similar in massing to the earlier phases of Broadgate to the south (see no. 408), with a lifeless glass-roofed galleria between the two. The whole development is built on a slab over the railway lines leaving Liverpool Street and there are suggestions that land to the north will soon be similarly developed. For this latest phase, SOM abandoned the neoclassicism of earlier phases in favour of a silver, near Hi-tech, modernism. Some

parts of the framing system are clad and expressed to add visual interest to the slick glass cladding. The tower is a thin parallelogram so at least it appears slender from some viewpoints.

Performing Arts Building, St Marylebone School (489)
2006–2007
Marylebone High Street, W1;
tube: Baker Street
Gumuchdjian Architects

The school occupies a very cramped, inner urban site with no real opportunities for expansion. It is, however, an old and very popular school, which found itself lacking the sort of facilities now considered essential. The only way of achieving some improvement was to occupy part of the tiny playground. To minimise the impact of this, the new double height gym is sunk into the ground alongside a canopied light well with a cheerily painted steel access stair; these areas are formed behind beautifully constructed in-situ concrete walls. Above is a three-storey concrete framed classroom block with glass and glass block infill and corten steel spandrel panels. The east end boasts a corten clad stair tower with a clock at the top. It is a very satisfying and ingenious little building.

Rivington Place (490)
2006–2007
Rivington Street, EC2; tube: Liverpool Street,
train: Shoreditch High Street
Adjaye Associates

The building houses two immigrant arts organisations offering exhibition spaces and a library as well as offices. The site is a tight urban corner in recently fashionable Shoreditch, on which the black clad foursquare block has a sombre presence. The building has four storeys, although this is disguised by small windows with more than one row to each storey; the windows alternate in a chequerboard pattern with dark grey concrete cladding. The sawtooth roof is also dark grey, a theme that persists inside, where there is a double height entrance hall and exhibition space at ground floor level and a further exhibition space and attractive library above. Private offices fill the upper storeys.

Office Building, 189 Oxford Street (491)
2006–2007
Oxford Street, W1; tube: Oxford Circus
Future Systems

The project involved the re-cladding of four storeys of a 1950s office building over shops on Oxford Street. Small though it is, it is an interesting little piece of architecture. The walls have been completely replaced with a series of interlocking, elongated, hexagonal frameless glass blisters. The effect is

truly crystalline and jewel-like. It is reminiscent in its shapes of Czech cubist architecture of the 1920s, perhaps no great surpise consdering that Future Systems partner Jan Kaplický was born and raised in Prague, except that Future Systems' rhetoric has usually been disdainful of the past.

Reiss Headquarters and Shop (492)
2006–2008
Barrett Street, W1; tube: Bond Street
Squire and Partners

Reiss are a London fashion house and this building just off Oxford Street provides two floors of retail space, four floors of offices, studios and cutting rooms and a penthouse flat recessed on the top floor. The principle façade to Barrett Street

faces south and is fully glazed. Except for a large opening around the store doors, this façade is obscured by a 'rain screen' formed of large clear acrylic slabs, which have been textured with ribs and grooves

formed across the surface and are supported on a steel frame. The cladding does provide the desired impact, appearing like a shimmering fabric, and is especially effective when illuminated at night. It does, however, obscure all views out of the building, which might be desirable in a shop but is surely less so in offices. The building also features a cranked concrete stair in a super high strength compact concrete composite, a material little used in Britain to date.

Bridge Academy (493)
2006–2008
Laburnam Street, E2;
tube: Old Street, train: Haggerston
Building Design Partnership

Located on a canal side site, the school is composed of three parts. The main six-storey horseshoe-shaped block contains classrooms wrapped around a library that is suspended over the central hall and sits underneath a plastic covered atrium. This is joined by a three-storey Performing Arts block and a two-storey sports hall. The outer walls of the main block are cranked in section and lined with timber boards with a red, rendered,

attic recessed storey; the arms of the horseshoe step down to form terraces with render and glass faces. The Performing Arts building is an irregular polygon rendered in red with a wire network for creepers. The sports building is a simple blue brick box with a long slit window. If it all sounds a little like a frenetic jumble then it is, but in a lively sort of way.

Apartment Building, 177 Tower Bridge Road (494)
2006–2008
Druid Street, SE1; tube: London Bridge
Glas Architects

A cheerful little tower overlooking the railway lines on the approach to London

Bridge Station, the building accommodates five floors of flats above a café. The plan shape is an irregular rectangle to fit the site, with a slight projection marking the stair tower. All the corners are rounded to reflect the characteristics of the cladding, which is corrugated metal sheeting. The cladding sheets are coloured in three different greys and bright orange and are arranged, most effectively, in a dazzle camouflage pattern. Most of the ground floor is shop front for the café.

Parkside Housing (495)
2006–2008
Seven Sisters Road, N4;
tube: Finsbury Park
Sergison Bates Architects

Situated overlooking the park, the three blocks of flats take their cue for massing and form from the Victorian Parkside Villas. They are very austere and even sombre. The slab edges are expressed as

concrete bands, all the windows are full height, the roof very shallowly pitched and the cladding is brick. The front elevations have a couple of slightly chamfered steps and there is some slight stepping in the wall thickness. It is remarkable how much presence these buildings establish with such simple, undemonstrative means. The two blocks on the road have five and six storeys and the block to the rear only three. The flats are well planned and lit and each flat has a recessed balcony.

Monsoon Office Building   (496)
2007–2008
Nicholas Road, off Olaf Street, W11;
tube: Latimer Road/Wood Lane
Allford Hall Monaghan Morris

This seven-storey headquarters building for the fashion chain is sited in a somewhat neglected and unloved part of town

next to a motorway. The structure is a concrete diagrid, which manifests itself at roof level as a characterful sawtooth profile. The core is mostly a separate element on the south side and the floors are virtually square, cut away to form a dramatic atrium space with stairs all the way up the building. The cladding is glass with bright yellow spandrel panels and vertical white louvres. The area around the building is being developed by the same client and architect team,

but the speculative buildings are not of the same standard.

Office Building, 10 Hills Place   (497)
2008–2009
Hills Place, W1; tube: Oxford Circus
Amanda Levete Architects

Amanda Levete added three upper storeys to an existing office building and clad the whole structure in a super sleek skin. The site is almost hidden in an alley off Oxford Street and the shiny façade is calculated to catch people's eye as they pass along the busy street. The ground floor is clad in sheets of glass backed with steel mesh and a dichroic film, which glows when illuminated at night. The upper floors are finished in silver tongue and groove aluminium slats, bent around four large eye-like windows tilted upwards to the sky. The effect is most striking. There is nothing of great interest in the interiors, except around these amazing windows. The charming little building with carved reliefs on the corner of Hills Place was the central London outpost of the Festival of Britain and was created by Ronald Ward and Partners in 1951.

Forthcoming Developments (498)

The London Olympic bid specifically forswore extravagant monuments, aware that these often embarrass later. Designed by HOK Sport, the principle stadium is modest and will become more so when the upper tiers are removed, leaving a capacity of only 25,000. Zaha Hadid's promising aquatics centre has been downsized with clumsy temporary seating tacked onto the sides. A handball arena by Make Architects and a velodrome by Hopkins Architects promise to be decent rather than stunning buildings. Elsewhere, a bridge by Heneghan Peng provides some hope for excitement. The Olympic Village is being designed by some reputable architects but, rising to thirteen storeys, it seems developers have had the ear of the promoters. It is to be hoped that the Lower Lea Valley, now one of London's dirty little secrets, will be left much the better for the Olympic experience.

London has been growing in recent years and feels noticeably full. The Thames Gateway, a long and poorly-defined stretch of the Thames and its banks, has been identified as the place for further expansion. The landscape is flat, marshy, atmospheric and by no means welcoming. The construction of a vast shopping centre at Stratford surrounded by a mini Dallas or Croyden of commercial towers and residential development is underway. A new town for 40,000 people is also being constructed at Ebbsfleet, chillingly reminiscent of Thamesmead, a failed 1960s new town ten kilometres away. Both Stratford and Ebbsfleet are on the high speed rail link to Paris and this, it is hoped, will guarantee the success of the developments.

An extension to the East London line with four new stations just east of the City is set to open in 2010 and looks to be architecturally 'modest'. Work has also started on Crossrail, an east-west heavy rail link across the whole city; there will be no new stations but significant alterations will be required to existing ones. A spur off the Northern line has been proposed to serve the new American Embassy at Nine Elms and Battersea Power Station.

Jean Nouvel's 'One New Change' to the east of St Paul's and Renzo Piano's

London Olympics, Aquatics Centre.

Central Saint Giles are nearing completion; published drawings and early views into the sites suggest that these are not their authors' best efforts. Rem Koolhaus's new headquarters building for N M Rothschild & Sons, a fifteen-storey glass tower behind St Stephen Walbrook, looks more promising.

The final frenzy of the late boom inevitably brought a spate of office tower projects and the fate of these is not entirely clear. Forty-four storey Heron Tower is currently going up, as are Renzo Piano's tapering 'Shard' at London Bridge and Kohl Pederson Fox's 'Pinnacle'. Richard Rogers' tapering 'Cheese Grater' and Rafael Viñoly's loathesome 'Walkie Talkie' appear to be on hold.

Beyond the City there a number of projects located on significant sites with long and contested histories. Hackney Council have recently adopted a development plan for the Bishopsgate Goods Yard site in Shoreditch. Viñoly has finally submitted a planning application for the Battersea Power Station development and new masterplanners have been appointed for the huge Chelsea Barracks site. It remains to be seen how these projects will progress but if the past is any guide then it will be slow going.

Since the National Lottery was established in 1994, most of London's cultural buildings have received funding for refurbishments or extensions and there would seem little left to do. However, funding has been confirmed for a brick ziggurat extension to the Tate Modern by Herzog & de Meuron, new galleries for the British Museum by Richard Rogers and a new building on the South Bank for the British Film Institute. Next door, Jubilee Gardens themselves were the subject of a design competition won by West 8. A long awaited London debut for Zaha Hadid is anticipated for 2010 in the shape of a new school building in Brixton.

The latest Lord Mayor has scrapped his predecessor's '100 Public Places' initiative for new or improved outdoor spaces, although two schemes which were part of the initiative will continue. Improvements to Exhibition Road and Euston Road by Dixon Jones and Terry Farrell respectively are much needed and eagerly awaited.

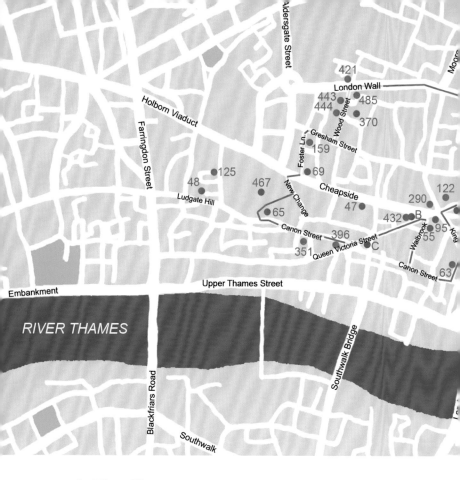

1. The City

Duration: 1hr. 40 min

Tips for a break!
George & Vulture, Castle Court, Cornhill (A)
Le Coq d'Argent, No.1 Poultry (B)
Sweetings, Queen Victoria Street (C)
Lamb Tavern, Leadenhall Market (D)

The 'square mile', as it implies, is small but very dense; much of the medieval street pattern remains with many tiny and architecturally interesting passages and courts. During the week the City bustles with workers, but is deserted at the weekend as no one lives there. Buildings date from the Norman period up to today, although Victorian and Modern office buildings dominate along with largely redundant Renaissance churches.

From the Tower (3) Trinity Square Gardens lie to the west with the Port of London Building (280) and Lutyens' monument to the Merchant Navy; beyond is the fascinating All Hallows Barking (21). Continuing westwards, Nos. 33–35 Eastcheap is Roumieu's absurd Gothic fancy (193), while a larger and more absurd Gothic fancy is Minster Court (412) in Mincing Lane heading north. At the top is Fenchurch Street with Lloyd's Register of Shipping (249); Lime Street heads north from Fenchurch to the atmospheric Leadenhall Market (218). Beyond are the Lloyd's (402) and Commercial Union (376) buildings in Leadenhall Street. On a loop around Creechurch, Bevis Marks and Bury Street are three of the City's oldest churches: St Andrew Undershaft (28)

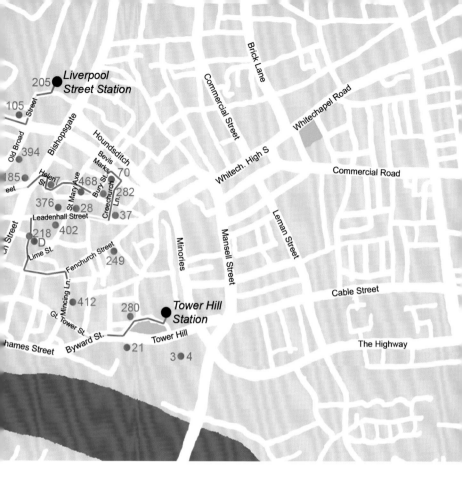

205 ● **Liverpool Street Station**

105

Old Broad Street

Bishopsgate

Houndsditch

Bevis Marks

394 ●

185 ●

eet

Helen St ● 7

St Mary Axe

468 ●

Bury St

Creechurch Ln.

70

282

376 ● St ● 28

37

402

218 ●

D

Lime St.

Fenchurch Street

249

Mincing Ln.

Gt. Tower St.

412 ●

280

● 21

Byward St.

Tower Hill

Minories

Mansell Street

Leman Street

● **Tower Hill Station**

3 ● 4

hames Street

Leadenhall Street

Commercial Street

Brick Lane

Whitechapel Road

Whitech. High S

Commercial Road

Cable Street

The Highway

St Katharine Cree (37) and St Helen Bishopgate (7) as well as the oldest synagogue, Bevis Marks (70), Berlage's Holland House (282) and the Gherkin (468).

Over Bishopsgate west down Threadneedle Street, there are Natwest banks new and old (185, 394). At the end is Mansion House Street, the most important nexus of the City, and home to St Mary Woolnoth (82), Mansion House (95), Bank of England (122), Royal Exchange (170), Midland Bank (290) and No.1 Poultry (432). On a cramped road junction it is an impressive display. Two unmissable Wren churches are on a loop down King William Street, Abchurch Lane, Cannon Street and Walbrook: St Mary Abchurch (63) in its atmospheric little yard and Wren's masterpiece, St Stephen Walbrook (55).

Queen Victoria Street and Cannon Street go west towards St Paul's (65) past Credit Lyonnais (396) and Bracken House (351), two of the City's more charismatic office buildings. North of the cathedral is Paternoster Square (466) with Amen Court (48) and the Stationer's Hall (125) a little to the west. At the north east corner of the cathedral is Cheapside with views of the tower of St Mary-Le-Bow (47). St Vedast alias Foster (69) and Goldsmiths' Hall (159) lie to the north on Foster Lane with Wren's St Anne and St Agnes at the top. Eastwards into Gresham Street leads to Wood Street with its enigmatic Police Station (370) and a plethora of new office buildings (421, 443, 444, 485) – Aldermanbury House is the best. London Wall heads east to the younger George Dance's exquisite All Hallows-on-the-Wall (105), to the north of which is Liverpool Street Station (205) and a well-earned break.

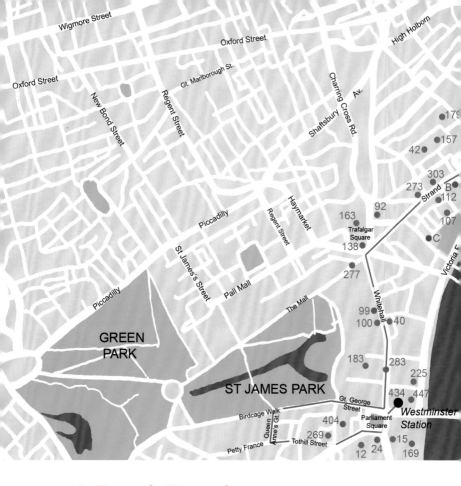

2. Towards Westminster

Duration: 1hr. 40 min

Tips for a break!
Ye Olde Cheshire Cheese, Wine Office Court, Fleet Street (A)
The Coal Hole, Strand (B)
Gordon's Wine Bar, Villiers Street (C)
Somerset House Terrace Café, Strand (D)

Ludgate Hill, Fleet Street and Strand form a continuous thoroughfare linking the twin cities of London and Westminster. The area is predominantly in commercial or institutional use and nothing remains of the large aristocratic residences lining the Strand in the 17th and 18th centuries. Buildings from all eras line the streets to either side and are some of the most charming in London.

St Martin, Ludgate (60) lies west of the cathedral and St Bride, Fleet Street (52) down Bride Lane to the south. Fleet Street itself has many interesting office buildings from the Victorian period on-

wards, of which the Daily Express (304) and the Daily Telegraph (295) buildings are the best. A rare half-timbered, jettied building on the south side is the entrance to the Inner Temple (17, 35); there are lovely walks around this and Middle Temple with fine examples of medieval architecture in Temple Church (9) and Middle Temple Hall (31). North across Fleet Street from the Temple is Lincoln's Inn (17) approached via Chancery Lane with the Public Record Office (178) and Holden's Law Society Building (160). Lincoln's Inn itself has pleasant gardens, Hall (20), Chapel (36) and Library (171).

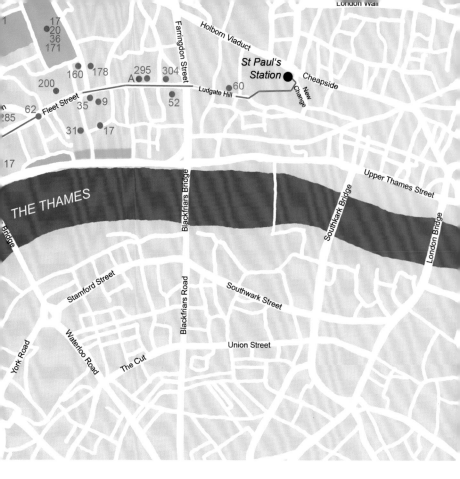

Farringdon Street

Holborn Viaduct

St Paul's
Station ●

Cheapside

160 178   295 304
A ●●
200   ●60
Ludgate Hill   New Change

62 Fleet Street 35 ●9   52

31●   ●17

17
20
36
171

●85

31●   ●17

17

THE THAMES

Blackfriars Bridge

Southwark Bridge

Upper Thames Street

London Bridge

Bridge

Stamford Street

Blackfriars Road

Southwark Street

Waterloo Road

The Cut

Union Street

York Road

In Lincoln's Inn Fields is the incompara-
ble Soane Museum (121).

The end of Fleet Street and the City and
the start of Strand and Westminster is
marked by the spikiest of gryphons and the
Royal Courts of Justice (200) followed by St
Clement Danes (62) and St Mary le Strand
(90). North of St Mary is the Aldwych
with Bush House (285) and to the south
the wonderful Somerset House (117) and
Waterloo Bridge (336). Beyond the bridge,
south of the Strand lies the Savoy Chapel
on Savoy Street, an interesting survivor
from the 1510s. Further west, in John Adam
Street, is the Royal Society of Arts (112) and
other Adelphi fragments (107). North of
the Strand, approached via Southampton
Street, is Covent Garden with church (42),
Market (157) and Opera House (179). The
most interesting buildings on the Strand
itself are the Savoy and Adelphi Theatres
(298, 303) and Zimbabwe House (273) near
the west end. The stuccoed terraces at the
west end are Nash improvements.

The Strand ends in Trafalgar Square
(138) with the National Gallery (163), St
Martin in the Fields (92) and Admiralty
Arch (277). Whitehall runs south from
here with an array of royal and government buildings, the best being Jones' Banqueting House (40), Horse Guards (99),
the Cenotaph (283), Dover House (100)
and the Foreign and Commonwealth Office (183). Off to the east on Derby Gate
is New Scotland Yard (225). Whitehall
ends in Parliament Square and Broad
Sanctuary, a Unesco World Heritage
site, with Westminster Hall and Palace
(15, 169), Westminster Abbey (12) and St
Margaret's Church (24). Methodist Central Hall (269) and the Queen Elizabeth
II Conference Centre (404) overlook the
same space; behind these is the beautiful
Queen Anne's Gate with its pre-Georgian
brick townhouses. North of Westminster
Hall is Hopkins' Portcullis House (447)
and Underground Station (434).

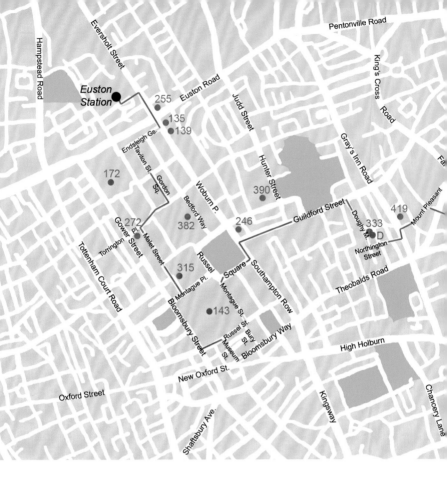

3. Clerkenwell, Holborn & Bloomsbury

Duration: 2hrs.

Tips for a break!
St John Bar and Restaurant, St John Street (A)
Jerusalem Tavern, Britton Street (B)
The Green, Clerkenwell Green (C)
The Duke, Roger Street (D)

Clerkenwell is one of London's oldest districts beyond the old wall and Holburn too appears early in London's history, although was only systematically developed in 17th and 18th centuries.

The well disguised entrance to the Barbican Arts Centre (392) can be accessed from Moorgate tube via Union and Silk Streets; from here the rest of the vast complex (381) can be accessed including sections of London's Roman Wall, St Giles Cripplegate (25) and the Museum of London (391). Silk Street runs into Whitecross Street; at the top is Hawksmoor's St Luke's Church (87) and, before

that, Fortune and Fann Streets run east between the Barbican and Golden Lane Estates (353). Off Aldersgate, Carthusian Street runs west through Charterhouse Square, with the Charterhouse (30) and Florin Court (330), and alongside Smithfield Market (188). To the south of the market lie London's oldest church, St Bartholomew the Great (5), and Britain's oldest hospital, St Bart's (94). St John Street, Lane and Square to the north lead to Clerkenwell Green, site of the Marx Memorial Library, and are home to St John's Gate (256) and St John's Priory (6), both remnants of the Knights Hospi-

taller's Clerkenwell Priory. Clerkenwell
Close runs north off the Green past St
James's Parish Church into Pear Tree
Court Peabody Estate (219). Over Far-
ringdon Road Ray Street leads into a
picturesque network of streets – Lon-
don's 19th-century 'Little Italy'. Warner
Street and Mount Pleasant head west to
Gray's Inn Road, the ITN building (419)
and Holborn.

Across Gray's Inn Road; Northington
Street heads west to John's and Doughty
Mews. On the former is a 1930s mixed-
use scheme (333) with a wonderfully
preserved pub. Doughty Mews is the site
of some recent, very small-scale domestic developments. Guildford Street west
from the end of the Mews passes the
Brunswick Centre (390) and Great Ormond Street Children's Hospital ending
in Russell Square. The Square retains
some of its Georgian character despite
subsequent development; most strident
is the manic Russell Hotel (246).

South from the Square, Montague
Street passes the British Museum (143).
The parallel Bloomsbury Street returns
north through Bedford Square, the
best preserved and loveliest of central
Georgian Squares. Malet Street goes
further north into the heart of the university district with the Senate Building (315), University College (172), the
Institute of Education (382), the School
of African and Oriental Studies Library,
Dillons Bookshop (272) and Gordon
Square. North of the square Taviton
Street is home to the eccentric School
of Slavonic and Eastern European Studies. Endsleigh Gardens runs east to the
junction of Woburn Place and Euston
Road. This generally unattractive street
has some delightful buildings: Woburn
Walk (139), St Pancras New Church (135)
and Euston Road Fire Station (255) along
with Euston Station.

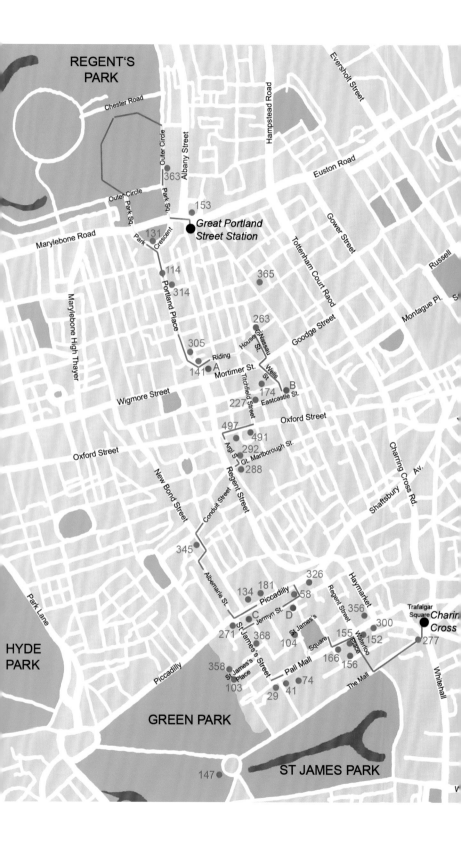

4. The West End

Duration: 1hr. 50 min.

Tips for a break!
The Heights Bar, St Georges Hotel, Langham Place (A)
The Champion, Wells Street (B)
Wiltons, Jermyn Street (C)
The Red Lion, Duke of York Street (D)

Soane's most lavish church, Holy Trinity (153) is outside Great Portland Street tube station; just north is the Royal College of Physicians (363) and Regent's Park with its various Nash developments. The north end of the Nash route is Park Crescent (131) bisected by Portland Place (114) on which are some Adams' houses as well at the Royal Institute of British Architects (314) and Broadcasting House (305). Portland Place turns into Langham Place around Nash's All Souls Church (141). Riding House Street runs east from the church to York House (263) and a little knot of streets are home to a number of fanciful fin de siècle buildings; the Post Office Tower (365) looms overhead. Wells Street going south passes All Saints, Margaret Street (174) with the curious Welsh Baptist Chapel (227) on Eastcastle Street. Great Titchfield runs south to Oxford Street.

Across Oxford Street is one interesting Future Systems façade (491); a little way to the west on Hills Place is another (497). Ideal House (292) and Liberty's Department Store (288) lie on Great Marlborough Street to the south. Across Regent Street, Conduit Street has an interesting collection of commercial buildings including one by Treadwell and Martin at No. 20; at the end is the Time Life Building (345) with its Henry Moore sculptures.

Piccadilly crosses the bottom of Albemarle Street; to the east are Burlington Arcade (134), the Royal Academy (181), St James's Church (58) and Simpsons (326) as well as Shaw's mutilated Piccadilly Hotel and an exuberant 'Wrennaissence' bank by Luytens. Jermyn Street runs parallel with Piccadilly towards St James's Street. At the top of St James's is the subtle Royal Insurance Office (271). Below is the equally subtle Economist Building (368) next door to John Crunden's Boodle's Club. St James's Place, a narrow cul-de-sac to the west, houses both Spencer House (103) and Lasdun's apartment building (358). The south end of St James's Street is a longstanding royal precinct with St James's Palace (29), the Queen's Chapel (41) and Marlborough House (74). Pall Mall eastwards was the centre of London's club land with the Reform Club (166), the United Services Club (152) and the Athenaeum (155). Further east are the Crane Bennett Office (300) and New Zealand House (356). St James's Square north of Pall Mall is the oldest in the West End, laid out in 1665, and has some fine 18th-century houses such as Lichfield House (104) at No. 15. The last leg of Nash's ceremonial route, Waterloo Place, goes south to St James's Park past the Duke of York Column via a mighty flight of steps bisecting Carlton House (156). At the foot of the steps is the Mall with Buckingham Palace (147) and Admiralty Arch (277) with Trafalgar Square and Charing Cross station beyond.

5. Finsbury & Islington

Duration: 2hrs. 10 min.

Tips for a break!
Three Kings, Clerkenwell Close (A)
The Peasant, St John Street (B)
The Crown, Cloudesley Road (C)
Moro, Exmouth Market (D)

Islington, like many modern London suburbs, was once a village outside the City and a place of escape. It soon assumed the character of a suburb as more people chose to live there and was thoroughly developed in the 18th and early 19th centuries. It is now a most decorative and desirable residential area with many Georgian streets and squares.

Finsbury was a marshy waste lying northeast of the City. It was drained for use as a recreation area in the 17th century and developed in the 18th. It has some Georgian houses, but the area is less coherent than Islington with more commerce and areas of poverty.

Kings Cross St Pancras (177, 191) is the capital's biggest rail and tube interchange. Kings Cross Road and Vernon Street head southwest to Percy Circus, off which is Bevin Court (348). This atmospheric part of town was the scene of Arnold Bennett's novel *Riceyman Steps* and retains something of the lost air that haunts the book. East across the very handsome Lloyd Square is Amwell Street on which is the unusual, for Britain, expressionist brick, Charles Rowan House of 1930. Over Roseberry Avenue is the now defunct Edwardian Finsbury Town Hall, behind which is Exmouth Market. At the west end are the Church of the Holy Redeemer (222) and, just to the south along Pine Street, Tecton's ground-breaking Finsbury Health Centre (328).

East along Bowling Green Lane are good examples of both early and late Victorian Board Schools (204, 236). St John Street runs north up to Angel Islington passing the Spa Green Estate (340) and Sadler's Wells Theatre (442).

Upper Street, a lively shopping and night life street, continues northwards; to the west of it lies Islington's Georgian residential district. The suggested route is just one through a pleasant and interesting area. Theberton Street runs west across Gibson Square and Liverpool Road into Cloudesley Square and charming Cloudesley Road. Richmond Avenue at the top of Cloudesley Road was developed slightly later and shows signs of early Victorian eclecticism. On Thornhill Square just to the north is Beresford Pite's exquisite Edwardian branch library (265). The top of Upper Street is accessed via Bewdley Street and Islington Park Street; here is the Union Chapel (211), which now has a double life as a place of worship and a most interesting gig venue. Beyond is Canonbury Square, perhaps the handsomest of all the Islington squares. To the east via Canonbury Road and Grove is a glimpse of the future in the shape of the Hauer-King House (427). Willow Bridge Road to the north runs into Balls Pond Road which ends at Highbury and Islington station to the west.

6. The Near East:
Spitalfields, Whitechapel, Shoreditch

Duration: 1hr. 40 min.

Tips for a break!
Pride of Spitalfields, Heneage Street (A)
Tayyab's, Fieldgate Street (B)
The Golden Heart, Commercial Street (C)
Dino's Grill, Commercial Street (D)

The East End can present a rather bedraggled spectacle. Waves of immigrants, various industries and the Blitz have come and gone as have planning, social engineering and slum clearance. The outcome of this eventful past is a highly disrupted urban fabric. There are beautiful fragments scattered amongst grim social housing blocks, forlorn waste grounds and ruined industrial hulks. If it is short on conventional urban beauty and structure, it has plenty of atmosphere, variety and, in places, an air of lonely mystery.

Royal Mint and Cable Streets lead east from Tower Hill tube station; Cable Street is famous for the violent confrontation with the British Union of Fascists in 1936. To the south along Ensign Street and Graces Alley is Wilton's Music Hall (180). Further east is Cannon Street Road; at the south end is St George in the East (80) and the forlorn Tobacco Warehouse (129). Further south lie the old dockside districts of Shadwell and Wapping, which retain some old dock buildings alongside much soulless recent development. Cannon Street Road runs north to Commercial Street – at the west end is Whitechapel High Street and the recently refurbished Whitechapel Art Gallery (247).

Brick Lane, running north, is the historic principle street of Spitalfields, named for the medieval brick fields in the vicinity. Later it became identified with weaving brought by the Huguenots in the 18th century and was worked by East European Jews in the 19th century

and Bangladeshis in the 20th. Some remnants of this history can still be seen. The touching Christchurch School (203) is still in use. A Huguenot church (97) became a Synagogue and is now a Mosque. Hanbury, Fournier and Princelet Streets to the west of Brick Lane form a tight quarter of impressive proto-Georgian terraces built by the Huguenots as homes and workplaces. Hawksmoor's domineering Christ Church (79) is opposite Spitalfield Market (221) on Fournier Street, while Princelet Street hides an evocative semi-derelict synagogue (196). Beyond Bethnal Green Road at the top of Brick Lane is Arnold Circus, centre of the Boundary Street Estate (238).

Calvert Avenue runs west past Dance the elder's St Leonard's, Shoreditch. Over Shoreditch High Street is Rivington Street running west into Shoreditch. Since the Local Authority permitted the use of derelict industrial buildings in this area for other things, the area has been transformed into a major residential, creative industry and entertainment district. Rivington Place is a particularly interesting new arts building (490). Curtain Road goes south to Worship Street and Webb's lovely row of shops and houses (182). An old steel bridge leads to Bishopsgate with its eponymous Institute (235). Folgate Street to the east is lined with more fine Huguenot weavers' houses; just to the south is a picturesque tangle of lanes around Artillery Passage. To the west of Bishopsgate are the various phases of Broadgate (408, 488) and Liverpool Street Station (205).

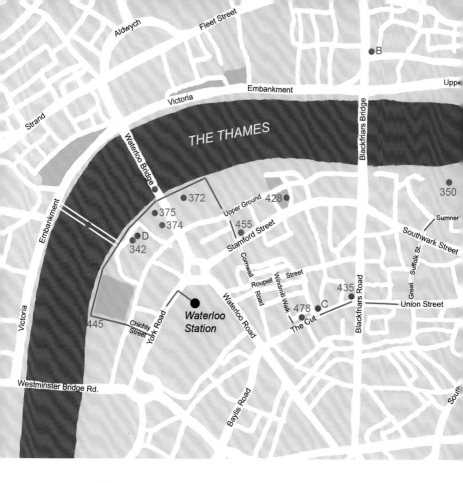

7. The Borough and Southwark

Duration: 1hr. 50 min.

Tips for a break!
The George Inn, George Inn Yard, Borough High Street (A)
The Black Friar, Queen Victoria Street (B)
The Anchor and Hope, The Cut (C)
Skylon, Royal Festival Hall, Belvedere Road (D)

There was a settlement at the south end of London Bridge almost from London's inception. It was not within the boundaries of the City and not therefore bound by any of the City's rules and regulations. In the Middle Ages it exploited this freedom to trade without the City Guilds' restrictions and to provide services that were unavailable over the bridge. The most renowned of these were in the entertainment sector: fighting with various animals, prostitution and the Theatre were all Southwark specialities. Later it was mostly given over to industry and infrastructure. However, the riverside sites, destroyed in the Blitz and easily accessible from the north bank, have gradually been filled with high profile structures. In the wake of the Festival of Britain, many of these are cultural and so Southwark, at least a strip of it, has resumed its old role as an entertainment district, albeit with fewer chickens and painted ladies.

The Thames' daftest crossing, Tower Bridge (220), is outside Tower Hill station. To the east of the bridge are Philip Hardwick's St Katherine Docks of 1828; direct and powerful, their use as retail and leisure facilities since the

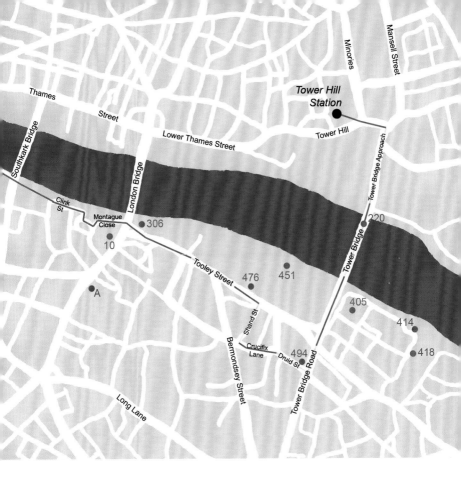

1970s does not do them justice. On the south bank a digression east along Shad Thames passes by Horsleydown Square (405) then between mighty brick Victorian warehouses to the Design Museum (414) and the David Mellor Building (418). West of the bridge is City Hall (451) and the rest of the unappealing 'More London'. Further south in Druid Street is Glas Architects' chirpy tower (494). To the north west, Shand Street ends at Tooley Street where the Unicorn Theatre (476) and the wonderful St Olaf House (306) can be found. Tooley Street heads west under the end of London Bridge and into the atmospheric little knot of streets around Southwark Cathedral (10) and Borough Market. Clink Street with its 12th-century fragment of Winchester Palace continues the route westward and gives way to the bankside footpath, which ends at the Millenium Bridge (446) with the Globe Theatre (413) and Tate Modern (350).

Park, Sumner and Great Suffolk Streets lead back south to Union Street which, heading west over Blackfriars Road, becomes The Cut, home to the new Southwark Station (435) and the Young Vic Theatre (478). A passage, Windmill Walk, on the north side of The Cut goes under Waterloo East Station and into the entirely charming Roupell Street area of the mid 19th century. Cornwall Road leads north to Upper Ground and the admirable Coin Street developments (428, 455). An un-named service road at the end of Cornwall Road carries on to the riverside embankment. To the west are, in turn, the National Theatre (372) the Hayward Gallery (374) Queen Elizabeth Hall (375) and last, but by no means least, the Royal Festival Hall (342). Overhead are two of the most interesting river crossings, Waterloo (336) and Hungerford (467) Bridges, and the Millennium Wheel (445).

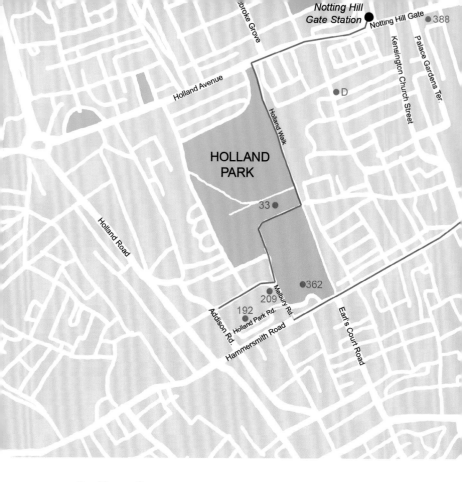

8. Kensington

Duration: 1hr. 50 min.

Tips for a break!
Daquise, Thurloe Street (A)
Victoria and Albert Museum Café, Exhibition Road (B)
The Orangery, Kensington Palace (C)
Windsor Castle, Campden Hill Road (D)

From as early as the 11th century Kensington was a small country village with a scattering of large houses on its outskirts. The 18th century saw some small scale development but it was only in the 19th that Kensington was subsumed into the city. The catalyst was the Great Exhibition of 1851 in Hyde Park. Much of the proceeds were used to create a great range of cultural and educational institutions inspired by Prince Albert (hence 'Albertopolis') on land south of the exhibition site. The arrival of the underground railway in the 1860s was an added spur to residential development.

The architecture was mostly stuccoed Italianate, sometimes lively but more often formulaic.

South Kensington tube station (270) with its little shopping arcade is one of the best of the Edwardian Leslie Green stations. At the south end of the arcade Pelham Street runs east to the cheerful Michelin Building (279). Brompton Road to the north arrives at the Brompton Oratory (213) with the Victoria and Albert Museum (250) and then the Natural History Museum (202) to the west along Cromwell Road. Between the two museums Exhibition Road runs north

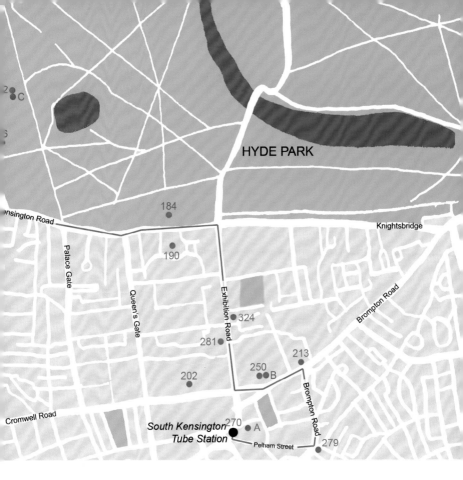

HYDE PARK

184

190

324

281

250 B

213

202

270 A

279

Knightsbridge

ensington Road

Palace Gate

Queen's Gate

Exhibition Road

Brompton Road

Cromwell Road

South Kensington
Tube Station

Pelham Street

Brompton Road

to Hyde Park. Along here are the Science Museum (281), Imperial College with its Business School by Norman Foster fronting the street, an interesting 1930s apartment block (324) and Shaw's Lowther Lodge at the top. In the park is the Serpentine Gallery, which in recent years has commissioned annual temporary pavilions by designers who have not previously worked in Britain. Also in the park is Patrick Gwynne's Dell Restaurant, a 1960s period piece. Kensington Gore progresses westward into Kensington High Street passing the Albert Memorial (184) and the Royal Albert Hall (190). Behind the Hall are the stocky Royal College of Music and the eccentric and enjoyable Royal College of Organists by Henry Cole (1876). A final Albertopolis institution, the Royal College of Art, is west of the Hall.

Further west along Kensington High Street on the north side is the entrance to Kensington Palace (66), originally envisaged as a country retreat when it was extended by William and Mary. In the grounds is Hawksmoor's Orangery (72). Beyond the Palace, Kensington High Street turns into a shopping street with erstwhile department stores Barkers (329) and Derry and Toms with its roof gardens. In Holland Park the dilapidated Commonwealth Institute (362) awaits developments. To the west are Melbury and Holland Park Roads with a fantastic collection of 19th-century artists' houses (192, 209). Notting Hill Gate and its station can be reached by traversing Holland Park, passing Holland House (33) on the way. Just beyond the station in Kensington Palace Gardens are the Czech and Slovak embassies (388).

HYDE PARK

Knightsbridge Station · Knightsbridge · A · 426

Kensington Road

Exhibition Road

Brompton Road · 239

Sloane Street

Pont Street · 400

Cadogan Square

Cromwell Road

South Kensington Station · 270

Eaton Square · 224

Old Brompton Road

Onslow Square · Onslow Gardens

Fulham Road

Sydney Street

King's Road

Sloane Square · B · 316 · 223

325

Leonard's Terrace

Royal Hospital Road

Chelsea Bridge Road

64

Glebe Place

Old Church Street

194 · 395 · D · 26 · 248

18

Cheyne Walk

207 · C

Chelsea Embankment

Tite Street

RIVER THAMES

98

301 →

BATTERSEA PARK

9. Chelsea

Duration: 1hr. 50 min.

Tips for a break!
Harvey Nichols Fifth Floor Café, Sloane Street (A)
Royal Court Theatre Bar, Sloane Square (B)
Tangerine Dream Café, Chelsea Physic Garden, Swan Walk (C)
The Phene Arms, Phene Street (D)

Chelsea as a small riverside hamlet pre-dated the Norman Conquest. Through the Middle Ages it was surrounded by large country houses, which have subsequently been replaced by late 17th and 18th-century residential development of terraces. By the 1880s when Chelsea was filled in, people had grown tired of the white Italianate stucco and the new fashion was for red brick Dutch, Queen Anne tall gabled houses, the style known as 'Pont Street Dutch'. The western part of Chelsea was also never connected to the rail or tube networks so development was smaller in scale, piecemeal and more individualistic. This area became a favoured abode for 19th-century painters and writers, most notably Turner, Whistler and Carlyle. Chelsea has remained largely residential except for the principle throughways, which are all upmarket shopping streets, and a number of large hospitals.

The immediate surroundings of Knightsbridge tube station are an orgy of traffic and retail. Harvey Nichols (426) is immediately opposite and Harrods (239) just around the corner. Sloane Street is quieter with only very expensive, very hushed emporiums. To the south is Arne Jacobson's Danish Embassy (400). To the west are Pont Street and Cadogan Square with many examples of 'Pont Street Dutch'; Nos. 62, 68 and 72 in the Square are by Shaw and Nos. 50 and 52 by Ernest George. The bottom of Sloane Street is marked by Sedding's Arts and Crafts masterpiece, Holy Trinity (224). Sloane Square is home to the Royal Court Theatre (223) and the early Modernist

Peter Jones department store (316). Further west along King's Road are the Georgian Duke of York's Barracks; this has now been commercially developed incorporating a home for the Saatchi Gallery. Across the Square at the centre of this development and down Franklin Street is Wren's Royal Hospital Chelsea (64) along with Soane's stable block.

West of the hospital, Tite Street runs south to the Embankment. Some of the many 19th-century artists' studio houses remain and a new somewhat forbidding one has recently been added by Tony Fretton. The stretch of Thames here is one of the pleasantest in London with Chelsea Bridge and Battersea Power Station (301) to the east, Battersea Park directly opposite, Albert Bridge (198) to the west and magnificent trees overhead. Westwards are a series of fine Queen Anne houses including Shaw's Swan House (207). Beyond Albert Bridge are more fine houses, particularly Charles Ashbee's Nos. 38 and 39 (248). At the end of Cheyne Walk is the Old Church (26) and Crosby Hall (18).

Old Church Street runs northwards and resembles in parts a lane in a country town. The little knot of streets to the east is picturesque and home to a beautiful house by Webb (194) and Mackintosh's London home. Old Church Street itself has the intriguing Inner Court (395) and, beyond King's Road, some early Modern houses (325). Onslow Gardens and Square, typically pleasant Chelsea thoroughfares, lead to South Kensington tube station (270).

10. Hampstead & Highgate

Duration: 2hrs. 20 min.

Tips for a break!
The Buttery Café, Burgh House, New End Square (A)
The Flask, Flask Walk (B)
The Brew House, Kenwood House, Hampstead Heath (C)
The Flask, Highgate West Hill (D)

Of all the villages subsumed into London, Hampstead and Highgate best preserve a rural village air. The street plan is rambling and informal, the buildings heterogeneous and there is much greenery. Unusually for London, the topography involves some ups and downs. All these picturesque qualities make for attractive places to wander at less visited times. There were small settlements in the vicinity in the Middle Ages but it was in the 18th century that they began to take on their current form with much development particularly in Hampstead. The area was popular because of the open spaces, its elevation and its rural character in contrast to London. As transport links with the city centre improved, it became an increasingly attractive place to live. From the start, existing residents were fighting against would-be incomers and developers to maintain the area's established character. Battles have been lost and battles won and the war continues to this day. The greatest victory for Londoners has been the preservation of so much green space so close to the centre of the city. On the other hand, both Hampstead and Highgate are surrounded by Victorian and Edwardian suburbs and the historic cores have had various additions. In the 20th century this pattern has yielded some regrettable constructions but also a good number of important Modern buildings, particularly from the early Modern 'white' period. Both suburbs have long been associated with artist and writer residents.

A little south of Belsize Park tube station Downside Crescent runs north into Lawn Road on which are the newly re-furbished Isokon Flats (322). Fleet Road goes north across South End Green – with a bookshop where George Orwell worked, now a burger joint –into South End Road and then Willow Road, at the bottom of which are Nos. 1–3 (334). At the end of Willow Road on New End Square is Burgh House, a very fine townhouse of 1703 now an arts centre and museum. Flask Walk connects to the west with Hampstead High Street, over which is Perrin's Lane leading into Ellerdale Road; No. 6 is the house Norman Shaw built for himself. There is another Shaw house at 39 Frognal, one street to the west, built for children's book illustrator Kate Greenaway in 1884. Opposite the house are some attractive school buildings by Arnold Mitchell of 1907. Frognal Way off Frognal to the east is the site of the Sun House (323). Church Row, which returns to the centre of Hampstead, can be reached via a path at the end of Frognal Way. From there, Holly Hill and Hampstead Grove head north to the Heath; Fenton House (67) stands near the top.

The Heath is crisscrossed by a network of paths. Broadly to the north and a little east is the Adam Brothers' Kenwood House (106) with its considerable art collection. From the House, Millfield Lane runs south east off which, to the north, are Merton Lane and Holly Terrace which lead to the centre of Highgate. Highgate Cemetery (167) is down Swains Lane to the south of the centre. To the north along Northwood Street are the iconic Highpoint I and II (320). Park Walk and Southwood Lane go north from here to Highgate tube station.

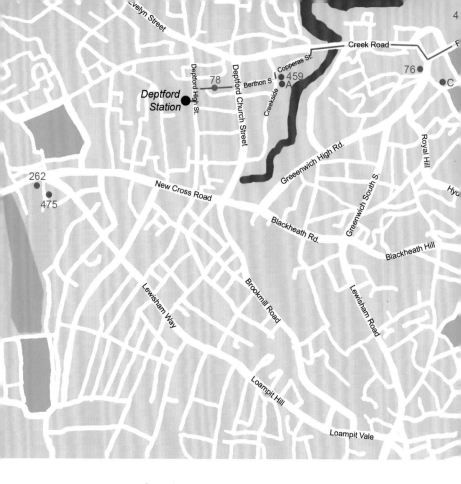

11. Deptford, Greenwich & Blackheath

Duration: 2hrs. 15 min.

Tips for a break!
Laban Theatre Café and Bar, Creekside (A)
Trafalgar Tavern, Park Row (B)
Spread Eagle, Stockwell Street (C)

Accessible both on the river and on the Roman Road to Kent, Greenwich was perhaps the first unoffending country town to be wrapped in London's dusty coils. It is no surprise to find that the first ever suburban steam rail service was the London and Greenwich Railway completed in 1838. A Royal Palace had been built in Greenwich as early as 1447, replaced by the Royal Naval Hospital for sailors at the end of the 17th century, initiating Greenwich's 200-year association with the Royal Navy. At the same time Greenwich began to be developed as a comfortable suburb, with fine houses built in the 17th,

18th, and early 19th centuries. Lying just to the south, Blackheath followed a similar pattern, while neighbouring Deptford has a related but very different history. A small fishing village on the banks of the Thames, it became an early industrial centre with the establishment of the first Royal Dockyard in the early 16th century. Four hundred years of industrial and maritime endeavour finally petered out at the end of the 20th century. Its long and fascinating past is likely to be matched by a interesting future.

Alighting at Deptford station offers the possibility of a detour with Deptford Town

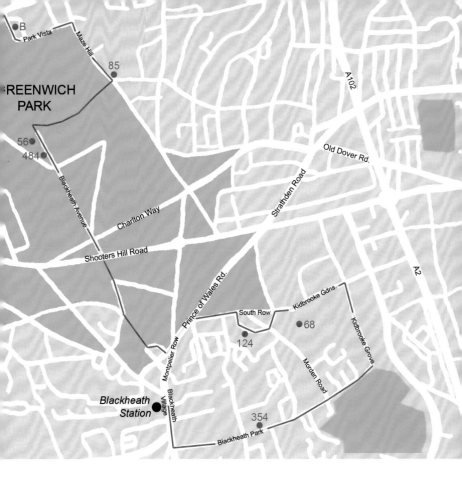

Hall (262) and the Ben Pimlott Building (475) down Deptford High Street and west into New Cross Road. The Town Hall is worth a walk even in such unpromising territory. Alternatively, the entrance to St Paul's Churchyard (78) is east off Deptford High Street a little to the north of the station. The shimmering enigmatic form of the Trinity Laban Dance Centre (459) can be seen to the east from the churchyard. Copperas Street and Creek Road lead eastward to the centre of Greenwich, now a UNESCO World Heritage Site. Here can be found Hawksmoor's St Alfege's (76), the Naval Hospital (44), the Queen's House (39) and West Wing (127) as well as, from 2011, a restored Cutty Sark with an intriguing new Interpretation Centre by Youmeheshe. The area is also home to the south end of the seemingly ancient Greenwich foot tunnel and some beautiful Georgian streets clustered around the bottom of Greenwich Park. Park Vista runs east along the south side of the Queen's House; at the east end is Maze Hill, the location of Vanburgh's very own mad castle (85). Westward across the park are the Royal Observatory (56), the Peter Harrison Observatory (484) and some fine views of the City from a rare high point. Running south from the observatories, Blackheath Avenue approaches the heath itself, which is surrounded by some fine housing, the most dramatic of which is the Paragon (124). East of this along Kidbrooke Gardens is Morden College (68), beyond which Kidbrooke Grove goes south to Blackheath Park. This road and the surrounding streets have a total of twenty-one wonderfully flimsy and optimistic Span Housing Developments (354) of the 1960s and 1970s. Blackheath Park also has Modernist houses by Patrick Gwynne at No. 10 and Peter Moro at No. 20. At the west end of Blackheath Park, Lee Road runs north into mildly picturesque Blackheath Village with its station.

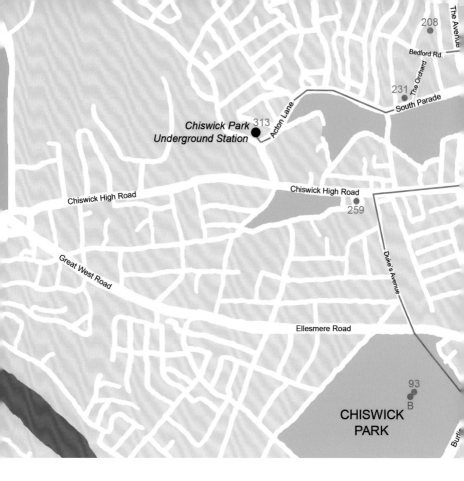

12. Chiswick

Duration: 2hrs.

Tips for a break!
The George and Devonshire, Burlington Lane (A)
Chiswick House Café, Burlington Lane (B)
The Tabard, Bath Road (C)

Like Chelsea, Chiswick was a longstanding riverside village centred on its medieval church. It was developed further in the 18th century with both terraced housing and larger freestanding country houses. The coming of the tube to Turnham Green in 1869 stimulated further development north of the old centre along the tube line. One early developer, Jonathan Carr, was set on building a new type of development; perhaps influenced by Nash's Park Village West, he and his architects constructed the first garden suburb, which was to influence suburbs the world over. Certainly the informal

layout and 'old English' architecture of Bedford Park was highly influential for the late Victorian and Edwardian development of Chiswick. In the 1920s and 1930s Georgian Chiswick, centred on Chiswick Mall by the river, was isolated from the newer Chiswick, centred around Chiswick High Road, by the construction of the Great West and Great Chertsey Roads.

The extensive and impressive old Royal Masonic (now Ravenscourt Park) Hospital (307) is just to the east of Stamford Brook tube station along Ravenscourt Gardens. Ravenscourt Park runs south

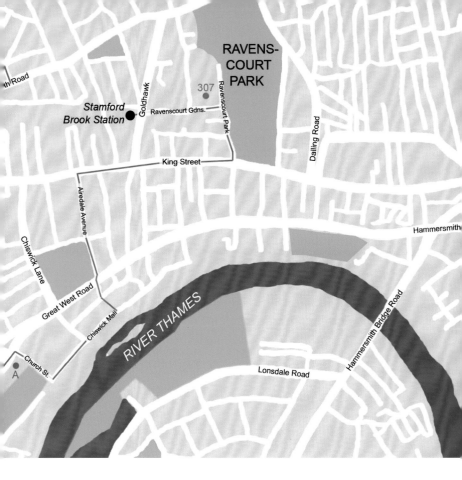

back to King Street. To the west is the impressive tram shed and power station of what was the depot of the London United Electrical Tramway Company, built at the very end of the 19th century. Airedale Avenue runs south to Chiswick Mall, with its fine Georgian houses. At the west end is the church of St Nicholas; the tower is 15th century and the rest of the church was rebuilt by Pearson in the 1880s. Further west on Burlington Lane is Chiswick's chief glory, Chiswick House and Gardens (93). Nearby Hogarth Lane is the site of the Hogarth museum housed in the artist's one-time home, a substantial 17th and 18th-century house.

Duke's Avenue connects to the north with the High Road passing Barley Mow Passage and Sanderson's Wallpaper Factory (259). East along the High Street, Turnham Green Terrace runs north to Bedford Park (208). On Bath Road are Norman Shaw's Church of St Michael and All Angels (215) and the Tabard Inn and stores (216). Various walks can be taken around Bedford Park but a semi-circular route around Rupert Road, Bedford Road and The Orchard gives a good idea of what the suburb is like. The Orchard ends on South Parade, which runs along the edge of Acton Green and Chiswick Common. Just to the west of The Orchard is Voysey's Tower House (231). At the west end of Acton Green Common is Chiswick Park Underground Station (313), one of the best of the inter-war Holden stations.

APPENDIX

Index of Objects

The black numbers listed in the index refer to the property numbers.

INDEX OF OBJECTS

APPENDIX

Index of streets

APPENDIX

INDEX OF STREETS

APPENDIX

INDEX OF STREETS

Index of architects

INDEX OF ARCHITECTS

INDEX OF ARCHITECTS

APPENDIX

Picture credits

All pictures witch are not separately listed in the following, stem from Henning Klattenhoff. If not otherwise indicated reference is made to the consecutive numbers of the properties.